LIGHT IN THE
DARKNESS

LIGHT IN THE DARKNESS

STUDIES IN THE GOSPEL OF JOHN

HOMER A. KENT JR.

BAKER BOOK HOUSE
GRAND RAPIDS, MICHIGAN

To DAN

with a father's prayer
that he will always follow
the Good Shepherd

Acknowledgments

The contributions of many have made possible this little volume, from the numerous writers past and present who have stimulated the author's thinking, to the students at Grace Theological Seminary who have provided the laboratory for refining the views set forth. In addition, the author wishes to express his special appreciation to the following:

Mr. Robert D. Ibach, Jr., who once again came to the author's aid by preparing the maps, charts, and the temple diagram with his usual meticulous care.

Dr. James L. Boyer, faithful colleague in the Department of New Testament and Greek, for allowing portions of his New Testament Chronological Chart to be adapted for inclusion.

The author's wife, Beverly, who read the manuscript and assisted in the choosing of photographs.

Dr. Herman A. Hoyt, president of Grace Theological Seminary, in whose course on the Gospel of John the author sat as a student twenty-five years ago, who read the manuscript and made helpful suggestions.

The Board of Trustees of Grace Theological Seminary, who granted the author a sabbatical leave that he might pursue further study in Israel and complete the manuscript of this book.

Contents

Illustrations

Picture Credits

Fondation Martin Bodmer, Bibliotheca Bodmeriana, CH-1223
    Cologny-Genève, Switzerland
The John Rylands University Library of Manchester, Deansgate,
    Manchester, England
Levant Photo and Design Service, P.O. Box 1284, Santa Cruz,
    California 95060

Photographs not otherwise credited are by the author.

Transliteration Table

Whenever possible, Hebrew and Greek words have been transliterated according to the following form:

Greek	Hebrew Consonants	Hebrew Vocalization
a — a	א — '	— ā
ϵ — e	ב — b, b̲	— a
η — ē	ג — g, g̲	— e
o — o	ד — d, d̲	— ē
ω — ō	ה — h	— ê
ζ — z	ו — w	— i
θ — th	ז — z	— î
ξ — x	ח — ḥ	— ŏ
υ — u	ט — ṭ	— o
ϕ — ph	י — y	— û
χ — ch	כ — k, k̲	— u
ψ — ps	ל — l	— ( )e
' — h	מ — m	
$\dot{\rho}$ — rh	נ — n	
$ą$ — āi	ס — s	
$\etą$ — ēi	ע — '	
$\omegą$ — ōi	פ — p, p̲	
$\gamma\gamma$ — ng	צ — ṣ	
$\gamma\kappa$ — nk	ק — q	
$\gamma\xi$ — nx	ר — r	
$\gamma\chi$ — nch	שׂ — ś	
	שׁ — š	
	ת — t, t̲	

Abbreviations

ANF	*Ante Nicene Fathers*
ASV	American Standard Version, 1901
KJV	King James Version, 1611
LXX	Septuagint (Greek translation of the OT)
NASB	New American Standard Bible, 1971
NEB	New English Bible, 1961
NT	New Testament
OT	Old Testament
RSV	Revised Standard Version, 1952
TDNT	*Theological Dictionary of the New Testament*

Preface

No Gospel of the New Testament is more greatly loved than the Gospel of John. Among young and old alike its profound message, beautiful imagery, and simple language have won their way into countless hearts. The familiar words of John 3:16 are among the first to be memorized by children in Sunday school, and yet the implications of that statement never cease to thrill even the most mature who have come to know in a personal way the Christ about whom John wrote.

The careful expositor knows, however, that the simplicity of vocabulary and grammatical structure of John does not mean that interpretation is easy. The relations of the Father and the Son, the activity of the Holy Spirit, and the "abiding" of believers in Christ are just a few of the topics in this Gospel which are presented in the simplest language, but whose depth offers the severest challenge to the student who would probe their meaning.

The method of treatment in this volume was prevented by limitations of space from being a verse-by-verse exposition. Nor was it possible to examine minutely all divergent interpretations in these pages. For a thorough study of that character, the work by Leon Morris, *The Gospel According to John* (1970) is perhaps the best recent treatment from a conservative standpoint. The aim of the present writer has been to discuss the Gospel of John paragraph by paragraph, centering attention upon problem areas. Each section of these studies should be read along with the Biblical text. Photographs, maps, diagrams, and charts have been used to assist the reader to place the message in its historical and geographical setting. It is my hope that all who read this volume in conjunction with the Gospel may be able to say with the disciples, "We have seen the Lord" (John 20:25).

Homer A. Kent, Jr.

Winona Lake, Indiana

Introduction

A brash young idealist once met Jesus and was enthralled by the encounter. He became an avid follower of our Lord and defender of the truths he was learning. In his zeal to protect his Master and uphold the standards of righteousness which Jesus taught, this young firebrand wanted to call down fire from heaven to consume those in Samaria who had shown discourtesy to Christ (Luke 9:54).

But with the passing of the years he absorbed more of the spirit of his Master, and understood that Jesus had come to die not just for a few believers, but even for those who were presently rejecting him (I John 2:2). Years later he had not forgotten the words of Jesus on personal retaliation, for he recorded them in his book: "If any man hear my words, and believe not, I judge him not: for I came not to judge the world, but to save the world. He that rejecteth me, and receiveth not my words, hath one that judgeth him: the word that I have spoken, the same shall judge him in the last day" (John 12:47-48). This disciple, of course, was John, the "son of thunder" (Mark 3:17). He had learned that those who would truly follow Jesus must be proclaimers of a message of hope, not dispensers of final judgment, for that task belongs to God at a future day.

John, however, never lost his forthrightness. He always understood that in the final issue, men are either in light or in darkness, and that God's judgment is certain upon those who reject the light. At the end of the second century Irenaeus related an incident which reveals John's firm belief in God's judgment upon rejecters of spiritual truth.

> And there are those who heard from him [Polycarp] that John the disciple of the Lord went in Ephesus to bathe and, when he saw Cerinthus within, rushed out of the bath house without having bathed, saying: "Let us flee lest even the bath house cave in, for Cerinthus, the enemy of the truth, is within."[1]

When John wrote the Fourth Gospel, he reflected the same clear understanding of men's relationship to God:

[1]*Against Heresies*, 3.3.4, in *Ante-Nicene Fathers*, ed. Alexander Roberts and James Donaldson (Grand Rapids, reprinted 1950), I, 416.

He that believeth on him is not condemned: but he that believeth not is condemned already, because he hath not believed in the name of the only begotten Son of God. . . . He that
believeth on the Son hath everlasting life: and he that believeth
not the Son shall not see life; but the wrath of God abideth on
him. (John 3:18, 36)

Canonicity and Authorship

Before one examines the message of the Gospel of John, several
matters of historical background must claim the attention.

There is little doubt about John's right to a place in the New
Testament canon. All of the earliest and most important uncial
manuscripts contain it—Sinaiticus, Vaticanus, Alexandrinus,
Ephraemi, Bezae, Washington, and Koridethi. It appears in the
more recent papyrus finds, such as P^{45}, P^{66}, and P^{75} (Fig. 1), and
the earliest manuscript still surviving from any New Testament
book (P^{52}) is a second-century fragment from the Gospel of John
(Fig. 2). The earliest versions contain it, and the Muratorian
Canon, our oldest surviving list of New Testament books (A.D.
170), names John as the fourth Gospel.

The acceptance of the canonical status of this Gospel and of its
authorship by John is supported also by the writings of Christian
leaders from the second century. Irenaeus (A.D. 120-202) and
Theophilus of Antioch (ca. A.D. 115-188) are the earliest writers
whose works have survived who also assert that John was the
author of this Gospel. Irenaeus said:

. . . . even as the Gospel and all the elders testify; those who
were conversant in Asia with John, the disciple of the Lord,
[affirming] that John conveyed to them that information.[2]

Afterwards, John, the disciple of the Lord, who also had leaned
upon His breast, did himself publish a Gospel during his
residence at Ephesus in Asia.[3]

Then, again, the Church in Ephesus, founded by Paul, and
having John remaining among them permanently until the
times of Trajan, is a true witness of the tradition of the
apostles.[4]

[2]*Against Heresies,* 2.22.5.

[3]*Against Heresies,* 3.1.1.

[4]*Against Heresies,* 3.3.4.

Fig. 1. *A page from Papyrus Bodmer XV (P75), showing the end of Luke and the beginning of John. This important papyrus contains John 1-5, 8-9, and portions of 6-7 and 10-15. It is dated somewhat earlier than A.D. 200.* Courtesy, Fondation Martin Bodmer, Bibliotheca Bodmeriana

As for the reliability of Irenaeus, Eusebius says that his authority was Polycarp who had personally heard the apostles.[5] He quotes Irenaeus as saying he had heard Polycarp, who in turn had personally known John:

> For, while I was yet a boy, I saw thee in Lower Asia with Polycarp. . . . so that I can even describe the place where the blessed Polycarp used to sit and discourse . . . also how he would speak of his familiar intercourse with John, and with the rest of those who had seen the Lord; and how he would call their words to remembrance.[6]

Theophilus of Antioch wrote regarding the authorship and canonicity of John's Gospel:

> And hence the holy writings teach us, and all the spirit-bearing [inspired] men, one of whom, John, says, "In the beginning was the Word, and the Word was with God. . . ."[7]

The identification of the author of the Fourth Gospel has been complicated by a perplexing statement of Papias (A.D. 70-155) which is cited by Eusebius:

> . . . but if ever anyone came who had carefully followed the presbyters, I inquired as to the words of the presbyters, what Andrew or what Peter said, or what Philip or what Thomas or James or what John or Matthew or any other of the disciples of the Lord, and what Aristion and the presbyter John, the Lord's disciples, were saying. For I did not suppose that information from books helped me so much as that from a living and abiding voice.[8]

Some scholars have concluded from this statement that "John the apostle" must be distinguished from "John the presbyter," and that the latter may have been the author of the Gospel. However, there is no other clear evidence for this shadowy figure, and even the statement of Papias is capable of explanation without necessitating two persons named John.[9]

[5]Eusebius *Ecclesiastical History* 4.14, in *The Fathers of the Church: Eusebius Pamphili, Ecclesiastical History*, trans. Roy J. Deferrari (Washington, 1969), I, 230-233.

[6]*Letter to Florinus*, ANF, I, 568.

[7]*To Autolycus*, 2.22, ANF, II, 103.

[8]Eusebius *Ecclesiastical History*, 3.39.

[9]See Donald Guthrie, *New Testament Introduction: Gospels and Acts* (Chicago, 1965), pp. 241-243; Everett F. Harrison, *Introduction to the New Testament* (Grand Rapids, 1964), pp. 209, 210.

The traditional view which ascribes the authorship to the apostle John thus has very early support, going back well into the second century and through Polycarp reaching even to the first. We must now look at the Gospel itself for information as to its author.

In no passage of the Gospel does the author give his name. Nevertheless there are three direct statements where the author is specifically indicated. The first is John 1:14, where the author writes, "We beheld (*etheasametha*) his glory." Of the twenty-two occurrences of the verb *theaomai* in the New Testament, not one is used of a mere mental or spiritual conception. It always denotes a visible happening. The aorist indicative form refers here to a past event, again more appropriate to a historical occurrence than to a present spiritual condition. The same verb is used in I John 1:1, where the sense of physical beholding is unquestioned. In distinction from its synonyms, this term emphasizes a longer, warmer, more intimate viewing.[10] Hence the author is claiming to have been an *eyewitness* of the glory of the Word who became flesh, the Lord Jesus Christ.

It is tempting to interpret the author's statement as referring to Christ's glory that was displayed at the Transfiguration. This in turn would limit the possible authors to Peter, James, and John, the only witnesses of that event who could have written this Gospel. However, it is not at all certain that the author had that event specifically in mind, for he later states that the miracle of changing the water into wine was also a manifestation of Christ's glory (*doxa*, John 2:11). In fact, the Gospel of John does not even contain the account of the Transfiguration. Hence the most that can be concluded is that the author was an eyewitness of Christ's glory which was displayed on various occasions throughout our Lord's ministry.

The second direct statement of the author about himself is John 19:35: "And he that saw it bare record, and his record is true: and he knoweth that he saith true, that ye might believe." Here the author ("bare record" means "wrote this Gospel") tells his readers that he was present at the Crucifixion. Elsewhere in

---

[10]Wilhelm Michaelis, "Theaomai," in *Theological Dictionary of the New Testament,* ed. Gerhard Kittel, trans. Geoffrey W. Bromiley (Grand Rapids, 1967), V, 344, 345.

the context we are informed that the disciple whom Jesus "loved" was one of those present (19:26).

The third reference is John 21:24: "This is the disciple which testifieth of these things, and wrote these things: and we know that his witness is true." In the same context the author has also been called "the disciple whom Jesus loved" (21:20), and has been differentiated from Peter. Inasmuch as some of the disciples in this incident were named, the one "whom Jesus loved" would in all likelihood be among the unnamed ones—either a son of Zebedee or one of the "two other of his disciples" (21:2). From other passages we know that three of the disciples were the most intimate in their associations with Christ: Peter, James, and John. Yet Peter is distinguished from "the disciple whom Jesus loved" (21:20-24), and James died too early for the report to circulate that he would not die (21:23, cf. Acts 12:2). Thus John is left as the most likely candidate, and this agrees with the earliest historical testimony from external sources.

Many have followed Westcott's pattern of noting indirect testimony from the book itself in pointing to John as the author. He demonstrates in an ever-narrowing circle how the writer reveals himself to be a Jew (through expression of many Jewish opinions, customs, and writing style), a Palestinian Jew of the first century (knowledge of Jerusalem and other geographical data which were subsequently destroyed in A.D. 70), an eyewitness (familiarity with details), an apostle (aware of apostles' private words), and finally the apostle John.[11] It has been objected that an author would hardly have referred to himself as "the disciple whom Jesus loved," but as Leon Morris counters, it is not a very natural way for an author to describe someone else either.[12] The objection, therefore, is not as weighty as it might first appear. The evidence from the Gospel itself, both direct and indirect, thus supports the testimony of early Christian history that the author of the Fourth Gospel was the apostle John.

[11]B. F. Westcott, *The Gospel According to St. John* (Grand Rapids, reprinted 1950), pp. v-xxv.

[12]Leon Morris, *The Gospel According to John* in The New International Commentary on the New Testament series (Grand Rapids, 1971), p. 12.

The Apostle John

John and his family. The known family of John consisted of four persons. In addition to John, there was his father Zebedee, who was a fisherman on Lake Galilee (Mark 1:19-20; Matt. 4:21). His mother was named Salome, as a comparison of the parallel passages Matthew 27:55-56 and Mark 15:40 will show. If John 19:25 is compared with Mark 15:40, there is revealed the strong possibility that John's mother was a sister of the mother of Jesus. John also had a brother named James, who was probably older since he is always named first. James was the first of the Twelve to be martyred (Acts 12:2).

The family occupation was fishing on Lake Galilee, where they were in partnership with Simon Peter and Andrew (Luke 5:10). The business was large enough to use hired servants (Mark 1:20) and was sufficiently prosperous to allow Salome to assist with the financial support of Christ and his party (Luke 8:3; Mark 15:40-41). John also seems to have been acquainted with the high priest, a fact which suggests some social importance (John 18:15).

John and Jesus. If, as many believe, John was the deliberately unnamed disciple in 1:35, 40, then he had been a follower of John the Baptist until he came in contact with Jesus. After our Lord began his public career, John was chosen out of the larger group of disciples to be one of the Twelve (Luke 6:12 ff.). He was also one of three apostles to whom were granted special confidences (raising of Jairus's daughter, Transfiguration, Gethsemane). At our Lord's death it was apparently John who was given responsibility to care for Mary (John 19:26-27).

John's later ministry. After Pentecost, John appears with Peter on two occasions: at the Beautiful Gate of the Temple in Jerusalem and at Samaria (Acts 3, 8). He was recognized as one of the pillars in the Jerusalem church (Gal. 2:9). Late in his life he was banished for a time to the isle of Patmos (Rev. 1:9). Ancient tradition associates John's final years with a ministry at Ephesus.[13]

[13]Irenaeus *Against Heresies,* 3.1.1; 3.3.4.

Date and Place of Writing

There is no direct evidence in the book as to the date of writing or the place of composition. Certain indirect indications suggest that John wrote for readers unacquainted with Jewish customs, and at a distance from the scenes about which he wrote. Some passages emphasize the wide scope of the gospel, a scope not recognized by the apostles at first. In 11:51-52, John interprets the unconscious prophecy of Caiaphas and shows the spread of the gospel beyond Judaism—a development that took considerable time as the Book of Acts reveals. For the erroneous report about John's personal future to circulate abroad considerable time may also be implied (21:23-24). John refers to Mary of Bethany in terms that may infer his readers' previous knowledge of the Synoptic accounts (John 11:2).

The dominant early tradition names Ephesus as the place of John's later residence and his writing of the Gospel.[14] Inasmuch as there is no evidence of John's being in Ephesus as early as the mid-sixties (Paul's writings place Timothy there, not John[15]), that would seem to mark the earliest possible date. The discovery in Egypt of a papyrus fragment of John from the early second century (Fig. 2) prevents any second-century dating (except at the very beginning). Accepting the authorship of John the apostle (who died, says Irenaeus, during Trajan's reign, 98-117 A.D.[16]), one is confined to a date somewhere during the last three decades of the first century.

Special Features

The Gospel of John has many distinctive features which will become apparent through careful study of its message. A few of the more noteworthy are the following:

1) It differs decidedly from the Synoptic Gospels (Matthew, Mark, and Luke). The first three Gospels are largely a compilation of historical data, particularly of Christ's most striking acts and words with little editorial comment. John, however, pauses

[14]*Ibid.*

[15]I Tim. 1:3; II Tim. 1:18.

[16]Irenaeus *Against Heresies*, 3.3.4; Eusebius *Ecclesiastical History*, 3.18; 3.20; 3.23.

Fig. 2. *Rylands Greek Papyrus 457 (P⁵²). This fragment, written on both sides, is the oldest portion of a New Testament manuscript now extant. It contains part of John 18:31-33, 37-38, and comes from the first half of the second century.* Courtesy, John Rylands University Library of Manchester

frequently to explain or apply (11:51-52 and 12:37-41 are two examples). The Fourth Gospel is not so much a biography of Christ as the others, for it is limited chiefly to what happened in Judea, and to the experiences of approximately thirty selected days.

2) The vocabulary is generally simple, but the terms have great intrinsic worth. Such words as *truth, light, darkness, life,* and *love* are frequent, and the breadth of their connotation challenges the greatest intellects.

3) Two great themes are contrasted throughout the book: faith and unbelief. Time and time again John points out that those who were confronted by Christ made either the one response or the other. He further shows that these two responses were made even at the very beginning of the ministry, and both faith and unbelief developed side by side till the end. This theme is suggested in 1:11-12, and is traced throughout the book.

4) John clearly and formally states the purpose of his Gospel in 20:30-31. That purpose was to convince his readers that Jesus was

the Messiah, the Son of God, and that personal trust in him imparts true life.

5) John has arranged his Gospel around a selected group of signs performed by Jesus. He tells us this was his method (20:30-31). Included were eight miracles performed by Jesus,[17] the resurrection of Christ, and perhaps the cleansing of the temple (2:18-23). By these signs our Lord demonstrated his authority and provided encouragement for men to trust him.

[17]Water to wine, nobleman's son, impotent man, feeding 5000, walking on water, man born blind, Lazarus, catch of fish.

Chapter 1

Prologue

(John 1:1-18)

"In the beginning was the Word." With this stately pronouncement[1] reminiscent of the opening words of Genesis, John begins his Gospel. In some respects this Prologue is the thesis and digest of the book. In it the author lays down his proposition that Christ, whom he calls the Word, is deity, was intimately involved at Creation, and has entered into human life so as to bring eternal life to as many as receive him. The rest of the Gospel is the unfolding and demonstrating of this truth.

Before proceeding far in a study of this passage, one must understand what John meant when he called Jesus Christ "the Word." This was by no means a common title for our Lord,[2] and yet John uses it without explanation, assuming that his readers would understand the sense. The Greek word in the original text is *Logos*, a term which denoted sometimes the faculty of reason or thought, and sometimes had the meaning of speech or word (that is, the expression of thought).

The employment of *Logos* as a term in Greek philosophy goes back at least as far as Heraclitus (535-475 B.C.), who explained all diversity in the universe by a unitary principle which he called variously God, Reason, Justice, Fire, or *Logos*.[3] It was more common among later philosophers, however, to use *Logos* more

---

[1]The highly literary form of the Prologue leads some to conclude it was an early Christian hymn adapted to serve as the opening to this Gospel. For an example of an attempt to divide it into stanzas, the reader should consult Raymond E. Brown, *The Gospel According to John* (i-xii) in The Anchor Bible series (Garden City, 1966), pp. 3, 4.

[2]Other NT uses are confined to the Johannine writings: I John 1:1; Rev. 19:13. The Byzantine text also has it in the textually doubtful portion of I John 5:7.

[3]Archibald Alexander, "Logos," *The International Standard Bible Encyclopedia* (Grand Rapids, reprinted 1946), III, 1912.

abstractly as "reason." There was little if any understanding of *Logos* as a personal being.

In the Old Testament there are a number of passages which indicate that God acted by his "word." He created by his word (Gen. 1:3; Ps. 33:6), and sometimes God's word is spoken of semi-personally (Ps. 107:20; 147:15). The Old Testament also spoke of God's wisdom as an almost personal entity in such passages as Proverbs 8 (especially verse 22 and following).

Palestinian Judaism employed the Aramaic term *Memra* ("word") in the Targumim (translations of the Hebrew Scriptures into Aramaic) in place of the name of God. This seems to have come about as the result of special concern to avoid using the name of God lest they break the Third Commandment. Nevertheless it indicates that Jewish people were accustomed to "the Word" as referring to God. The Jewish philosopher Philo of Alexandria (born 20 B.C.) used the term *Logos* more than 1300 times in his writings, but primarily in the abstract sense of Reason or Divine Intelligence. Leon Morris concludes: ". . . he saw the Logos as a philosophically respectable bridge between a transcendent God and this material universe."[4] Strongly affected by Greek philosophy, Philo could not bring himself to use *Logos* in the fully personal sense which John asserts.

It should be clear that when John wrote of "the Word," he was using a term which all of his readers, Jew and Gentile, would grasp with at least some measure of understanding. They should have understood that just as words are the expression of thoughts, so to call Christ the Word was to regard him as the communication of the Divine Wisdom, the personal revelation of the truth of God. He was not just the communicator but the communication itself. He did not merely tell God's truth. He *was* the truth (John 14:6). But however full or meager the understanding of his readers may have been, John proceeded in the Prologue to enrich the title with the explanation that Jesus Christ is

---

[4]Leon Morris, *The Gospel According to John* in The New International Commentary on the New Testament series (Grand Rapids, 1971), p. 121.

JESUS' PUBLIC MINISTRY

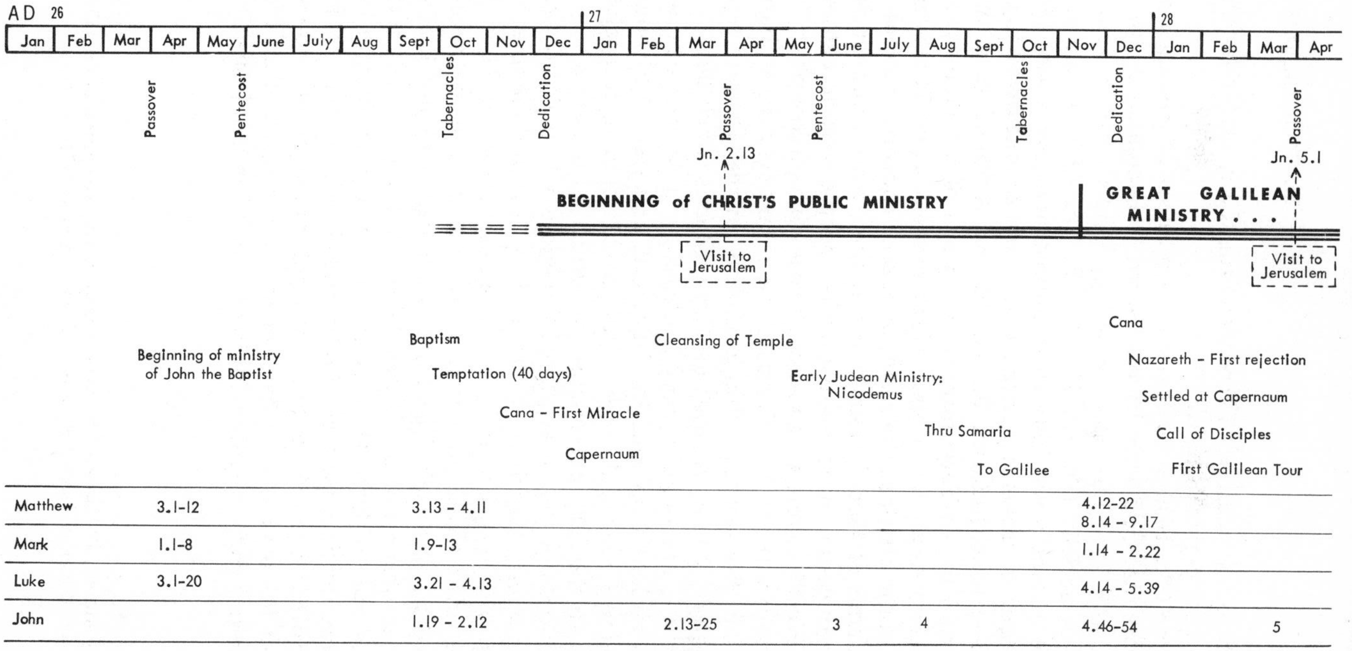

AD 26 — | Jan | Feb | Mar | Apr | May | June | July | Aug | Sept | Oct | Nov | Dec | 27 | Jan | Feb | Mar | Apr | May | June | July | Aug | Sept | Oct | Nov | Dec | 28 | Jan | Feb | Mar | Apr

Feast markers (top scale): Passover · Pentecost · Tabernacles · Dedication · Passover · Pentecost · Tabernacles · Dedication · Passover

Timeline events:

- Beginning of ministry of John the Baptist
- Baptism
- Temptation (40 days)
- Cana – First Miracle
- Capernaum
- BEGINNING of CHRIST'S PUBLIC MINISTRY
- Jn. 2.13 Passover — Visit to Jerusalem
- Cleansing of Temple
- Early Judean Ministry: Nicodemus
- Thru Samaria
- To Galilee
- Cana
- GREAT GALILEAN MINISTRY . . .
- Jn. 5.1 Passover — Visit to Jerusalem
- Nazareth – First rejection
- Settled at Capernaum
- Call of Disciples
- First Galilean Tour

Matthew	3.1-12	3.13 – 4.11	4.12-22 / 8.14 – 9.17
Mark	1.1-8	1.9-13	1.14 – 2.22
Luke	3.1-20	3.21 – 4.13	4.14 – 5.39
John	1.19 – 2.12	2.13-25 · 3 · 4	4.46-54 · 5

Fig. 3.

God expressed in genuine human flesh, and has embodied in his own person the fullest revelation of God to man.[5]

I. The Word and God (1:1-2)

A. The Word Is Eternal with God.

"In the beginning" (*en archēi*) reminds us of Genesis and was probably so intended. There is this difference, however, that in Genesis the expression is used regarding the time of creation, whereas here the reference is unrestricted. The Word is said to be already existing when creation began (1:3). John does not say that in the beginning the Word began, but that in the beginning the Word already "was." The imperfect tense form *ēn* implies timelessness in this statement. Thus the Word antedates time and goes back to eternity past with God.

B. The Word Is Personally Distinct from God.

"The Word was with God." This assertion identifies the Logos as a separate entity from "God." Thus he must not be considered as a mere attribute of God nor an emanation from God. The word "with" (*pros*) is used here in the sense of "in the presence of, " as for example its use in Matthew 13:56 and Mark 6:3. A distinction of some sort must be drawn between the Word and the being called "God." That distinction was not one of essence, however, but of personality as the next clause makes clear.

C. The Word Is Identical in Essence with God.

"The Word was God." This statement answers the question as to whether the distinction to be drawn between the Word and God makes the Word somewhat less than God. In the original text the word "God" (*theos*) appears first in the clause without the article and before the verb, and "the Word" (*ho Logos*) follows the verb and uses the article. This does not mean, however, that "God" is the subject of the verb. It is quite normal for predicate

---

[5]For further study of John's use of the Logos designation, see Morris, *John*, pp. 115-126; C. K. Barrett, *The Gospel According to St. John* (London, 1967), pp. 127-129; Brown, *John*, 519-524.

nouns which precede the verb to be used without the article, and it would be most strange for "the Word," which does have the article, to be the predicate noun in a clause in which the subject was without the article.[6] By placing *theos* first in the clause, John gave it the emphatic position, and by employing it without the article he stressed the qualitative sense of the noun. His point was: "The Word was deity." The distinction in person between the Word and God expressed previously did not mean that the Word was not equally God. Although the Logos was not the same as God the Father personally, they were the same in quality or essence. Both are deity. Grammatically this was the best way John could have expressed this thought. If he had used the article with *theos*, he would have expressed the error of Sabellianism which held that the Son and the Father were one person, and thus would have contradicted his previous statement which distinguished them. Jehovah's Witnesses miss the point of the passage altogether when their *New World Translation* renders "the Word was a god," for John is not demonstrating that Christ is some semi-deity but that he is no less than very God in essence. There are four other places in John 1 where *theos* appears without the article (vss. 6, 12, 13, 18), and not even the *New World Translation* renders these "a god."[7]

Verse 2 summarizes the previous three assertions. Yet as C. K. Barrett observes, it is not mere repetition, for it clarifies the point that "the Word does not *come to be* with God; the Word *is* with God in the beginning."[8]

II. The Word and Creation (1:3)

"All things were made by (*dia*) him." Thus we are to understand that at creation, "God said" (Gen. 1:3) implies the presence

---

[6]See E. C. Colwell, "A Definite Rule for the Use of the Article in the Greek New Testament." *Journal of Biblical Literature,* Vol. 52 (January 1933), pp. 12-21; F. Blass and A. Debrunner, *A Greek Grammar of the New Testament and Other Early Christian Literature,* trans. Robert W. Funk (Chicago, 1961), Section 273, p. 143.

[7]A helpful recent discussion of the erroneous treatment of John 1:1 by Jehovah's Witnesses can be found in Edmond C. Gruss, *Apostles of Denial* (Newhall, CA, 1970), pp. 115-119.

[8]Barrett, *John,* p. 130.

and activity of the personal Word, Christ himself. Of course, this does not mean that the Father was not involved in creation, for I Corinthians 8:6 indicates that the Father is the ultimate source (*ex hou*, "out of whom"). However, both I Corinthians 8:6 and John 1:3 say that creation occurred "through" (*dia*) Christ. Thus the Word is viewed as more than a passive instrument of the Father. Every created thing (*panta* without the article looks at all things individually rather than collectively) passed through the intelligence and will of the Son of God (cf. also Col. 1:16-17).

The first part of the verse states the fact positively. The last part restates the truth in a way that emphasizes there are no exceptions. Every created thing came into being through the creative activity of the Word. It should be clear that Christ himself must thus be uncreated inasmuch as he personally created everything which has come into being.[9]

III. The Word and Mankind (1:4-13)

In this grand statement, John has challenged his readers with the greatest concepts they could possibly entertain. He has related the Word first to God, and then to the universe, the most encompassing entity which man can perceive with his senses. Now he moves to the most important aspect of creation: mankind. What he has to say in these verses is a digest of what the rest of this Gospel is about.

A. The Word Was the Life and Thus the Light of Men. (1:4)

"In him was life." It is common for this verse to be interpreted in the highest and most restricted spiritual sense of eternal life, and thus to see here that which is true only for believers. However, several factors should caution us against restricting John's meaning arbitrarily. 1) The word "life" (*zōē*) does not always mean spiritual life or eternal life. The term is used of the life

---

[9]Textual editors question whether the closing words of 1:3 (*ho gegonen*) really belong with verse 3 or should be the beginning of verse 4. The oldest uncials (Aleph, B) contain no punctuation and thus provide no help. The earliest Fathers appear to attach the words to what follows, although later the trend developed to relate them to the preceding statement. The sense is more readily grasped if the words are attached to verse 3, as in KJV, RSV, and NASB.

which God has given to all men (Acts 17:25), of the earthly life of a lost man (Luke 16:25), and of the present life in contrast to the life to come (I Tim. 4:8), in addition to its many uses denoting spiritual life. Hence the term is a broad one and can denote all kinds of life. 2) In this passage the light which resides in the Word is not said to be given to men directly by the Word, but is granted somewhat indirectly through the life which they have: "the life was the light of men." Thus a relationship of the Word to mankind generally may be in view. 3) Verse 9 supports this wider reference, for Christ is called the light "which lighteth every man" (not just believers).

It is probably better, therefore, to understand John as declaring that all life of whatever sort came into being because the creative force resided in the Word. And whatever kind of life one possesses provides that person with "light." The highest kind of life to be received from Christ is eternal life (*aiōnios zōē*), and this provides the greatest spiritual light. But all men possess some kind of life from their Creator, and their human life provides them with the light of reason and conscience (Rom. 1:19-20; 2:14-16; Acts 14:17). This light alone was not enough to save them, but it was enough to leave them without excuse (Rom. 1:20). Believers, however, have received spiritual life in addition, and thus possess far more light as to the knowledge of God and his will for men.

B. The Word Was Unreceived by Men Generally. (1:5-11)

The problem is that the light had to contend with darkness (1:5). "Darkness" refers to the realm of spiritual evil, the state of the world under Satan's sway since the Fall. It is because men are sinful, and live in a world of spiritual darkness, that they are not guided by the light of reason and conscience. Their imaginations and thoughts are evil (Gen. 6:5; Rom. 1:21). The darkness, however, could not extinguish the light. Scholars disagree as to whether the verb *katalambanō* should be understood in the sense of *attain, appropriate,* or *comprehend,* or in the hostile sense of *overtake, seize, overcome.* Either translation makes sense, for the darkness did not understand nor appropriate the light; neither did it succeed in overcoming it. On the whole, the latter sense

Fig. 4. *The Jordan River, whose waters were used by John the Baptist in his baptizing ministry.* Levant Photo and Design Service

seems preferable, and fits John's other uses of *katalambanō*, all of which are with the hostile sense.[10] Hence John is understood to say that the light and the darkness exist presently together. The light that men have through the life they possess has not abolished the darkness. Nor has the darkness blotted out the light. This helps us to understand the response which occurred even when the Word became flesh.

The sad spiritual condition of mankind is shown clearly in the response to the ministry of John the Baptist (1:6-8). The rather detailed references to John in this Gospel (1:6-8, 15-39; 3:23-36; 4:1) may be partly accounted for by the need to correct wrong opinions regarding him that were held by some of his supporters. We know that earlier at Ephesus, where this Gospel was written, there were believers who had been strongly attached to the ministry of the Forerunner (Acts 19:1-7), and perhaps this influence persisted.

[10] John 6:17; 8:3; 8:4; 12:35.

John the Baptist came as a man authorized by God for the giving of testimony regarding Christ. The author carefully sets John apart from Christ by precise wording. William Hendriksen shows in tabular form how John "came" (*egeneto*), was a mere man, was commissioned by God, testified to the true light, and was the agent through whom men were brought to believe the light; whereas Christ "was" (*ēn*) from all eternity, is the Word, is himself God, is the true light, and is the actual object of belief.[11]

Furthermore, John was a good witness and by his life he gained the respect of the people, for "all hold John as a prophet" (Matt. 21:26). Some apparently even thought he was Messiah (John 1:21). He personally disclaimed such ambitions for himself, and was content to bear his witness to Jesus as the Light in order that through his testimony[12] men might believe in Christ.

Jesus the personal Word, however, was the true or real Light who lights every man (1:9). It is grammatically possible for the phrase *erchomenon eis ton kosmon* (coming into the world) to refer either to "every man" or to "the true Light." Thus KJV treats it as the former, and NASB as the latter. If the former is meant, the phrase seems somewhat unnecessary (what other kind of men are there?), unless it is intended to mark the time of this enlightenment as when men are born. Supporters, however, are able to point to rabbinical usage of the phrase in the simple sense of "men." It seems better to construe the phrase with "the true Light" which John then asserts was coming into the world. This accords well with 1:10 which stresses the fact that the Light was in the world. Furthermore, the expression that light has come into the world is used elsewhere in John to describe Jesus, not men (3:19).

The unhappy fact is, however, that in spite of the witness of John the Baptist, the entrance of the Light into the world by the incarnation was unrecognized by men generally (1:10-11). Even

---

[11]William Hendriksen, *Exposition of the Gospel According to John* (Grand Rapids, 1953), p. 76.

[12]"Through him" refers to John, not Jesus. The pronoun "him" has the subject of the sentence as its antecedent. Men are called upon to believe "in" Jesus, but not "through" him. Thus men were asked to believe in Jesus through the witness of John.

though the world had been created by him, it failed to recognize and acknowledge its Creator. The "world" (*kosmos*) here is the world system of mankind, lost in sin, and unresponsive to the Light whom God sent. The spiritual blindness of men is brought into even sharper focus by the statement: "He came unto his own [*ta idia*], and his own [*hoi idioi*] received him not." The first phrase is neuter, and is used elsewhere in the sense of "home" (i.e., one's own belongings). This is the way the words are translated in Acts 21:6. The second use of the phrase is masculine and means "his own people." The reference is to Christ's homeland and the Jewish people. As God's chosen nation and the recipients of his direct revelation in their Scriptures, they of all people should have welcomed Jesus. But it was they who crucified him.

C. *The Word Was Received by Some.* (1:12-13)

Although national Israel rejected the Light when he came into the world, some Jewish individuals did not. Those who "received him" are explained as those who "believe in his name." They were the ones who recognized Jesus Christ as the One whom the Father had sent, who had fulfilled the ancient prophecies and had come to be their Savior. They had accepted his message as from God and had responded favorably to his invitation. To "believe in" (*pisteuousin eis*) involves not only intellectual assent but also personal appropriation and commitment. Those who received him accepted Christ's message about his person and the purpose of his ministry, and entrusted themselves to him. "Name" is a common expression to denote the entire person, including what he stands for and represents (see John 15:21; 17:26; Acts 4:12).

All such persons have become "children of God"[13] on the authority[14] of Christ. They are sharers of his life on the highest

[13]The Greek expression is *tekna theou*, and should not be rendered "sons of God" as in KJV. "Children" (*tekna*) denotes a sharing of nature, whereas "sons" (*huioi*) denotes position as heirs.

[14]Greek: *exousian*. The word denotes right, authority, or permission, as distinct from *dunamis* which denotes intrinsic ability. Werner Foerster, "Exousia," *Theological Dictionary of the New Testament*, ed. Gerhard Kittel, trans. Geoffrey W. Bromiley (Grand Rapids, 1964), II, 562.

spiritual plane. This relationship to God is not the experience of all men, however, for it comes about only in those who receive the incarnate Word by faith. It is not the product of natural birth but of the direct intervention of God. This truth will be further presented when John records the interview with Nicodemus (3:1-21). Persons who are born of God through faith in Christ the Word are thus not simply the product of physical descent ("blood").[15] Nor can their new relationship to God be explained on the basis of mere sensual desire which operates in physical reproduction ("will of the flesh"), or the action of a man in planning or executing procreation ("will of man").[16] What is referred to is a new spiritual relation to God that comes about solely through the action of God who has offered to men his Son. No human endeavor can achieve the spiritual birth here described. God alone can perform this feat, and he has offered to provide this new birth to all who will receive the revelation given by his Son and entrust themselves to him for eternal life.

Occasionally one encounters the interpretation that regards verse 13 as referring to Christ rather than to believers.[17] If legitimate, this would provide a strong statement supporting the virgin birth of our Lord. Such an understanding requires that the pronoun "who" (KJV "which") be read as singular rather than plural. However, there is not one Greek manuscript supporting the singular pronoun. The view is first encountered in Irenaeus,[18] and Tertullian stated that the plural reading was an invention of Valentinian Gnostics.[19] The absence of Greek manuscript evidence makes this alternative most unlikely.

---

[15]The Greek text uses the plural *haimatōn* ("bloods"), and has been explained either as the mingling of blood from father and mother, or as depicting the long line of physical generation through one's ancestors.

[16]The word "man" in the Greek text is *andros*, denoting a male human, not *anthropos*, mankind.

[17]For example, R. C. H. Lenski, *The Interpretation of St. John's Gospel* (Columbus, 1942), pp. 63-70.

[18]Irenaeus *Against Heresies*, 3.16.2, 3.19.2, in *Ante-Nicene Fathers*, ed. Alexander Roberts and James Donaldson (Grand Rapids, reprinted 1950), I, 441, 449.

[19]Tertullian *On the Flesh of Christ*, XIX in *ANF*, III, 537.

IV. The Word and the Old Testament System (1:14-18)

Prior to the Word's entrance into the world through the incarnation, the Old Testament had revealed God's way of dealing with men. The Jewish nation had been brought into a covenant relation with God, and the Mosaic Law provided the framework whereby men could live pleasing to God. John's Prologue must now show how the coming of the Word into the world fits into this plan of God's operation.

It is explained that the Word became man through incarnation (1:14). To say that the Word who has already been shown to be God (1:1) "became flesh" does not imply that he ceased to be God. Rather he added the condition of humanity to what he already was. "Flesh" is used here in the sense of physical life, human nature. Perhaps this particular term was chosen, rather than "man," to refute more directly certain docetic heresies which were current in John's day and claimed that Christ's "humanity" was only an appearance.

"Dwelt" (*eskēnōsen*) comes from a verb that meant literally "to live in a tent." Used metaphorically as here, it could suggest the temporary nature of Christ's earthly presence "among us." However, to a Jewish mind the verb could easily have evoked the concept of the tent or tabernacle in the wilderness where the Divine Presence (the Shekinah) manifested himself. Thus the statement asserts the presence of the Word in human flesh, in language strongly reminiscent of God's presence with his people in Old Testament times.

At this point the author testifies to his own experience as an eyewitness of these things. What he saw as he was with Christ was the very glory of God the Father displayed through the person, words, and deeds of Jesus. (See the Introduction, p. 4, for additional discussion of verse 14). The Word is described as "the only begotten (*monogenēs*) of the Father," but this should not cause us to think primarily of the birth process, for such a meaning will not fit all cases where this term is used in the New Testament.[20] In addition to those instances where it is used of children who were the only offspring of their parents (Luke 7:12;

[20]See the author's discussion in *The Epistle to the Hebrews* (Grand Rapids, 1972), p. 230.

8:42; 9:38), it is used also of Isaac who was not the only son born to Abraham (Heb. 11:17). We should rather understand the term in the sense of "unique," for this sense will apply to all cases where an only child is meant, and also in the case of Isaac (who was born of the free wife Sarah, in contrast to Ishmael and Hagar). In the case of Christ, his unique relation to the Father has been made clear (in distinction from believers who also are called "sons" and "born of God").

"Full of grace and truth" epitomizes the Word as the revealer of the Father.[21] Grace suggests God's matchless mercy and favor toward men, and truth depicts his fidelity to his promises.

The Word was witnessed to by John the Baptist, last of the Old Testament prophets (1:15). After four hundred years of no direct revelation, the Spirit of God came upon John that he might bear witness to the Jewish people regarding Jesus. Our Lord indicated him to be the last of that Old Testament prophetic line (Matt. 11:13; Luke 16:16). In his testimony John said, "He that cometh after me is preferred before me." He meant that Jesus, who was six months younger than he and began his ministry later, was really of higher rank than he. The reason is found in Christ's preexistence: "For he was before me." Thus the revelation in Christ is shown to be connected to the Old Testament system. He was the One for whom that dispensation provided the foundation.

Furthermore, Christ the Word is the fullness of that which the Law could only foreshadow (1:16-17). These seem to be the words of the author (not John the Baptist). The Mosaic Law (which stands here for the entire Old Testament economy) is contrasted with the new revelation in Christ. The author of the Epistle to the Hebrews makes a similar comparison of the two dispensations by discussing Christ and Moses (Heb. 3:1-6). Christ's fullness is

[21]The noun which "full" (*plērēs*) modifies is uncertain. As to form, the nominative adjective would appear to go with "the Word" (*ho logos*), and this is doubtless what prompted the KJV translators to put the intervening material in parentheses. However, papyrus usage indicates that *plērēs* was often treated as indeclinable, and thus it could be regarded as modifying "glory" or "the Father." See Blass-Debrunner, *Greek Grammar*, Section 137, p. 76. The difference in meaning is slight, inasmuch as the Word is said to be displaying the Father's glory. Thus "grace and truth" is characteristic of both Christ and the Father.

the very fullness of divine power (Col. 1:19; 2:9), and by becoming children of God by faith, believers share in this fullness of power and blessing sufficient for every need (Eph. 3:19; Col. 2:10). Grace follows upon grace from the divine supply. The author does not mean that grace and truth did not exist under the Mosaic Law (see Exod. 34:6), but that these characteristics of God became embodied in human flesh when Christ came.

The Prologue reaches its grand conclusion with the proclamation that Christ the Word is the fullest revelation of the Father (1:18). No mere man has ever seen God's face or his essence. Even the various theophanies were at best only the "back parts" of God (Exod. 33:23). In Christ, however, we have the highest revelation of God, so that Christ himself could say, "He that hath seen me hath seen the Father" (John 14:9). "In the bosom" suggests the closest intimacy. One could compare the cases of Lazarus in Abraham's bosom (Luke 16:22) and John himself in Jesus' bosom (John 13:23).

The most ancient manuscripts of John have the words "only begotten God" (*monogenēs theos*) rather than "the only begotten Son" in verse 18.[22] If this should be the original reading, and the evidence for it is strong, it is a striking assertion of the deity of Christ. With this statement the Prologue reaches its climax. John has related Christ to the grand sweep of God's dealings with the universe and with men. It now remains for him to demonstrate the thesis just set forth, and this will be done in the remainder of the Gospel.

Questions for Discussion

1. What ideas was John conveying by calling Christ "the Word"?
2. How can the Word be *with God* and also *be God*?
3. In what ways does Christ "light" every man?
4. What is the difference between physical birth and being born "of God"?
5. What did John the Baptist understand his own ministry to be?

---

[22]P66, Aleph. B, C, L. P75 is the same except for the addition of the article.

The
Public
Ministry
(John 1:19–12:50)

Chapter 2

Early Belief in Judea and Jerusalem
(John 1:19–2:25)

John begins demonstrating the truth of his thesis that the Light has come into the world, and that those who received Christ experienced new life as children of God, by concentrating on the beginnings of faith. He takes his readers in the opening sections of his book to all areas of the land of the Jews, and shows how people responded to Jesus in Judea, Samaria, and Galilee. The emphasis upon the exercise of faith in Christ permeates the first four chapters of John (1:37, 50; 2:11, 23; 3:16, 36; 4:39, 41-42, 53).

I. The Testimony of John (1:19-36)

A. *To Officials from Jerusalem* (1:19-28)

The ministry of John the Baptist was creating a tremendous stir among the populace of Israel. From the throngs who came to hear him preach and the multitudes who responded to his call to baptism, it must be concluded that many felt a spiritual lack and were ready to do something about it.

It was the responsibility of the Jewish leaders, however, to check on all religious teachers who moved among the people.[1] In Deuteronomy 13:1-5 and 18:20-22 there was laid upon the nation the responsibility of examining every prophet who came, to see whether or not he was of God. In the days of Jesus this function was exercised by the Sanhedrin, the highest official body in Israel, which had jurisdiction over internal affairs by permission

---

[1]Verse 19 contains the first of nearly 70 references to "the Jews" (*hoi Ioudaioi*) in this Gospel, compared to 5 in Matthew, 6 in Mark, and 5 in Luke. In many of these uses, such as the one in 1:19, the term refers to the religious authorities. R. E. Brown concludes: ". . . the Fourth Gospel uses 'the Jews' as almost a technical title for *the religious authorities, particularly those in Jerusalem, who are hostile to Jesus.*" *The Gospel According to John* (i-xii) in The Anchor Bible Series (Garden City, 1966), p. LXXI.

of Rome. Thus the Sanhedrin sent out a committee of priests and
Levites who belonged to the Pharisee party (vss. 19, 24).[2] In
answer to their question, "Who art thou?" John clearly explained
his own position in relation to the Messiah.

He categorically denied that he himself was Christ, that is, the
Messiah (1:19-20). The delegation next questioned whether he
would claim to be Elijah (1:21a). The prophecy of Malachi 3:1 and
4:5 predicted that Elijah would come again at the outset of the
Day of the Lord. Many Jews, therefore, expected Elijah to reap-
pear bodily to announce salvation and to anoint the Messiah.
The question put to John meant: "Are you the Old Testament
Elijah who has returned to the earth?" To this John replied,
"No."

We must, however, reckon with Matthew 11:14 and 17:10-13,
where Jesus said: "If ye will receive it, this is Elijah, which was
for to come." Apparently we must harmonize by understanding
that John was Elijah only in the sense that he ministered in "the
spirit and power of Elijah" (Luke 1:17) and did an Elijah-like
work. Israel could not blame their failure to believe on the absence of Elijah, but God in his foreknowledge knew that at
Christ's first coming Israel would not be ready for Elijah's final
ministry. Therefore John was sent "in the spirit and power of
Elijah."

The question, "Are you the prophet?" (1:21b), doubtless reflects Deuteronomy 18:15, a prediction by Moses that "the Lord
thy God will raise up unto thee a Prophet from the midst of thee,
of thy brethren, like unto me." The identification of this prophet
was a matter of disagreement among the Jews. Some thought the
prophet was Messiah himself. Others thought he was Jeremiah
(Matt. 16:14) or someone else. The Qumran group which lived
near the Dead Sea during the years of New Testament history
held to three Messiahs, of whom "the prophet" was one.[3] We
now know from Peter (Acts 3:22-23) and Stephen (Acts 7:37) that

[2]Because of the dominance of the Sadducees in the Sanhedrin, it is strange to
find this delegation composed of Pharisees. Perhaps the greater scrupulous-
ness of the Pharisees regarding the interpretation of Moses accounts for their
presence in this investigating committee.

[3]The Manual of Discipline, ix, 8-11, in T. H. Gaster, *The Dead Sea Scriptures*,
Anchor Books (Garden City, 1956), p.58.

Christians understood the prophecy to refer to Christ himself. Thus John spoke correctly when he denied that he was this prophet.

John then quoted Isaiah 40:3 and explained his identity by telling of his mission (1:22-23). He was the one who was announcing the arrival of Messiah. It was customary in the East before the visit of a sovereign for advance preparations to be made in leveling the roads so that the event could be accomplished successfully. John was calling upon the nation to prepare itself morally and spiritually for the coming of her King.

He emphasized the preparatory and symbolic nature of his ministry by explaining his baptism (1:24-26). This baptism was not Christian baptism, for that was not instituted until after Christ's resurrection. Although the idea of baptism was not new to his contemporaries, John's baptism was different in its purposes and its subjects. It was not proselyte baptism. It did not initiate one into Judaism. But it did provide opportunity for men to testify in a public act to their desire for cleansing and their readiness to receive the Messiah. In relation to such a person, John placed himself in a most subordinate position (1:27-28). He felt unworthy even to perform the menial task of a slave in view of the majesty which belongs to Christ.

The author has located this incident for his readers as occurring on the east side of Jordan, at a place called Bethany in the most ancient manuscripts. (Bethany beyond Jordan must, of course, be distinguished from the Bethany near Jerusalem on the east slopes of the Mount of Olives.) No trace of this site can be identified today. The alternate readings Bethabara and Betharaba are less well regarded by most students of the text. In the third century Origen traveled in this region and was aware of both readings. He was unable to find any place called Bethany beyond Jordan although he admitted it was the reading in most manuscripts.[4] His influence did much to popularize the alternate "Bethabara," but the original was most likely "Bethany."

---

[4]Origen, *Commentariorum in Evangelium Joannis*, VI, 40, in A. E. Brooke, *The Commentary of Origen on S. John's Gospel* (Cambridge, 1896), I, 157-158.

B. To the Crowds (1:29-34)

On the day following the interview with the Sanhedrin delegation, John announced Jesus to be the Lamb of God (1:29-31). The particular audience addressed is not identified, but it is assumed to be the general crowd which frequently gathered to hear John. This incident must have occurred just as Jesus was returning to public view following the temptation. (It should not be concluded that Jesus' baptism occurred at this time, for that had been followed immediately by the temptation, without time for the events mentioned in John 1:35—2:1. What is given here is John's report of that earlier event.)

What was John thinking of when he called Jesus the "Lamb of God"? Perhaps he had in mind Isaiah 53 with its description of the Suffering Servant who was led "as a lamb to the slaughter." John had quoted another passage from Isaiah the day before, so he was familiar with the prophecy (1:23). Or perhaps he was thinking of the Passover ritual in which the lamb was slain and the blood was sprinkled. Being the son of a priest (Zacharias, Luke 1), he would be well acquainted with the ritual, and in addition, Passover season was near (2:13). It does not seem possible to know precisely which Old Testament portion or ritual John was alluding to, but surely the idea of sacrifice must be part of the figure. Here then is testimony at the very beginning that Christ's coming would be for the redemption of lost men, and that suffering and sacrifice would be involved.

John also declared that Jesus was the One who baptizes with the Holy Spirit (1:32-33). Whether John and Jesus had ever met prior to the baptism is not certain. They were kinsmen through their mothers (Luke 1:36), but John had spent most of his early years in desert regions (Luke 1:80). Even if John might have known something about Jesus, he did not have the divine indication that Jesus was the Messiah until the time of the baptism. The descending Spirit in the form of a dove[5] at Jesus' baptism had been the prearranged sign to John that Jesus was the Messiah. He also knew from such passages as Isaiah 11:2 and 42:1

[5]Why the Holy Spirit should have appeared in the symbol of a dove is not explained in Scripture. The symbol is not dissimilar to the mention of the Spirit as hovering over the waters at creation (Gen. 1:2).

that the Messiah would be especially indwelt by the Spirit and thus could minister the Spirit to others. Hence John once again indicates that the ministry of Jesus would produce the reality of spiritual transformation in contrast to John's baptizing which was largely preparatory and symbolic.

John concluded this public witness by testifying that Jesus is the Son of God (1:34). "Messiah" thus meant to John much more than a merely political ruler. He was the divine King. At this very beginning stage, John recognized Christ's redemptive work (1:29), his preexistence (1:30), and his unique relationship to the divine Father.

C. To Two Disciples (1:35, 36)

The next day John was in the company of two of his own followers, and made the same pronouncement regarding Jesus as he had done before the crowd the day before (1:29). One of these disciples was Andrew (1:40), and it is probable that the unnamed one is John, the writer of this Gospel, who shows his characteristic reserve in not naming himself. In all subsequent lists of the Twelve, John is always grouped among the first four, along with Andrew, Peter, and James.[6] It was to be expected that Christ's earliest followers would come from the Baptist's ministry.

II. The Response of Some Disciples (1:37-51)

In this section the person of Christ was recognized by the disciples through their initial experiences with him. In each of these encounters the men saw something about Jesus which captured their profound interest.

A. Jesus Recognized as Teacher (1:37-39)

Andrew and the unnamed disciple immediately saw in Jesus the qualities of a superb teacher. They called him "Rabbi," which John translates for us by the Greek work for "teacher." They were so impressed that they desired to spend the rest of the day with him so as to learn from his lips.

What time of day was the "tenth hour"? If the common Jewish method of reckoning was employed, which began the number-

[6]Matt. 10:2-4; Mark 3:14-19; Luke 6:13-16; Acts 1:13.

ing of the hours of the day at sunrise, the tenth hour would be 4
P.M. However, this makes the comment strange that the disciples
abode with him "that day," inasmuch as there would have been
very little day remaining. Another possibility is to explain it after
the Roman method which began the civil day at midnight. Thus
the tenth hour would be 10 A.M. Of the four times John mentions
the hour of day (1:39; 4:6; 4:52; 19:14), the first three could
conceivably be interpreted by either scheme, but the last reference is brought into hopeless conflict with Mark 15:25 if the
Jewish mode is employed. Therefore, on the assumption that
John uses the same method throughout the Gospel, the Roman
scheme offers the best understanding in all the passages.[7]

B. Jesus Recognized as Messiah (1:40-42)

The preceding interview so impressed Andrew that he went at
once to share the news with his brother Simon and succeeded in
bringing him to meet Jesus. Even though the conception which
these men had of Jesus as Messiah grew immeasurably in succeeding years, they found enough at this first meeting to satisfy
their understanding of Old Testament prophecy regarding the
Messiah to come.

Our Lord recognized with prophetic insight what Simon
would become, and gave him the new name Cephas (Aramaic)
which translates into Greek as *Petros*, meaning "rock" or
"stone." During his years with Jesus, Peter did not always demonstrate the firmness of his name, but subsequent to the resurrection of Christ, his steadfastness for the faith caused all to
recognize his qualities of leadership.

C. Jesus Recognized as the Prophesied One (1:43-46)

Presumably Jesus is to be understood as the one who both
found Philip and then called him to be his follower. Philip was
from the town of Bethsaida, which is also said to be the home of
Andrew and Peter. The well-known Bethsaida-Julias was in
Gaulanitis, near the Sea of Galilee, just east of where the Jordan

[7]This is the view of B. F. Westcott, *The Gospel According to St. John* (Grand
Rapids, reprinted 1950), p. 282, and William Hendriksen, *Exposition of the
Gospel According to John* (Grand Rapids, 1954), pp. 104-105.

enters the lake. Inasmuch as Peter lived at Capernaum (Matt. 8:14; Mark 1:29; Luke 4:38), and Mark 6:45 implies that Bethsaida was near Capernaum (John 6:17), some have postulated two Bethsaidas. This would help to explain the expression "Bethsaida of Galilee" (John 12:21). The matter is still obscure, but a suburb of Bethsaida-Julias located on the west bank of the Jordan may be the best solution.[8]

Philip found in Jesus the One whose coming had been foretold in the Scriptures long before. He immediately bore witness to his friend Nathanael[9] and invited him to share his knowledge. By calling Jesus "the son of Joseph," Philip was merely telling what he knew at the time. It is most doubtful that Jesus told his disciples at the outset regarding his virgin birth. He preferred to let them discover his uniqueness from their contact with him. Of course, the statement is true as it stands, for legally Jesus was the son of Joseph, and on this fact rested his claim to the throne of David (Matt. 1:1-16).

Nathanael was not impressed by the reference to Jesus as being from Nazareth. He knew perhaps that no Messianic predictions were attached to Nazareth, a town not even mentioned in the Old Testament. Nevertheless he followed his friend Philip and went to see Jesus.

D. Jesus Recognized as Son of God and King of Israel (1:47-51)

As Nathanael approached Jesus after being invited by Philip, our Lord astounded him by revealing that he knew all about him and could even describe the scene where Nathanael had just been. Nathanael's response recognized the supernatural character of what Jesus had just done, and showed that he was ready to acknowledge him as the Messianic King who was also the Son of

---

[8]For discussion of the problem, see the articles in *The Interpreter's Dictionary of the Bible*, ed. George Arthur Buttrick (New York, 1962), I, 396-397, and *The New Bible Dictionary*, ed. J. D. Douglas (Grand Rapids, 1962), p. 145.

[9]Nathanael is presumably the same person called Bartholomew in the Synoptics. This identification is based upon the fact that he appears here among the others who became apostles. Furthermore, in three of the four lists of the twelve apostles (see footnote 6), the man called Bartholomew is next to Philip. Also John never mentions Bartholomew, and the Synoptics never mention Nathanael. It is likely that Bartholomew is a patronymic for Nathanael.

God. Such a response revealed an awareness of the Biblical prophecies regarding the Messiah (e.g., Ps. 2:6-8).

The description of Nathanael as "an Israelite indeed, in whom is no guile" reminds us of the Jewish patriarch Jacob ("supplanter") whose name was changed by God to Israel ("God strives"). Jesus thus characterized him as a true Israelite, a forthright man with no deceitful spirit of Jacob in him. In view of what Jesus went on to say (1:51), it is possible that Nathanael may have been meditating on his illustrious ancestor while he was sitting under the fig tree. Geographically this could have been near the place where Jacob had his dream of the ladder reaching to heaven (Gen. 28:10-22). To Jacob the dream revealed God's presence as open to him, with angels available to minister on his behalf. Our Lord revealed to Nathanael that the true basis of access to heaven is Jesus himself. He who is both Son of God and Son of man provides the perfect ladder whereby God and men can meet. The "seeing" to which Jesus referred was not a physical experience such as the Transfiguration (which Nathanael did not witness) or the Second Coming, but the spiritual comprehension which believers gain as they accept the revelation which God provides in Christ.

III. The Marriage at Cana (1:1-11)

A. The Setting (2:1-5)

The narrative now moves to Galilee (cf. 1:43), where on the third day from the last-mentioned event, Jesus and his new disciples arrived in Cana. This village was not far from Nazareth, and was the home of Nathanael (21:2). A marriage celebration was being held, and Mary the mother of Jesus was one of those present. It could be inferred that Mary was already there before Jesus and his disciples arrived. Perhaps she was a relative or had some responsibility for the proceedings. At least she took the initiative to approach Jesus about the problem and then to instruct the servants.

At this marriage feast a social catastrophe was impending, for the wine supply ran short. (It should not be blamed upon the unexpected arrival of Jesus and six disciples, for they had been invited.) To Mary's statement with its implied request, "They have no wine," Jesus responded, "Woman, what have I to do with thee? mine hour is not yet come." This enigmatic reply must not be misunderstood. To address his mother as "Woman" was not to show harshness nor disrespect. It was the same word our Lord used when he addressed Mary from the cross (19:26). In fact it was his usual polite term for addressing women (Matt. 15:28; Luke 13:12; John 4:21; 8:10; 20:13). The expression "what have I to do with thee"[10] is a Semitism which indicates a divergence between the thoughts of the persons involved. Jesus meant that in some sense what Mary was thinking was not his concern at the present. It must await his "hour." The "hour" of Christ is referred to elsewhere by John in 7:30; 12:23, 27; 13:1; and 17:1, and seems clearly to refer to the time of his suffering and death. It can hardly be that Mary was asking simply that a miracle be performed, for in some sense Jesus seems to be rejecting what Mary asked, and yet he proceeded with the miracle. It is better to understand that Mary was hoping for Jesus to give the supreme manifestation of himself, perhaps to remove the suspicion of impurity that must have hovered over her those many years. She doubtless had heard of John's recent testimony regarding Jesus (1:26-27, 29-34, 36), and of course she had pondered for years the significance of the supernatural events surrounding the conception and birth of her Son (Luke 1: 28-37; 2:19). Nevertheless Jesus knew that the full display of his glory to accomplish what Mary hoped would not come till Calvary and the Resurrection. It is to the credit of Mary that she did not take offense but left the matter in Jesus' hands. At the same time her instructions to the servants indicated that she was confident he would do something.

B. The Sign (2:6-10)

The house where the wedding was held had six stone waterpots, each holding from 20 to 30 American gallons.[11] Jewish families commonly used these for ritual purification (Mark 7:3-4).

---

[10]Greek: *Ti emoi kai soi;* literally, "What to me and to thee?"

[11]Greek: *metrētas duo ē treis,* "two or three measures." Each measure was about 10 American gallons; hence each waterpot contained 20-30 gallons. "Weights and Measures," *The New Bible Dictionary,* p. 1325.

Whether all the water in the six waterpots was changed to wine (120-180 gallons, a tremendous amount), or only that which was drawn out from the well after the waterpots were filled, is not certain.[12] Whichever occurred, the miracle was impressive and complete. Even the master of the feast[13] was visibly impressed and remarked to the bridegroom the unusual circumstances in serving the best wine last.

Some are troubled by our Lord's providing wine. Efforts to treat this wine[14] as unfermented seem contrived and usually unconvincing. It must be remembered that wine was the common beverage at meals in that culture. Drinking water was often impure. Furthermore, wine partaken of as a beverage was often diluted, especially in Roman times.[15] The social evils of drinking in modern America should not be read back into the culture of Biblical times.

C. The Effect (2:11)

As a result of this miracle the glory of Christ's omnipotence was revealed. The faith of the disciples increased, for faith rests upon knowledge, and as their knowledge of him enlarged, their trust in him deepened.

It should be noted that this was the "beginning" of Christ's miracles. Stories of childhood wonders performed by Jesus are thus pure fantasy and are categorically denied by this Scriptural statement. The miracle at Cana was not only the first of the "signs"[16] which Jesus did, but also was the first that John selected to demonstrate his thesis (20:30-31).

[12]Westcott holds the latter view on the basis that the verb *antleō*, "draw," usually means to draw from a well, not from a waterpot. He also questions the likelihood that Jesus would have utilized water for purification as the basis for the miracle. However, in such a view there is little reason for mentioning the six waterpots at all, so that the traditional understanding is still the most likely. Westcott, *John*, pp. 37-38.

[13]No Jewish literature helps to define the precise function of the *architriklinos*, the master of the feast. Inasmuch as he can summon the bridegroom, he could hardly have been a slave. He may have been similar to a modern toastmaster.

[14]The Greek term is *oinos*, the same word as found in Eph. 5:18, Matt. 9:17, Luke 1:15, I Tim. 3:8, and many other NT references.

[15]II Macc. 15:39.

[16]The term translated "miracles" in 2:11 is *sēmeiōn*, which looks at the event as a token, proof, indicator, or sign of something. In the case of Jesus, the miracles were signs of Christ's origin, person, and mission.

IV. The Cleansing of the Temple (2:12-25)

A. *The Setting* (2:12-13)

Jesus was still a member of the family circle at this time, and in the spring before the first Passover of his ministry the family made a visit to Capernaum, a city on the north shore of the Sea of Galilee. Eventually, this place would be Christ's headquarters during his ministry (Matt. 4:13). Absence of any mention of Joseph or Jesus' sisters (Matt. 13:56) probably implies that Joseph was dead and the sisters were now married with homes of their own.[17] When the annual spring feast of Passover arrived Jesus went up[18] to Jerusalem.

B. *The Action* (2:14-17)

Upon entering the Temple precincts, Jesus found within a most unworshipful atmosphere. To make things more convenient for the worshipers, facilities were provided for the sale of animals and fowls and the exchange of Roman coinage for temple money. The outer court (Court of the Gentiles, see Figs. 5, 6) resembled a marketplace more than a sanctuary.

Jesus responded to this situation by dispersing the merchants and their wares. Fashioning a whip from small cords (perhaps these were lying around from the sale of bound animals), he drove out the sellers and the animals.[19] The whip was real, and the righteous anger of Jesus was genuine, but the force must

---

[17]The brothers of Jesus are named in Matt. 13:55, and there is no sufficient reason to understand them in any other sense than as children of Joseph and Mary. Efforts to make them cousins, or older sons of Joseph by a previous marriage usually stem from attempts to preserve the perpetual virginity of Mary. The strongest argument for this view is the second century tradition of Mary's perpetual virginity, but this is not sufficient to overthrow the normal sense of Scriptural statements.

[18]Although Jerusalem is south of Capernaum, one always is said to go "up" to Jerusalem regardless of the compass direction. This may be partly due to the fact that Jerusalem is on an elevation, so that one had to make an ascent to reach the city. Furthermore, the location of the temple at Jerusalem may also have encouraged this terminology from an ethical and spiritual standpoint.

[19]Although the Greek expression *ta te probata kai tous boas,* "both the sheep and the oxen," might suggest that only the animals were driven out, the use of the masculine form *pantas,* "all," makes it certain that the men were included.

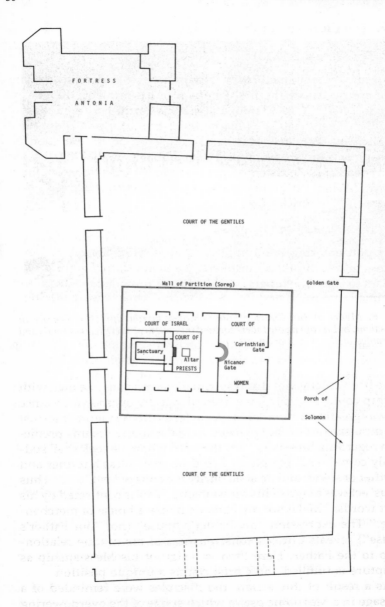

Fig. 5. *Plan of Herod's Temple.*

Fig. 6. *Model of the Court of the Gentiles surrounding the Temple in Jerusalem. In this open court were located the sellers of sacrificial animals and the tables of the moneychangers.*

have been chiefly moral and spiritual inasmuch as one man with a whip could certainly have been physically overpowered since he was greatly outnumbered. What Jesus did was more than just an impulsive act of indignation. In Malachi 3:1, 3 is this prediction regarding Messiah: "... the Lord whom ye seek shall suddenly come to his temple.... And he shall sit as a refiner and purifier of silver: and he shall purify the sons of Levi. . . ." Thus Jesus' act was a·sign of his Messiahship. This is confirmed by his next words: "Make not my Father's house a house of merchandise." The expression "my Father's house" (not "our Father's house") reveals Christ's consciousness of his unique relationship to the Father. Here then is a sign of his Messiahship as Scripture is fulfilled and Christ claims a unique position.

As a result of this action, the disciples were reminded of a passage in a Messianic psalm which spoke of the overpowering passion of Messiah for the things of God (Ps. 69:9).

C. The Response (2:18-22)

The Jewish authorities[20] accosted Jesus with the demand for some divine credential or sign giving him the right to act as he had done. He had just given them a sign but they were spiritually blind to its significance. Jesus then gave the veiled prophecy of his resurrection, the greatest sign which was yet to come (cf. Matt. 12:38-40 for another instance).

Christ's reference to "this temple" was capable of a double meaning, and turned upon the fact that the physical structure symbolized the divine Presence, but Christ the Logos was the actual Presence of God among men. Not only did the Jewish authorities miss the point, but even the disciples failed to grasp the meaning until after the resurrection. The Jewish leaders' failure to acknowledge the rightness of Jesus' act makes it understandable why they did not prevent the return of these merchants and thus made necessary a similar cleansing by Jesus three years later (Matt. 21:13).

The mention of forty-six years helps to date this event. Inasmuch as the temple was not completed until just before the Roman-Jewish War of A.D. 66-70[21] the statement in 2:20 must mean "forty-six years was the time used to build the temple to this point." Herod began the building in the eighteenth year of his reign, which was 20/19 B.C.[22] The forty-sixth year would be A.D. 26/27. Hence this Passover was presumably the spring of A.D. 27.

D. The General Effect (2:23-25)

John closes his discussion of this incident by a summarization of Jesus' ministry in Jerusalem at this time. Our Lord performed other "signs" which are not described but which brought immediate response from many. However, John notes that "Jesus did not commit himself unto them." The text actually uses the word "believe" (episteuen) in 2:24, just as in 2:23 (episteusan). The sense is: "Many believed in Jesus, but Jesus was not believing in

---

[20]See Footnote 1 (this chapter).

[21]Josephus Antiquities of the Jews, Book XX, Sect. 219 (XX.9.7).

[22]Josephus Antiquities of the Jews, Book XV, Sect. 380 (XV.11.1).

them." Their faith was superficial, being based only on miracles they had seen. Jesus knew that unless faith is made to rest in his person, it will not endure (cf.4:48; 11:47-53).

Questions for Discussion

1. Why did John the Baptist deny that he was Elijah when Jesus in Matthew 17:12-13 said he was?
2. In what way did Nathanael "see" angels ascending and descending upon the Son of Man?
3. What should John's hearers have understood when he called Jesus the Lamb of God? Why?
4. What did Jesus' presence and action at the wedding in Cana imply as to his attitude toward the institution of marriage?
5. In what ways was the cleansing of the temple a sign of Jesus' Messiahship?

Chapter 3

Nicodemus and the New Birth
(John 3)

The Gospel of John continues its presentation of material not given in the other Gospels[1] by recounting the remarkable conference between Jesus and Nicodemus. Jesus was in Jerusalem for the first Passover Feast of his ministry (2:13). During his stay he had entered the temple and had performed an act which to discerning eyes was a sign of his Messiahship. Apparently he had also performed other miracles or "signs" which caused great public interest (2:23). However, much of this popularity was superficial, and Jesus did not accept it at full value. He knew that in most cases those who followed were more impressed with the miracles than with Christ himself and his mission (2:24-25).

There was one man, however, whose interest in Jesus was of a sort which set him apart from most of the people in Jerusalem. In the original text there were no chapter divisions or versification, and in addition there is the word "but" (*de*) which ties 3:1 to 2:25: "But there was a man of the Pharisees, named Nicodemus." He was also one of those in Jerusalem, but he was different from those who followed Jesus simply because they were entertained by the miracles.

The interest of Nicodemus was aroused by something deeper.

I. The Interview with Nicodemus (3:1-21)

A. *The Circumstances* (3:1-2)

Nicodemus belonged to the religious party called the Pharisees. This group had an honorable beginning during the Maccabean period of Jewish history.[2] Their movement was an

---

[1]B. F. Westcott has computed the material peculiar to John as constituting 92 percent of the book. *Introduction to the Study of the Gospels* (Boston, 1869), p. 201.

[2]The origin of the Pharisees is generally assumed to have stemmed from the Hasidim of the Syrian and Maccabean periods. H. L. Ellison, "Pharisees," *New Bible Dictionary*, ed. J. D. Douglas (Grand Rapids, 1962), pp. 981-982.

effort to call the people back to their Mosaic Law and to resist the apostate elements within the nation. Unfortunately, the passing of time resulted in the Pharisees' elevating the traditions of the elders to a point where the traditions sometimes contradicted the Scriptures (cf. Matt. 15:2, 9). The Pharisees were, however, the most orthodox party among the Jews.

Politically, Nicodemus was a ruler of the Jews. He was a member of the highest ruling body within the nation, the Sanhedrin (cf. 7:50). Professionally, Nicodemus was a teacher. The original text of 3:10 actually reads: "Are you *the* teacher of Israel?" Thus he may have been unique in some respect, perhaps as the most popular lecturer of his day.[3]

He came to Jesus at night, perhaps in order to have a private interview without interference from the crowds. (It seems a bit harsh to accuse Nicodemus of cowardice on no more evidence than this. Other references to him in this Gospel show him to be a man of considerable courage; cf. 7:50-51; 19:38-40.)

The specific subject which Nicodemus wanted to discuss must be a deduction, but there are indications from the context and from Jesus' statements as to what was on Nicodemus's mind. Jesus had given a sign of Messiahship by cleansing the temple (Mal. 3:1, 3). This had been followed by his claim of a unique relationship to God ("my Father's house," 2:16). These things occurred in the temple, and since the high priest of the temple was also president of the Sanhedrin (of which Nicodemus was a member), they could hardly have escaped the notice of this distinguished teacher. He must have wondered whether Jesus really could be the Messiah. If he were, then the prophesied kingdom must be about to appear.

Furthermore, John the Baptist had been creating great popular fervor with his preaching: "The kingdom of heaven is at hand" (Matt. 3:1-6). Thus Nicodemus wanted to learn from Jesus about the Messianic kingdom. Jesus, however, knew exactly what was on his mind and broached a more personal problem: Nicodemus' personal relation to the kingdom.

---

[3]It is possible, of course, that "the teacher" is an instance of the generic use of the article, with the sense, "You occupy the position of the teacher, not the pupil; hence you should know these things."

Fig. 7. *The Old City of Jerusalem, looking east toward the Mount of Olives. The Second Temple once stood on the site now occupied by the Moslem Dome of the Rock.*

B. The Discussion (3:3-21)

Two main subjects were discussed in this interview: the importance of new birth in order to enter the kingdom, and the experiencing of new birth through believing in Christ.

1. New Birth Is Essential for Entering God's Kingdom. (3:3-12)

Christ's opening assertion went right to the heart of the problem (3:3). Jesus, who knew the thoughts of his visitor, said in effect: "If we are to talk about my Messianic claims and the Messianic kingdom, let's start at the beginning. Let's talk about how one enters that kingdom." Thus Jesus said, "Except a man be born again, he cannot see the kingdom of God." (It is true that "born again" can also be translated "born from above," but the usual translation seems preferable in the present context. This is what Nicodemus would probably have understood at this stage of the discussion. Of course, to be "born again" is to be "born from above" as Jesus went on to explain.)

The kingdom of God mentioned here should not be confused with the universal kingdom of God which has always been operative (Ps. 103:19). Rather, it is the Messianic kingdom which was predicted by the Old Testament prophets. Herman A. Hoyt states:

> This kingdom will thus consist of three things: the rulership of God mediated through His appointed King, the Lord Jesus Christ; the realm of God's rule, the earth restored to its Edenic splendor; and the function of this rule exercised among those who are redeemed.[4]

Although the ultimate establishment of this kingdom will be on earth, at present believers are participating in a limited sense in certain aspects of that kingdom (Col. 1:13). They acknowledge Christ as their king, they enjoy the presence of the Spirit in their hearts, and they experience some of the powers of the age to come (Heb. 6:5). However, Jesus pointed out that Nicodemus could expect no participation at all in the kingdom of God unless he would be born again.

Nicodemus immediately faced a problem (3:4). He cited the obvious impossibility of physical rebirth. But to start life anew in the moral or spiritual realm is no less difficult. All of life's experiences have contributed to one's moral character. To wipe the slate clean and begin again may be a wistful desire, but is humanly impossible to attain.

Jesus then explained that the new birth about which he spoke was not physical but spiritual (3:5-8). And it was not the result of human effort, but was the product of the Holy Spirit. To be a part of God's kingdom, one must be born "of water and of the Spirit." The similarity of this passage to Ezekiel 36:25-26 is striking. There God foretold what would someday happen to Israel when she finally would forsake her sin and turn to God. "I will sprinkle clean water upon you, and ye shall be clean: from all your filthiness . . . and a new spirit will I put within you." The water symbolized the cleansing aspect of this experience, and the new spirit referred to the impartation of new life by the entrance of the Holy Spirit into the life.

Although there is general agreement that the reference to "Spirit" in 3:5 denotes the Holy Spirit, considerable difference of

[4]Herman A. Hoyt, *The New Birth* (Findlay, OH, 1961), p. 36.

opinion surrounds the interpretation of "water." One common view explains it as referring to water baptism, noting the juxtaposition of water baptism and Spirit baptism in the announcement of John the Baptist (1:33).[5] A variant of this view interprets the water not as John's baptism but as Christian baptism. Such explanations labor under the difficulty that this "water" is made an absolute requirement for new birth, and Nicodemus was expected already to know about it (3:9). Yet Christian baptism had not yet been instituted. Furthermore, the Greek expression *ex hudatos kai pneumatos* ("out of water and Spirit") uses two nouns without articles and joined by *kai* as objects of one preposition, thus suggesting that they are not entirely separate but are aspects of one concept.[6]

Another view interprets "water" as referring to procreation, either as natural birth, or figuratively in close connection with "Spirit" so as to yield the sense of "spiritual seed."[7] Holders of this view usually point to non-Biblical instances where the male semen is called "water," "rain," or "dew." However, interpreting "water" as natural birth results in a truism that seems unlikely in this instance. It was hardly necessary for Jesus to tell Nicodemus that in order to be born again he first needed to be born physically. If the term is interpreted as "spiritual seed," any distinctive sense of "water" virtually disappears.

In view of the fact that Nicodemus was expected to know something about new birth (3:10), the conclusion seems inescapable that it must have been revealed to some extent in the Old Testament. It is significant, therefore, that the connection of "water and Spirit" is made more than once in Scripture. In addition to Ezekiel 36:25-26 (cited previously), Isaiah 44:3 says:

> For I will pour water upon him that is thirsty, and floods upon the dry ground: I will pour my spirit upon thy seed, and my blessing upon thine offspring.

The New Testament also uses the concept of water in close association with salvation, and frequently this is used in the

[5]C. K. Barrett, *The Gospel According to St. John* (London, 1967), p. 174.

[6]Hoyt, *The New Birth*, pp. 45-48.

[7]Leon Morris, *The Gospel According to John* (Grand Rapids, 1971), pp. 216-218.

sense of cleansing and is to be ministered to men through the divine word.

> Now ye are clean through the word which I have spoken unto you. (John 15:3)

> . . . Christ also loved the church, and gave himself for it: That he might sanctify and cleanse it with the washing of water by the word. . . (Eph. 5:25-26).

In certain passages the terminology of washing is omitted, but the mention of the word of God is retained.

> Of his own will begat he us by the word of truth. (James 1:18)

> Being born again, not of corruptible seed, but of incorruptible, by the word of God, which liveth and abideth for ever (I Peter 1:23).

Hence it is concluded that new birth involves the cleansing action of God's word which shows man his sin and announces salvation in Christ. When a man believes, God's Spirit imparts to him new life—the life of God. These two aspects of the word and the Spirit ("incorruptible seed") are seen together in I Peter 1:23.

Jesus made the assertion that spiritual birth requires the action of God's Spirit, on the principle that all forms of life reproduce after their kind. Natural life ("flesh") is capable of reproducing itself but nothing higher. Thus the Spirit of God must intervene if man is to be born again with spiritual life. Of course, there is much of mystery here. Hence Jesus used the wind with its uncertain origin and its unpredictable path to illustrate that God's working in regeneration is not explainable by laws presently known.[8]

Our Lord was astonished that Nicodemus had no understanding of these things (3:9-12). The Old Testament was not unclear about the need for a spiritual relationship to God. Mere ritual was never enough to satisfy God, as the prophets proclaimed time and time again. Surely Nicodemus, from his position as teacher in Israel, should have known these things. Alas, he did not, and in his spiritual blindness he was typical of the vast majority in the nation who had long ago lost sight of God's

---

[8]If "wind" (pneuma) is translated in 3:8 as "Spirit," the assertion is not an illustration but a statement: "The Spirit breathes where he wishes." However, pneuma can be used in either sense (see Heb. 1:7, NASB for another NT use as "wind"), and the common rendering is usually preferred.

spiritual dealings, and had substituted perfunctory performance of religious ritual and observance of rabbinical traditions.

Shifting to the plural "ye" and "we" in 3:11, Jesus goes beyond Nicodemus to include the rest of the Jewish people, most of whom had not been persuaded by John's ministry and had been only superficially attracted to Jesus (2:24-25). By "we" Jesus refers not just to his own testimony given in Jerusalem, but to the preaching of John before him, and to the long line of Old Testament prophets who likewise had endeavored to point men to the saving grace of God and to make them aware of the vital place of God's Spirit in making possible a genuine relationship to God. The writer John later used the words of Isaiah to characterize the national response to Jesus (John 12:37-41).

What Jesus had been telling Nicodemus consisted really of "earthly things" (3:12). They had to do with God's revealed plans for regenerating men upon earth.[9] Certainly Nicodemus should have understood something of this from the Old Testament revelation. He should have known that God wants to impart his Spirit directly to men on earth and share his life with them. If even this was unreceived, how could Nicodemus hope to understand such "heavenly things" as God's eternal plan for man's redemption as mentioned in the succeeding verses? The full revelation of the incarnate Son from heaven (3:13), and his work of uniting men with the Father in heaven, are parts of a grand scheme that can never be understood apart from that spiritual rebirth that Nicodemus, as well as all mankind, needed.

2. New Birth Is Experienced Through Faith in Christ. (3:13-21)

Christ showed Nicodemus the incomparable importance of being born again. The question remained: how is this new birth to be experienced by men? Jesus dealt with this matter by first explaining that he was offering himself to the world as its Savior (3:13-17). Inasmuch as new birth must come from God, not man, then one must look to God for revelation about it. And no mere man has ever ascended to heaven to bring back an authoritative

---

[9]"Earthly things" can hardly be restricted to the matters of physical birth and the wind, for there is no warrant for supposing that Nicodemus was ignorant of them.

word from God. We are totally dependent, therefore, upon the revelation provided for us by Jesus, the Son of Man, who has descended from heaven by the incarnation. Here is the first statement from the lips of Jesus revealing his own awareness of his preexistence. The additional phrase "which is in heaven" (KJV) is found in later manuscripts, but is not generally regarded as original.[10]

The illustration of Moses and the brazen serpent should have been most instructive to Nicodemus, the expert in Old Testament history. Numbers 21:4-9 gives the account of a plague of poisonous snakes which came among the Israelites in the wilderness and caused many deaths. Relief came when Moses at God's instruction made a brass serpent and mounted it on a pole. All who had been bitten were spared from death if they looked upon that elevated serpent. The Israelites were under threat of physical death, but were asked to believe God's word and look upon the serpent which was lifted up in their midst and thereby receive healing. So Jesus, the Son of Man on a far higher plane, offers healing from spiritual death. Men perishing with spiritual death are asked to believe God's revelation and look in faith to Christ who would be lifted up on a cross and would ultimately ascend to the Father's right hand. The blessed result for believing men would be eternal life. Here then is the way to receive new birth—by entrusting oneself to Christ who died as man's Savior.

The Gospel of John often intersperses the evangelist's comments along with the narrative, and this may be the case beginning at 3:16. Many interpreters feel that the words of Christ end with 3:15.[11] It is noted, for example, that the statement in 3:19, "men loved (ēgapēsan) darkness," sounds more like John was looking back on the situation rather than reporting Jesus' own comment. Jesus would more likely have said, "men love dark-

---

[10]If this questionable reading is genuine, the sense is that even the incarnation did not denude heaven of the Son's presence, for the Son is ever in the bosom of the Father (1:18). Another explanation is that the phrase should be interpreted as the author's parenthetical comment, noting the fact that Christ has now returned to heaven.

[11]Morris, *John*, p. 228; Hoyt, *New Birth*, p. 82; B. F. Westcott, *The Gospel According to St. John* (Grand Rapids, reprinted 1950), p. 54.

ness." On the other hand, some interpreters insist that these are the direct words of Jesus to Nicodemus through 3:21.[12] No change of speaker is indicated in the text. Regardless of which view is taken, the words are part of God's inerrant revelation to men, and thus are equally true whether spoken by Jesus or John.

The basis of this incomparable provision for man's need was the love of God (3:16). He so loved mankind, whom he had created for fellowship with himself, that he provided his unique Son as the substitute to die for sinners. And we must never suppose that Christ was an unwilling victim, for he freely offered himself (Heb. 9:14). The purpose of God's gift of his Son was to bring salvation to men (3:17). Condemnation was not the object, although it is the inevitable result to those who reject him.

The result of the offering of Christ as Savior is shown to be twofold (3:18-19). To those who looked to him in faith as the heaven-sent One who would bear their guilt, the result was removal of all condemnation. The message of God as announced by Jesus provided for cleansing of all sin and impartation of new life by the Spirit (cf. "born of water and the Spirit," 3:5). Thus, believing in Christ is the way to experience the new birth.

On the other hand, unbelief in God's provision leaves one in his former condition of condemnation by God. Such persons have turned away from the gracious offer of God. They have preferred their sinful lives rather than the pure light of righteousness as displayed in Christ.

Why is it that some do not respond to the light provided in Christ (3:20-21)? This question is answered by placing the responsibility upon man's own character. Men reject the light because their character is evil. Those who engage in the practice of evil actually hate the pure light of God's revelation in Christ. The reason is that they do not want their sins exposed.

The picture is not totally black, however, for some come "to the light." These are the ones who are "doing the truth" (*poiōn tēn alētheian*). This statement is commonly explained as though it said, "Those who come to the light do the truth." However, this is not how the text reads. "Doing the truth" is antecedent to

---

[12]Raymond E. Brown, *The Gospel According to John* (i-xii) in The Anchor Bible series (Garden City, 1966), p. 149; William Hendriksen, *Exposition of the Gospel According to John* (Grand Rapids, 1953), pp. 139-145.

"coming to the light," and the interpretation must take this into account. To "do the truth" is to act in accordance with what God has revealed to be the truth. Here it describes the person who accepts God's standard of righteousness and God's estimate of man's sinful condition. Such a person "does the truth" when he responds with appropriate action to God's revelation and accepts the light of the gospel as proclaimed in Christ. By accepting and acting upon God's truth, he comes to the light. It is not indicated, however, that this latter person is intrinsically better that the unbeliever or that he has any reason to boast before God or men. Rather, when he has come to the light in Christ, it is a demonstration that God has been already working in his life, and thus he has been born of God, for "his deeds," that is, his "doing the truth" and "coming to the light," have been "wrought in God." To God belongs all the glory.

II. Further Testimony of John the Baptist (3:22-36)

The concluding portion of the chapter presents the further witness of John the Baptist regarding the person of Christ, his provision for men, and the relative positions of John and Jesus. The passage confirms the previous teaching about the new birth by showing that man's eternal destiny depends upon faith in Christ.

A. The Circumstances (3:22-26)

Jesus left Jerusalem and engaged in a ministry in other portions of Judea. John the Baptist was also preaching in this area. The baptizing which Jesus performed (though his disciples did the actual rite, 4:2) must have been of a type similar to John's. It could not have been Christian baptism in the full sense, for that was not instituted until after the resurrection (Matt. 28:19-20). The growing popularity of Jesus, which was beginning to overshadow that of John (3:26; 4:1), provoked certain questions.

The parallel ministries of John and Jesus are not recounted in the Synoptics. From Mark 1:14 and Matthew 4:12 one might conclude that John was imprisoned immediately after the temptation of Jesus, and that our Lord withdrew at once to Galilee. Only the Gospel of John records this early Judean ministry and the simultaneous preaching of John and Jesus.

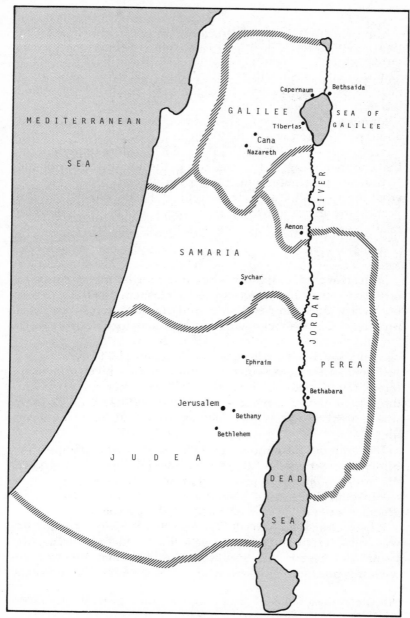

Fig. 8. *New Testament Palestine.*

The exact location of Aenon and Salim cannot be fixed today with certainty. Several sites are proposed by experts in Palestinian geography. Donald J. Wiseman concludes that Tell Sheikh Selim, eight miles south of Bethshan, is the most likely, lying near several springs which might have provided the name "Aenon" (from *'ayin*, "spring").[13]

Manuscript evidence is divided over whether the discussion about purification was with "the Jews" (KJV, P[66] Aleph Theta), or with "a Jew" (ASV, NASB, P[75] A B K L). More important for the understanding of the passage is the identification of the "purification" around which the question revolved. In view of what John's disciples reported to him, it seems likely that the particular purification rite at issue was water baptism, and the relative merits of the baptisms of John and Jesus.

B. *John's Testimony About Himself* (3:27-30)

John answered his followers by explaining his own position in relation to Jesus Christ. As far as John was concerned, there was no rivalry between Jesus and himself. John's position as a prophet of God was acknowledged by him as a gift from heaven. He had no authority to change it in any way. He had earlier denied explicitly that he was the Messiah (1:20). Rather, his position as the forerunner was itself a God-given function, foretold in the Old Testament (Isa. 40:3; Mal. 3:1) and restated in the angelic announcement to John's father (Luke 1:13-17). John was content to occupy the place that God had marked out for him.

The supreme place, however, belonged to Christ. He was the Bridegroom who would claim the bride. John was the friend of the Bridegroom, ready to assist him in any way he could, but destined to decrease in his influence while Jesus, the Bridegroom, would grow in importance to the people.

When John called himself "the friend of the bridegroom," he was using terminology from a well-known custom to make his point. This person was similar to the "best man" in present wedding tradition. In cases where a bride might be forsaken

---

[13]Donald J. Wiseman, "Salim," *New Bible Dictionary*, p. 1125; *The Macmillan Bible Atlas*, ed. Yohanan Aharoni and Michael Avi-Yonah (New York, 1968), p. 227.

before the marriage, ancient Mesopotamian law forbade any marriage between the friend of the bridegroom and the rejected bride.[14] A case in point was Samson and his Philistine fiancee (Judg. 14:1—15:6). Samson was enraged when his best man married the bride who had been pledged to Samson.

C. The Testimony About Christ (3:31-36)

Here is another place where there is uncertainty about the speaker. Are the words of 3:31-36 the continued testimony of John the Baptist (there is no clear indication of a change in speaker), or are they the comment of John the Evangelist as he reflects upon these things many years later? Some have even suggested that they are the words of Jesus, although such a view assumes that the text has been disarranged, a circumstance without any manuscript evidence. Either of the first two explanations is preferable to the third, and the solution is not essential to the interpretation of the passage. Certain similarities between the thoughts here and those of the Evangelist in the Prologue may make the second view slightly more probable (see below).

The explanation is given that Christ alone was capable of expressing perfectly to man the nature of God, the program of God, and the responsibility of all men to God. How tragic that men generally did not recognize the One who came from heaven. ("No man receiveth his testimony" is a generalization similar to 1:11, but is quickly modified in 3:33 to allow exceptions, just as in 1:12.) Yet this failure on man's part did not change the fact that Christ was bringing divine truth, and those comparatively few who did respond have set their seal of approval upon the revelation Christ brought.

Other prophets from ages past had brought segments of God's truth, but their revelation was only partial. This was because the Spirit's power which had come upon them to impart their message was granted them in measured amounts. The Spirit came upon them at stated periods. In the case of Christ, however, God

---

[14]A. van Selms, "Friend of the Bridegroom," *New Bible Dictionary*, p. 441.

"giveth not the Spirit by measure" (3:34).[15] Possessing the Spirit in unmeasured fullness, Christ was equipped to provide the highest revelation of the Father to men (Heb. 1:2).

Not only does Christ have a heavenly origin for his person and his message, but he also is the beloved Son of the Father and possessed a mandate from the Father to perform certain tasks (3:35). The person who responds to the message of Christ is placing himself in the care of one who is uniquely able to bring men into the place of favor before the presence of God.

It is evident, therefore, that the everlasting destiny of men depends upon their relationship to Christ (3:36). Acceptance of Christ brings the new birth with its everlasting life. Rejection, however, leaves the sinner to continue under the wrath of God, which someday will bring eternal destruction.

Questions for Discussion

1. Why did Nicodemus come to Jesus by night?
2. What is meant by being born "of water and of the Spirit"?
3. How does a person today become "born again"?
4. What are the implications of John's statement about "doing the truth"?
5. What is the present condition of persons who do not believe in the Christ as explained in Scripture?

---

[15]No subject is given for the verb "giveth" (*didōsin*, 3:34); hence three possibilities are: 1) God is assumed as the Spirit-giver who gives the Spirit to Christ in unmeasured fullness. This is supported by verse 35. 2) Jesus is the one who gives the Spirit to his disciples. It may be properly questioned, however, whether the unlimited nature of this giving is accurate when applied to the disciples, nor is this idea entirely clear in the context. 3) The Spirit does not make his bestowals by measure. The first view is preferable.

Chapter 4

Early Belief in Samaria and Galilee
(John 4)

This Gospel continues its presentation of the response that Jesus met in various parts of Palestine by moving now to Samaria and Galilee. Chapter 4 contains our Lord's clear teaching regarding his own identity and the gift which he imparts. It also illustrates how his word transcends barriers of prejudice and applies to the need of every person. It teaches the true nature of worship, the importance of even one individual in the eyes of Christ, and the need to view humanity as a harvest needing to be reaped.

I. The Interview with the Woman of Samaria (4:1-42)

A. *The Setting* (4:1-6)

1. *The Departure of Jesus from Judea* (4:1-3)

Several inferences may be drawn from the explanation regarding Jesus' departure. First, Jesus wished to avoid any appearance of rivalry between himself and John the Baptist. When he recognized that his increased popularity was being widely discussed, he withdrew from the scene. John's ministry of preparing the way for Messiah was fully in the plan of God, as was John's subsequent lessening of popularity (3:30). Jesus, therefore, wanted no confusion on this point to arise in the minds of the people. Jesus and John were not vying with each other to see who could achieve the greatest following. They were in a sense partners, not rivals.

Second, Jesus wished to avoid premature hostility against himself. He left when he found that the Pharisees were taking special notice of his actions. These were men from one of the religious parties of the nation. They were the most orthodox group, but because of their hidebound loyalty to their traditions, they became the most implacable enemies of Christ during his ministry. None were as frequently denounced by our Lord as they. (For example, see Luke 11:37-44.) They later became so intense in their opposition that plans were made to capture him at the first opportunity. Jesus did not wish that sort of hostility to develop this early in his ministry.

The baptizing which Jesus authorized[1] was actually performed by his disciples. Perhaps this was done so that none could claim a superior baptism on the grounds that it had been administered directly by Jesus.

2. *The Journey Through Samaria* (4:4-5)

John informs us that Jesus "must needs go through Samaria" (see Fig. 8). Geographically, the most direct route from Judea to Galilee passed through Samaria. Josephus, the first-century Jewish historian, informs us that Jewish pilgrims from Galilee went this way to Jerusalem.[2] Among the more scrupulous, however, it was not the usual route. Because there was such animosity between the Jews and the Samaritans (4:9), Jewish travelers frequently crossed to the east of the Jordan River and journeyed through Perea.

This mutual hatred between Jew and Samaritan was of long standing. It had its roots historically in the captivity of the Northern Kingdom. At that time the Assyrians removed the Jewish inhabitants and repopulated the territory of Samaria with people from other lands (II Kings 17:24 ff.). These people brought their own gods with them, and even though they eventually adopted the God of Israel, their worship was never a pure one. When the Southern Kingdom returned from the Babylonian Captivity nearly two hundred years later, the Jews refused any help from the Samaritans in rebuilding the temple at Jerusalem, and the hatred between the two peoples became intense (Ezra 4). Eventually the Samaritans built their own temple on Mount Gerizim, and had their own form of the Pentateuch.[3]

---

[1]On the nature of this baptism, see comment on 3:22.

[2]Josephus, *Antiquities of the Jews*, Book XX, Section 118 (XX.6.1).

[3]Present-day visitors to Nablus (ancient Shechem) are shown a scroll of the Samaritan Pentateuch, for which a fantastic age is claimed.

Fig. 9. *The presumed village of Sychar on the slopes of Mount Ebal, not far from Jacob's well.* Levant Photo and Design Service

Jesus, however, knew when to disregard tradition and prejudice. The fact that he "needed" to go through Samaria is best explained as Christ's supernatural knowledge that he had a spiritual ministry to perform in this oft-avoided region. He arrived at a place which was historically connected with the Old Testament figures Jacob and Joseph. The site was originally bought by Jacob and was given to Joseph, who was buried there (Gen. 33:18-19; 48:22; Josh. 24:32). Today the site of Sychar (mentioned only here in Scripture) is most likely to be identified with the village 'Askar, about half a mile from Jacob's well on the eastern slope of Mount Ebal. Efforts to identify Sychar with Shechem are confronted with the problem that Shechem was apparently not occupied in New Testament times.[4]

3. *The Resting at the Well* (4:6)

This well shaft still exists and may be visited by travelers. When Jesus arrived after a day of journeying through the hilly country of Samaria, it was evening (6:00 P.M., Roman time[5]), and he took the occasion to rest. This was the time of day when the women normally came to draw water (Gen. 24:11). Notice that the deity of Christ did not interfere with the normal characteristics of true humanity. Though possessing omnipotence as an attribute of his deity, Christ voluntarily laid aside the use of such attributes except for those occasions when it was specifically the Father's plan. His fatigue, therefore, was not an "act" but was a genuine condition.

B. *The Interview* (4:7-26)

1. *The Gift of God* (4:7-14)

A woman of Samaria[6] came with her waterpot to obtain water from the well, and Jesus established a point of contact with her

---

[4]*The Wycliffe Historical Geography of Bible Lands,* ed. Charles F. Pfeiffer and Howard F. Vos (Chicago, 1967), p. 142.

[5]For a discussion of John's mention of time, see comments on 1:39; 4:52; and 19:14.

[6]"Of Samaria" (*ek tēs Samareias*) must refer to the territory of Samaria, not the city of that name which was too far away and was called Sebaste at that time.

Fig. 10. *A spring of "living water." In contrast to a well or cistern which collects water, this flowing stream comes out of the ground from springs at Tel Dan, and is one of the sources of the Jordan River.*

by requesting a drink (4:7-9). He was alone with her because the disciples had gone to the village to obtain provisions. Our Lord's approach to the woman was a natural one, designed to lead easily into the subject and avoid abruptness and embarrassment. It also was an approach which provided for further discussion, and this is precisely what Jesus wanted. The thought that a Jewish man would deign to speak with a Samaritan, and a woman at that, was somewhat surprising to her and she was disposed to ask about it.

The observation that Jews "have no dealings with Samaritans" should perhaps be understood as "do not use [vessels] together with Samaritans."[7] This rendering suits the context better, for the disciples had obviously gone to a Samaritan village to have business dealings with some Samaritan merchants.

To this Samaritan woman Jesus announced the gift of God which was available to her (4:10). Actually he spoke of two gifts. The first was the "gift of God." We should notice that the "living water" is not said to be the gift of God (i.e., the Father) but is a gift which Christ would bestow. We would do well to translate 4:10 as follows: "If thou knewest the gift of God, even who it is that saith to thee. . . ." Thus the gift of God is Christ himself, whom the Father sent into the world (3:16). If the woman had known the true identity of Jesus, she would have come in faith to him.

The second phase of this gift is what Jesus would give. "Thou wouldest have asked of him, and he would have given thee living water." What is this "living water" which Jesus offered to her? When received, this water would refresh the thirsty soul and issue in eternal life. In 3:5 "water" was used as a symbol of God's word. In 7:37-39, where Jesus makes almost the same announcement, the "living water" is identified as the Holy Spirit. It seems probable, therefore, that as Jesus talked with the woman, he meant the following: "If you recognized who I am, you would accept my words as the word of God. Receiving by faith this word, you would find it made vital in your life by the action of the Spirit, and eternal life would be your possession."

[7]See the article by David Daube, "Jesus and the Samaritan Woman: the Meaning of *sunchraomai*," *Journal of Biblical Literature*, Vol. LXIX, Part II (June 1950), pp. 137-147.

At first the woman did not seem to be impressed (4:11-12). If Jesus could not even draw water from the well at hand, how could he be such an expert on water and wells that he could provide a better well than that of Jacob, a well that provided enough water for his cattle as well as his family. By referring to "living water," Jesus was deliberately using an expression which might be interpreted several ways, just as when he spoke of the "temple" in 2:19, and of being "born again" in 3:3. Living water could refer to a bubbling spring in contrast to water collected in a cistern or well.

The answer to the woman's question was that Jesus was not speaking of physical water at all, but of a spiritual gift which would provide a perpetual inner source of refreshment (4:13-14). This gift which Christ offered was his word which, when received by faith and empowered by the Spirit, would result in all the blessings of eternal life.

2. *The Woman's Need* (4:14-18)

Addressing Jesus as *kurie*, a word which may mean either "Lord" or "sir" (and at this stage in the encounter she probably meant the latter), the woman respectfully asked for a supply of the water which Jesus had mentioned. She was still thinking in terms of physical needs, and hoped to spare herself the long daily trip to the well. In a larger sense her whole life to this point had been a seeking of temporal and emotional satisfaction by yielding to physical impulse.

Jesus countered by asking her to call her husband. This request was not a changing of the subject nor a comment unrelated to the context. Our Lord was causing her to face the issue of her own spiritual need. He knew about her tangled domestic life. Her reply that she had no husband was honest as far as it went, but Jesus amazed her by revealing his supernatural awareness of her situation. She had been married five times, and now was living with a man without even the formality of marriage. The previous marriages could conceivably have been legitimate, each one following the death of the former spouse. The tenor of the passage, however, makes it more probable that she had been involved in at least several divorces.

There is no need to find some hidden meaning in the "five" husbands. To allegorize these "five" as a reference to the five cities from which the original Samaritan colonists were brought (II Kings 17:24), and then to identify them with five pagan gods which were brought with the colonists (II Kings 17:29-41), is totally foreign to the straightforward prose style employed here.[8]

3. The Problem of Worship (4:19-24)

The woman's exclamation, "Thou art a prophet," was an admission that Christ's description of her life was correct and probably supernaturally revealed. She then raised a problem, which was perhaps partly an attempt to divert the discussion to less personal channels. (How often the human heart does this, rather than face squarely the issue of sin and its solution.) However, this problem regarding worship did present real difficulties. If Jesus should insist that she acknowledge fully the God of the Old Testament, accept the Jewish Scriptures, and observe the sacrificial ritual, she could counter with the excuse, "You Jews won't let us Samaritans worship at your temple in Jerusalem."

"This mountain" is a reference to Mount Gerizim, upon which the Samaritans had erected their own temple because of Jewish refusal of their offers to participate in the rebuilding and worship at the temple in Jerusalem during the days of Ezra and Nehemiah.[9] The Samaritan temple was destroyed by John Hyrcanus in 129/128 B.C. during the Maccabean Period.[10] Thus it had been demolished more than a century and a half before Jesus met the Samaritans.[11] Josephus says the temple resembled the one at Jerusalem.[12]

---

[8]This view, however, is regarded as plausible by C. K. Barrett, The Gospel According to St. John (London, 1967), p. 197, although the literal interpretation is more widely held.

[9]Ezra 4:1-2; Neh. 4:1-2; Josephus Antiquities, Book XI, Sections 322-324 (XI.8.4.).

[10]Josephus, Antiquities, Book XIII, Section 255 (XIII.9.1).

[11]The Samaritan Pentateuch has the name "Gerizim" rather than "Ebal" at Deut. 27:4. The variant may have been an attempt to provide Scriptural sanction for their temple (cf. Deut. 27:1-7).

[12]Josephus, Antiquities, Book XIII, Section 256 (XIII.9.1).

Fig. 11. *Mount Gerizim.* Levant Photo and Design Service

Jesus answered the woman's question by going to its heart. He showed that worship itself is the essential thing. The place is secondary and of temporary significance (4:21). Though the Old Testament economy had specified certain geographical locations (Deut. 12:5; II Chron. 6:6; 7:12; Ps. 78:67-68), that era was about to be superseded. The reason is that God himself is spirit, and hence true worship is an act of the spirit (4:24). Dependence on ritual or physical environment to produce genuine worship of God is erroneous. The presence of Christ on earth made more direct worship possible (4:23). He was the highest and most complete revelation of the Father (Heb. 1:2). He is the image of the invisible God (Col. 1:15) and the One in whom we see the Father (John 1:18; 14:9). Thus Jesus could say to the woman: "The time now is."

Our Lord, however, did not avoid the question of Jew versus Samaritan. He told her that the salvation which men need was contained in Jewish Scriptures (4:22). The Samaritans as a religious group were wrong. But by his discussion Jesus showed that the problem was more basic than mere national tradition. It was a matter of recognizing God's truth and worshiping God with our spirits.

4. The Identity of Messiah (4:25-26)

The woman had just been given some most thought-provoking truths. She had listened intently, following his words, raising certain problems, but accepting his answers. One additional problem remained for her. She believed in a coming Messiah, but she did not know who he was. The Samaritans believed in a Messianic figure whom they called Taheb ("Restorer"). T. H. Gaster explains:

> The Taheb is not a messiah in the Jewish sense of an anointed prince. Rather is he the prophet foretold in Deut. 18:18—the eschatological guide and monitor mentioned also in the Dead Sea Manual of Discipline (9.11). . . . Known also as the Star, in accordance with Num. 24:17 . . . the Taheb will restore the temple on Gerizim, reinstitute the sacrificial cult, and obtain the recognition of the heathen.[13]

The woman thus had some background for the revelation Jesus was about to give. She did not yet, of course, know who Jesus was, nor the full import of Messiah as the Son of God.

To her Jesus made the categorical statement: "I that speak unto thee am he." Now she could understand the meaning of his words. This person who stood before her was the gift of God, the Messiah himself. He was qualified to offer this boon of living water. She need not defer until some far-distant future the solution of her spiritual needs. The Messiah was now present!

It is interesting to note that Jesus revealed himself to the woman of Samaria more specifically than he had to any other person up to this time. Others had recognized in Jesus their Messiah (1:41). But at least as far as the Gospels inform us, Jesus had not told them in so many words. But to this thirsting soul, Jesus precisely identified himself as the prophesied Messiah.

[13]T. H. Gaster, "Samaritans," The Interpreter's Dictionary of the Bible, ed. George Arthur Buttrick (New York, 1962), Vol R-Z, p. 194.

C. The Results (4:27-42)

1. To the Woman (4:27-30)

The woman continued to be the object of our Lord's conversation (imperfect tense *elalei*, "continued speaking"), and this feature amazed the disciples when they returned. They were more startled that Jesus would converse with a woman than the fact that she was a Samaritan. Jewish rabbis would not have done so in public, except in extreme circumstances. Rabbinical writings contain such statements as the following:

> Jose ben Jochanan of Jerusalem said, Let thy house be opened wide; and let the needy by thy household; and prolong not converse with woman. [14]

> R. Jose the Galilean was travelling on the road. He met Brurih (the wife of R. Meir) and asked her: "Which way must we take to the city of Lud?" She answered: "Thou Galilean fool! Did not our sages say, that thou shouldest not converse much with a woman? Thou shouldest have asked, Which way to Lud?" [15]

This remarkable interview so deeply impressed the woman that she left her waterpot behind and returned to the city. [16] The problem of drawing physical water now seemed not nearly so important. The spiritual satisfaction which she had found available in Christ eclipsed temporal concerns. She was particularly absorbed in the fact that Jesus knew all about her past and yet offered to her the blessings of "living water" (4:29). Though shunned, no doubt, by the respectable society of her day, she had met the Messiah and he had offered her eternal life through faith in his word.

The woman immediately wanted to give testimony to others of what she had found. But she did so with utmost tact. It would have been unseemly, presumptuous, and probably ineffective for this woman to attempt to teach the

[14]*Pirqe Aboth* 1.5 in Charles Taylor, *Sayings of the Jewish Fathers* (New York, 1969), p. 15.

[15]"Tract Erubin," *Babylonian Talmud*, ed. and trans. Michael L. Rodkinson (Boston, 1918), III, 121.

[16]It is possible that the woman deliberately left the waterpot behind for Jesus' use, expecting to retrieve it when she returned with the others from the city. See William Hendriksen, *The Gospel According to John* (Grand Rapids, 1954), pp. 171-172; Barrett, *John*, p. 201.

men of the city regarding spiritual truth. Her background hardly qualified her to speak with authority on religious and spiritual matters. Therefore, her statement to them was phrased in a deliberately cautious way so as not to arouse antagonism, and yet it suggested that they ought to see Jesus for themselves. She actually said: "Come, see a man who told me all things which I did. This man can't be the Messiah, can he?"[17] Their curiosity was stimulated and they proceeded to seek him out.

2. *To the Disciples* (4:31-38)

When the disciples returned from the village with their provisions (4:8), they naturally expected Jesus to eat. They were about to learn, however, the importance of spiritual values over physical ones (4:31-34). Jesus was willing to forego physical refreshment in order to perform a spiritual ministry. The doing of God's will was actually a satisfaction and nourishment to his own soul (Job 23:12).

The disciples were also taught to recognize the need of immediate harvest (4:35-38). As companions of Jesus they had been primarily engaged in a ministry of spiritual seed sowing. Yet they were taught by Jesus that they should also be sensitive to the harvest all around them. They need not wait until their own sowing matured. John the Baptist, the Scriptures, the working of God in providence as it illuminated the Scriptures, and even the conversation of Jesus with the woman during their absence—all of these factors and others had been sowing the seed of the Word of God. There were hearts even in their day which were ready to respond.

If the statement, "There are yet four months and then cometh harvest," is a proverb, then it merely points up the usual interval between sowing and harvesting, and offers no assistance for dating this incident. Although no other instance of this "proverb" has been found, it is sometimes suggested that the interval between the *end* of sowing and

---

[17]Her question used *mēti*, rather than *ou*, thus indicating a negative answer expected. To have phrased it otherwise would have doubtless aroused immediate opposition to such a bold assertion.

the *beginning* of harvest is about four months.[18] Absence of clear proof that it was a proverb, along with the fact that the normal growing season in Palestine was more like six months,[19] leads most interpreters to regard the statement as an indication that harvest season (April) was literally four months away, and thus the time of the incident was December.

3. *To the Samaritans* (4:39-42)

The testimony of the woman who had learned of Christ by personal interview resulted in faith on the part of many Samaritans. How often a radically changed life is particularly effective in bringing others to Christ. When Jesus himself ministered in the city, many more believed. Their faith now was dependent not on the testimony of another, but upon their own personal experience with Jesus.

These two days in the Samaritan village of Sychar did not, of course, accomplish the evangelization of all Samaria. Later in his ministry Christ instructed his disciples not to minister in this province (Matt. 10:5), and he himself encountered ill will there (Luke 9:52-53).

II. The Healing of the Nobleman's Son in Galilee (4:43-54)

A. *The General Situation* (4:43-45)

With his arrival in Galilee after the two days in Samaria, Jesus had now visited three major sections of the Jewish homeland. The reason for this itinerary of Jesus is given in the proverb, "A prophet hath no honor in his own country." This explanation has raised its own problems. What did Jesus regard as his own country? Once this is settled, how does this give the reason for Jesus' entering Galilee? Some have identified Jesus' own country as Judea, the place of his birth, explaining the lack of proper reception at Jerusalem as

---

[18]Barrett, *John,* pp. 201-202.

[19]Henri Daniel-Rops, *Daily Life in Palestine at the Time of Christ* (London, 1961), p. 233.

the reason for his return to Galilee.[20] However, 4:1-3 indicates that Jesus left Judea precisely because of too much popularity (superficial though it was). Much more likely is the view that Galilee is his own country.[21] This is consistent with all the uses of this proverb in the Synoptics (Matt. 13:57; Mark 6:4; Luke 4:24), two of which use it of Galilee generally, and one of Nazareth in particular.

Why, then, did Jesus enter Galilee if he could expect no honor there? A number of factors need to be included in the explanation. There had been too much superficial popularity in Judea (2:23-25; 4:1-3), but Jesus knew it would not be this way in Galilee. It has also been suggested that Jesus needed to build an initial reputation elsewhere before returning to Galilee where "familiarity breeds contempt,"[22] and it is true that Christ's reputation from Jerusalem did precede him and drew the crowds to him (4:45). Even more important, however, is the fact that by coming to Galilee Jesus would avoid the sort of "honor" which would provoke a premature confrontation with the Pharisees.[23]

B. A Miracle and the Growth of Faith (4:46-54)

1. Faith Based on Signs and Wonders (4:46-48)

Jesus began his Galilean ministry at Cana, where he was already known favorably because of the miraculous changing of water into wine (2:1-11). Here Jesus met a nobleman (*basilikos*, king's officer). The man was most likely a Jew, and may have been at Jerusalem for Passover when Jesus was (at least he is included among those who had seen signs and wonders, 4:48). He was probably in the service of Herod Antipas, the tetrarch of Galilee, who is called "king" in the New Testament (Matt. 14:9; Mark 6:14, 22).

[20]B. F. Westcott, *The Gospel According to St. John* (Grand Rapids, reprinted 1950), pp. 77-78; Barrett, *John*, p. 205.

[21]Hendriksen, *John*, pp. 178-180; R. E. Brown, *The Gospel According to John* (I-XII), in The Anchor Bible series (Garden City, 1966), pp. 186-187.

[22]R. C. H. Lenski, *The Interpretation of St. John's Gospel* (Columbus, 1942), pp. 343-344.

[23]Hendriksen, *John* pp. 179-180.

The faith in Jesus which brought the nobleman to seek our Lord's assistance was on the surface commendable. Yet Jesus appeared to disparage it with the words addressed to the man and the rest of the crowd, "Except ye see signs and wonders, ye will not believe." Jesus knew that faith based only on seeing miraculous deeds is superficial and requires a succession of miracles to nourish it (2:23-25). Those who followed him because of miracles alone soon drifted away (6:26, 66). Even in the case of the nobleman, at least two limitations in his faith can be noted: he thought Jesus must be bodily present in order to heal, and he thought Jesus could heal but not raise the dead.

2. *Faith Based on the Word of Jesus* (4:49-50)

The nobleman again asked Jesus to accompany him to Capernaum before the lad should die. Jesus, however, wanted this man to learn that there was a higher basis for faith than merely watching him perform a miracle. He gave the man his word, "Your son lives,"[24] with no further tangible signs. Nevertheless the man believed the simple promise of Jesus and acted upon it. He did not get precisely what he had asked for (*ie,* Jesus did not "come down" with him), but he believed the word regardless.

3. *Faith Placed in Jesus Himself* (4:51-54)

As the Gospel describes the scene, the nobleman's servants greeted his return with the very words which Jesus had uttered the day before. Inquiry revealed that the turn for the better occurred at 7:00 P.M.[25] the previous evening, the very time when Jesus had given his word.

As a consequence, the nobleman and all his household "believed" (*episteusen*). Certainly more is meant than simply that they believed Jesus' statement or accepted the miracle.

---

[24]The verb *zaō* ("live") can have the sense of "recover" when used of sick persons. See Mark 5:23.

[25]The "seventh hour" Roman time was 7:00 P.M. If Jewish reckoning were used, the time would have been 1:00 P.M., but if that were the case, one would have expected the nobleman to have returned home the same day. For more discussion of John's references to hours of the day, see 1:39; 4:6; and 19:14.

The former had already been believed (4:50), and the latter was now a matter of sight, not faith. The sense is that they became believers and followers of Jesus. Henceforth they would not need miracles, nor even statements from Jesus on every matter. They could trust Jesus himself. Such a faith looks to Christ for guidance, accepts without question everything our Lord has revealed, and leaves to him those things which we do not understand.

John notes that this was the second "sign" (*sēmeion*) which Jesus performed after coming to Galilee from Judea. It was not the second miracle in our Lord's career, for John has noted many others as occurring in Jerusalem (2:23; 3:2). It was the second one to be performed in Galilee, and in both of them Jesus was at Cana (2:1; 4:46) after coming from Judea (1:43; 4:43).

Questions for Discussion

1. Why did Jesus leave Judea at the time he did?
2. How does one worship God "in spirit and in truth"? What other ways are sometimes attempted?
3. What did Jesus mean when he spoke of "living water"?
4. What did Jesus' action with the Samaritan woman reveal about (a) social prejudice? (b) principles of personal witnessing?
5. Why is a prophet without honor in his own country?
6. What was Jesus' "own country"?
7. What stages of faith were exhibited by the nobleman?

Chapter 5

The Growth of Unbelief
(John 5)

At this point in John's narrative, the author begins tracing the growth of unbelief in relation to Christ's presentation of himself. In each remaining chapter of this section dealing with the public ministry, there is a direct mention of unbelief among the hearers of Jesus' teaching (5:38; 6:36; 7:47-48; 8:59; 9:22; 10:31; 11:53; 12:37). This unbelief is centered around three miracles, those of chapters 5, 9, and 11.

I. The Miracle at the Pool (5:1-9)

A. *The Setting of the Miracle* (5:1-5)

The time is set at "a feast of the Jews," but the feast is not otherwise identified (5:1). Although many manuscripts include the article, "the feast,"[1] most of our oldest sources omit it.[2] Even the presence of the article would not settle the identification, however, inasmuch as both Passover and Tabernacles are used with the article in 6:4 and 7:2, and Passover is used without the article in Matthew 27:15 (Mark 15:6). It may be implied that it was the occurrence of the feast which brought Jesus to Jerusalem, and this would point to Passover, Pentecost, or Tabernacles, the three feasts of the year which required attendance at Jerusalem. This would rule out Purim and Trumpets. Some have suggested that chapters 5 and 6 have been transposed,[3] and that this feast refers to the Passover of 6:4, but there is no manuscript support for such a view. If 5:1 is Passover, it must be the year following the Passover of 2:13 and prior to the Passover of 6:4. If it is Pentecost or Tabernacles, it would be in A.D. 28 following an unmentioned Passover.

[1] Aleph C L X and the Byzantine text-type.

[2] P66, 75 A B D K W Theta.

[3] J. N. Sanders, "John, Gospel of," *The Interpreter's Dictionary of the Bible* (New York, 1962), E-J, 935.

The place of the miracle was by a pool having five porches and called Bethesda. There is also some textual confusion about this statement. The word "pool" can be read in the uncial manuscripts as either a nominative ("there is by the sheep [gate or market] a pool which is called . . .") or a dative ("there is by the sheep pool a [place] which is called . . ."). Furthermore, the name appears variously among the manuscripts as Bethzatha, Belzetha, Bethsaida, or Bethesda.

Today the commonest identification of the site in Jerusalem is in the northeast part of the Old City beside the Church of St. Anne. This would be in the vicinity of the Sheep Gate mentioned by Nehemiah (3:1; 12:39). Confirmation for the name Bethesda comes from the Copper Scroll from Qumran which contains the words: "At Bet Eshdatayin, in the pool at the entrance to its smaller basin. . . ."[4] The dual form probably indicates the twin basins. Jack Finegan accounts for the name Bethzatha as a corruption when the Hebrew dual form was reproduced in Aramaic by the feminine plural and then transcribed into Greek.[5] Excavations reveal two large pools separated by a stone partition. Presently much of the construction is covered by other buildings. The five porches were apparently along the four sides and on the dividing partition (see Fig. 12).

The multitude present at the scene consisted of a variety of sick folk (5:3a). They had gathered at this spot because of the curative value which they felt was possessed by these waters.

The final phrase of 5:3 and all of 5:4 are textually doubtful.[6] In the light of 5:7, it may be that the disputed verses do represent the popular opinion regarding the pool and entered the text as a scribal gloss, but there is serious question that they ever formed a part of the original text. If the words are omitted, there is no Biblical statement that an angel actually stirred the waters (although there is no reason why such could not have occurred).

[4]Raymond E. Brown, *The Gospel According to John* in The Anchor Bible series (Garden City, 1966), Vol. 29, pp. 206, 207.

[5]Jack Finegan, *The Archaeology of the New Testament* (Princeton, 1969), pp. 142-147.

[6]Omitted in P66, 75 Aleph B C L. D includes the questionable portion of vs. 3, but omits all of vs. 4.

Fig. 12. *The Pool of Bethesda (model).*

Fig. 13. *Excavations at the Pool of Bethesda.* Levant Photo and Design

The phenomenon could have been due to bubbling springs.

The man who received Christ's miraculous ministration was an adult who had been an invalid for thirty-eight years (5:5). Being incapacitated for so long, he may have been well known in the community and was an ideal person for the miracle to have the greatest impact.

B. The Performance of the Miracle (5:6-9)

Jesus began with a simple question which can be rendered literally, "Do you want to become healthy?" (5:6) The answer would seem to be obvious, for that was ostensibly the reason for the man's being there. Furthermore, Jesus was aware that the man was accustomed to being at the pool, so that it would seem that the desire for healing would have been the consuming passion of the poor victim. The question served to focus attention upon the man's need, and also to reveal something about his hopeless condition as indicated by the response he made.

The discouraged answer from the man blamed others for his condition, and repeated the popular opinion about the bubbling waters (5:7). Insofar as his own resources were concerned, he was helpless and hopeless. He could not quickly enter the pool by himself, and when the waters were agitated no one would give up his own opportunity to help someone else. Apparently these people had cause to believe that the curative value of these waters extended only to the first person to enter the pool. Thus the man was reduced to whining complaint. If he were to be healed, it would not be because of his own strong faith in Jesus, for he seems to display none at all. In fact, he didn't even know who Jesus was (5:13).

The Lord's command, "Rise, take up thy bed, and walk," actually said nothing about a miracle, but was based upon the fact that a miracle was simultaneously occurring (5:8). The man could not have followed these instructions unless the healing had taken place. The utter simplicity of Jesus' ministration reminds us of his majesty and power. There was no need to plead for divine aid. He needed but to speak and it was done. From one standpoint, Jesus asked the man to do what was impossible. At the same time, it must be obvious that Christ did not require him to act without furnishing him the power when it was needed.

The obedience of the man to the command of Jesus demonstrated the completeness of the miracle (5:9). He was not only healed from his longstanding weakness, but he was also granted complete muscular coordination. He did not need any sort of therapy to strengthen unused muscles. When Jesus healed him, the restoration was total.

The narrative notes that this healing occurred on a sabbath day. A literal rendering of the statement ("and there was a sabbath on that day") suggests that it was not the regular weekly sabbath, but a feast day (5:1), certain of which were treated as sabbaths regardless of the day of the week on which they happened to fall. Passover and Unleavened Bread (Lev. 23:5-7), Pentecost (Lev. 23:16-21), Trumpets (Lev. 23:24), Atonement (Lev. 23:27-32), and Tabernacles (Lev. 23:34-39) were all to be regarded as sabbaths.

It should not be supposed that Jesus had forgotten what day it was, nor should it be regretted that "unnecessary" trouble arose because the miracle was performed on that day rather than on the day before or the day following. Surely our Lord, who knew all about the man's circumstances without having to ask him (5:5) also knew what day it was. We must rather understand that Jesus chose this day to cause men to see the sabbath in proper perspective (see Mark 2:23-28).

II. The Opposition from the Jews (5:10-18)

A. The Charge of Sabbath Violation (5:10-16)

Because the miracle had been performed on a sabbath, the occasion was provided for criticism of Jesus. The charge was leveled first against the healed man (5:10-14). "The Jews" is a reference to the religious authorities, who in this instance may have been Pharisees.[7] Seeing the man carrying his bed mat, they reminded him of his violation of rabbinical law (5:10). The Scriptural basis for these regulations was found in Exodus 20:8-11, Jeremiah 17:21, and Nehemiah 13:15. The rabbinical tract "Shabbat" lists forty less one acts of labor that are forbidden on the sabbath, and the last one is "transferring from one place to

[7]See footnote 1 in chapter 2 (on 1:19).

another."[8] Another regulation stated: "If he carried a person on a litter he is not culpable even of (carrying) the litter, because the litter is of no consequence to the person."[9] This last regulation implies that if the litter alone were carried, the act would be a sabbath violation. However, it should be noted that the Jeremiah and Nehemiah passages are inveighing against doing business on the sabbath, not such personal matters as carrying one's bed roll.

The man's excuse for his action was that his healer had told him to carry his bed (5:11). Even though he did not yet know his benefactor, he felt that the ability to heal should have constituted some sort of authority.

In all likelihood this was only Jesus' second visit to Jerusalem since beginning his ministry, and thus he would not have been immediately recognized by everyone. Furthermore, the crowds around the pool had apparently prevented Jesus from accomplishing any spiritual work with the man, so the Lord had slipped away (5:12-13). The Jews' question, "What man is that which said unto thee, Take up thy bed, and walk?" is enlightening as to their sense of values. They seemed to ignore utterly the healing which had occurred, and concentrated solely on the supposed sabbath violation.

At some unspecified later time, Jesus found the man in the temple (5:14). Perhaps he had gone there to give thanks to God and to make an offering. The Lord's words, "Continue sinning no longer (*mēketi hamartane*) lest a worse thing happen to you," imply at least that his physical ailment had been the result of sin in his life. This is by no means always the immediate cause of calamities, as Jesus himself declared on another occasion (9:2-3), but at times it may be so. Alcoholism, narcotics addiction, and sexual promiscuity are just a few examples of sins which often carry their own physical penalties.

The charge of sabbath breaking was next made against Jesus when the man informed the authorities of the identity of his benefactor (5:15-16). Certainly the man was not a malicious in-

---

[8]"Tract Sabbath," *Babylonian Talmud,* ed. Michael L. Rodkinson (Boston, 1918), I, 135-136.

[9]*Ibid.,* p. 177.

former. He may have been required to report to the authorities who his healer was in order to verify his own explanation that he had not carried his bed on the sabbath without due cause. This example of violation of rabbinical regulations by Jesus produced murderous hatred against him among the leaders, and helps explain why Jesus avoided Jerusalem during the next few years except for brief visits (7:1).

B. *The Charge of Blasphemy* (5:17-18)

Jesus explained his action on the sabbath as being consistent with the sabbath rest of God the Father. Even though the Father has enjoyed a sabbath rest ever since finishing the work of creation (Gen. 2:2-3; Heb. 4:1, 3-5), he is still engaged in doing good for men. Works of mercy are in accord with true sabbath practice, for the sabbath was made for man's benefit (Mark 2:27). When Jesus healed the man on the sabbath and instructed him to remove his bed from the porch of Bethesda, he was employing the sabbath in a perfectly legitimate way.

This explanation did not quiet the Jews. They pounced upon Jesus' words "My Father," and understood that he was claiming a unique relationship to God. They believed him to be saying that God was "his own father" (*patera idion*), and this was an assertion of equality with God. If this had been a mistaken inference by the Jews, Jesus could (and should) have corrected them at once. That he did not indicates that their understanding of his words was correct (although their rejection of his divine person made the conclusion of blasphemy they drew a false one). Thus the charge of blasphemy was added to the accusation of sabbath violation, and these two charges became the basis of the conflict against Jesus.

III. The Explanation by Jesus (5:19-47)

A. *The Son and the Father* (5:19-23)

Here Jesus gives an extended explanation of the tremendous claim he had just made. He first asserted an equality of action between himself as the divine Son and the Father in heaven (5:19-22). He made it clear that his claim of equality (5:17-18) did not in any sense imply rivalry or independent action. On the contrary, because the Son and the Father share the same nature, they share also the same purposes. By his very nature as holy God, the Son is unable to act in contradiction to his Father.

Nor is this submission to the Father's will an arbitrary or forced arrangement (5:20). It is based upon the fact that the Father loves (*philei*)[10] the Son and joyfully bestows upon him the knowledge of his plans and works so that the Son might reveal them to men. This included not only the miraculous work of healing just performed upon the man at the pool, but even greater works that would be displayed to men in due time.

As examples of the works greater than healing of physical ailments, Jesus claimed that the Father has shared with the Son the prerogatives of raising the dead and of executing divine judgment (5:21-22). It may be questioned whether 5:21 refers to the eschatological resurrection of the physically dead, or to the spiritual quickening of people by regeneration. Both kinds of resurrection are mentioned later in this passage (5:25, 28). Perhaps the statement was made purposely broad to cover both concepts, especially since they are not unrelated. The executing of divine judgment has been bestowed by the Father upon the Son, not in the sense that the Father has abandoned all participation in it (Dan. 7:9-14), but with the sense that the Father works through the Son.

These prerogatives which the Father has shared with the Son are intended to insure that the Son may share equally in the honor which men bestow upon the Father (5:23). Any words of praise made to God which ignore the revelation which the Father made through his Son are not truly honoring to God at all. To reject the Son is to dishonor the Father who sent his Beloved. It is not enough to believe in a Supreme Being if at the same time one refuses to acknowledge the command which He has given to men to receive his Son (6:28-29).

This explanation by Jesus to his hostile audience should have made it clear that he truly was claiming equality with God (5:17-18). However, this claim, stupendous though it was, was

---

[10]This is the only NT instance where *phileō* is used of the Father's love for the Son. The use of *agapaō* is more common (3:35; 10:17; 15:9; 17:23, 24, 26). On the assumption that the two verbs are to be distinguished in meaning, *phileō* emphasizes affection arising out of relationship.

not blasphemy, for it could properly be made by the Messianic Son who shared in a unique sense the nature of the Father.

B. The Son and Men (5:24-30)

This portion of the discussion not only provides information but is an implicit invitation to men to avail themselves of all that Jesus provides.

The first part speaks of the present (5:24-26). Those who listen to Christ's message, and heed it because they have believed that God has authorized him, receive eternal life and will not face a condemnatory divine judgment. If it be asked how one who is spiritually dead can hear and heed Christ's message, the answer can be found in the analogy with the physical situation of the impotent man at the pool. He could obey the words of Christ to rise and take up his bed roll only because the one who spoke the message also provided the enablement. In like manner Christ's message provides the power. The gospel is the power of God unto salvation (Rom. 1:16). Jesus not only shows the way to eternal life, he *is* the way (14:6).

Although 5:25 is similar to 5:28, the inclusion of the phrase "and now is," along with the absence of the mention of graves, makes it clear that regeneration is in view in 5:25, rather than physical resurrection. At present Christ is calling men from spiritual death (separation from God) into a condition of spiritual life (sharing of God's life forever) on the basis of trust in Christ's work on their behalf. The apostle Paul used similar terminology to describe regeneration as he wrote: "And you hath he quickened (*sunezōopoiēsen*), who were dead in trespasses and sins" (Eph. 2:1).

It must not be supposed, however, that Christ was a mere prophet who announced God's intention. He is the divine Son who has eternal life inherent in himself, and this was true even when he became man. Thus he can bestow it upon all whom he wishes (5:26, cf. vs. 21).

Jesus next spoke of his relation to men in the future (5:27-30). The actual execution of judgment was not a part of his earthly ministry (3:17), but it will be performed by him ultimately. The reason given is because Jesus is "Son of Man" (*huios anthrōpou*). Absence of the article before this expression leads some to stress the qualitative sense, and conclude that it is his humanness that is being emphasized: "because he is man." However, there must certainly be more involved than this, for humanity alone is hardly a sufficient qualification for one to act as judge. It is therefore more probable that the expression is to be regarded as an official title of Messiah (based perhaps on Daniel 7:13) and thus not requiring an article. It was because Jesus was the Messianic Son of Man that he was appointed to this task by the Father.

The judgment here in view must await the resurrection (5:28-29). As noted previously, the mention of the graves, as well as omission of the words "and now is," distinguishes this reference from the regeneration of 5:25. Nevertheless, Christ will also call the physically dead from their graves, just as he brings regeneration to the living who trust him. Both the righteous dead and the wicked dead will be resurrected by the voice of Christ, the righteous to enter fully into the bliss of eternity with glorified bodies, and the wicked to hear their doom pronounced.[11] Yet in no sense is the Son acting out of harmony with the will of the Father (5:30). Thus when Jesus was denounced for any of his actions (such as at the pool of Bethesda, 5:18), his critics were in reality opposing God.

C. The Son and the Witnesses (5:31-47)

1. John the Baptist (5:31-35)

To claim equality with God is an astounding assertion, and on the lips of anyone else it would be blasphemy. Christ, therefore, brought forth witnesses to support his claim. His statement, "If I bear witness of myself, my witness is not true" (5:31), is paradoxical in the light of 8:14. Numerous explanations have been offered. It seems best to regard the reference as meaning legal validity[12] (i.e., self-testimony without supporting witnesses is not legally valid) or else to regard it as qualified in some fashion

---

[11] Although this passage has been used to teach a general resurrection of all men at the same time, it actually states only the fact that all will be raised, without specifying whether there may be various stages by which resurrection will occur. One should consult Rev. 20:4-6 for a description of the phases of resurrection.

[12] So R. E. Brown, *John*, pp. 223-224.

as the following: "not true in your estimation because you would claim it was biased."[13]

Jesus then pointed to "another" (allos) who bears witness to him (5:32), but he did not at this time identify this witness. That it was not John the Baptist seems clear from the flow of thought in the verses immediately following.[14] Jesus accepts the testimony of this allos (5:32), but asserts that it was not from man (5:34). Apparently then, allos refers to the Father who is subsequently discussed in 5:37-38.

Nevertheless, John the Baptist did bear witness to the truth of Jesus' identity (1:26-27, 29-34, 36), and thus he did provide support for Jesus' claim (5:33). Our Lord had a greater witness than John and did not rest his claims upon John's authorization, but because many of his hearers had listened to John and had been caught up for a time in the enthusiasm and impact of John's ministry, Jesus mentioned him in the hope that some at least might come fully to the light and be saved (5:34-35). John had been a good witness. He had acted as a lamp to light the way to Christ. (The past tenses of the verbs in 5:35 imply that John's ministry was over.)

2. Jesus' Works (5:36)

Apart from Jesus' own claims about himself, there was the testimony of his miraculous works and his fulfillments of Old Testament Messianic predictions which served to confirm his identity. These supernatural performances should have demonstrated divine approval upon Christ's ministry (Acts 2:22), and thus were a greater testimony than John could give him.

3. The Father (5:37-38)

These verses are the explanation of whom Jesus meant by "another" in 5:32. God the Father had borne testimony to Christ's true identity both directly and indirectly. The voice of the Father had sounded from heaven at the baptism of Jesus (Matt. 3:17). The Father had also testified to the incarnation of his

[13]This is the view of William Hendriksen, Exposition of the Gospel According to John (Grand Rapids, 1953), pp. 205-207.

[14]Most commentators identify allos as the Father, among them Morris, Lenski, Barrett, Brown, Westcott, Reith, Tasker, and Godet.

Son through the miraculous events surrounding Jesus' birth. The greatest testimony of the Father regarding the Son was his Word enshrined as the Old Testament Scriptures. Yet the vast majority of Jesus' audiences were spiritually blind and deaf to God's presence and his workings, as evidenced by their almost total failure to receive God's own Son.

4. The Scriptures (5:39-47)

The final witness to be mentioned was the Scripture, in this instance the Old Testament. The verb "search" (*eraunate*) can be either imperative or indicative. Although either rendering is intelligible, most recent interpreters conclude that the indicative offers the smoothest sense in this context. Jesus is then understood to be making an assertion, "You are searching the Scriptures," rather than issuing a challenge to search, and laments the fact that in spite of this praiseworthy activity they have missed the real meaning of the written Word of God. The problem was not that the Scriptures were obscure, but that the readers were unwilling to follow where the light led them (5:39-40).

Such reliance upon technical study of the Torah is confirmed by rabbinical writings, such as this statement attributed to Hillel:

> He who has gotten a good name has gotten it for himself. . . .
> He who has gotten to himself words of Thorah [the Law], has
> gotten to himself the life of the world to come.[15]

These harsh words of Jesus were not uttered out of irritation because the Jews failed to congratulate him for his miracle-working power. He was not seeking glory from men (5:41). What distressed him was the clear indication from their attitudes that they had no experience of nor genuine interest in the saving love of God (5:42).

The tragedy was compounded by the fact that not only did they fail to respond properly to Jesus, the One who had come in the Father's name (involving perfect conformity to His will, 5:19, 30), but that they would show no such reluctance to follow others who had no divine authorization (5:43-44). "If another should come" (*ean allos elthēi*) is probably to be understood as a general

---

[15]*Pirqe Aboth* 2.8 in Charles Taylor, *Sayings of the Jewish Fathers* (New York, 1969), p. 32.

reference, not just to one individual. It could include such false messianic pretenders as Simon Bar-Kokhba,[16] leader of the Second Revolt in A.D. 132-135, or Anti-Christ, but it is not likely from the manner of the expression that Jesus had one certain person in mind. However, people who are more concerned with reputation and human opinion will not be greatly impressed with one whose sole concern is to do the will of God and thus get honor from above.

Although Jesus has explained his identity as the Divine Son, and asserted the guilt of his listeners for failing to receive him, he reminded them that it would not be necessary for him to be their accuser before the Father (5:45-47). They already stood condemned on the basis of the very Mosaic Scriptures which they professed to revere. A genuine acceptance of the Old Testament would have prepared them to recognize and respond to Christ. But their misguided concentration on the ceremonies and upon rabbinical additions and their failure to grasp the spiritual heart of the message (except for a comparatively small remnant), left the majority of the Jews incapable of seeing in Jesus the Messiah sent from the Father. His words met with no belief among such hearers.

Questions for Discussion

1. If 5:3b-4 is not a part of the original text, what did the impotent man mean by his reference to the troubling of the water in 5:7?
2. Why did Jesus choose the sabbath day to heal the man at the pool?
3. Are physical ailments and misfortunes the result of sin?
4. What two reasons are given in this chapter for the Jews' efforts to kill Jesus?
5. What is the meaning of Jesus' statement, "If I bear witness of myself, my witness is not true?" (5:31)

---

[16]Yigael Yadin, *Bar-Kokhba* (New York, 1971).

Chapter 6

The Feeding of Five Thousand
(John 6)

The feeding of the five thousand is the only miracle of Jesus which is recorded in all four Gospels (cf. Matt. 14:13-21; Mark 6:30-44; Luke 9:10-17). John differs from the others, however, in showing how the miracle provided the occasion for a remarkable discourse the next day in which Jesus explained that he is the true Bread which came from heaven. In John's Gospel, the miracle is preliminary to the main discussion.

The long Galilean ministry of Christ, which lasted over a year and a half (and if the period of the special training of the Twelve be included, the time is nearly two years), is dealt with by John only in chapter 6. Further description of happenings during this period is given in the other Gospels, and one should consult a harmony of the Gospels for the complete historical and chronological picture (see also Time Chart II, Fig. 14).

I. The Miracle of the Bread (6:1-14)

A. *The Setting of the Miracle* (6:1-9)

Jesus was now in the north of Palestine, by the Sea of Galilee. Sometimes this beautiful, mountain-rimmed lake was designated by the name of the city Tiberias on its western shore. Today it is called Lake Kinneret. "The other side of the sea" (*peran tēs thalassēs*) apparently indicates the eastern side in the vicinity of Bethsaida Julias (Luke 9:10) inasmuch as there was a recrossing of the sea to reach Capernaum and the eastern Bethsaida by the next day (Mark 6:45).[1] The traditional site of Tabgha near Capernaum on the northwest side of the lake does not seem to fit these circumstances.

The witnesses of the miracle were the multitudes who continually followed Jesus because of his miracles. The verbs of 6:2 in the original text stress the fact that this was their habitual

[1]On the question of the one or two Bethsaidas, see comment on 1:44.

activity. The crowd was "continually following him because they were continually beholding. . . ." This was the height of our Lord's popularity in Galilee. The time was Passover season (i.e., spring; note the mention of "much grass" in 6:10). One full year remained until the crucifixion.

A comparison with the parallel accounts (Matt. 14, Mark 6, Luke 9) suggests that something like the following must have occurred: Early in the day Jesus put the question to the disciples as to where they might obtain bread (John 6:5). Later, after considering the problem for many hours, the disciples could think of no alternative but to send the crowd away (Matt. 14:15). Thus the inadequacy of men to meet the need was clearly acknowledged. Philip felt there was no point in discussing *where* they might buy bread since they did not have enough money even if a market were nearby. Andrew mentioned that one little lad had a lunch[2] with him, but that would hardly suffice for such a crowd. Human inadequacy, however, is always an opportunity for the power of God to be demonstrated.

B. The Performance of the Miracle (6:10-14)

After arranging the people in seated groups (of fifty each, Luke 9:14), Christ proceeded to give thanks to the Father for the loaves and fish given by the lad. He then began to distribute these provisions to the disciples, and miraculously the supply continued to be adequate until all the five thousand men (women and children present would be in addition to this figure) were filled. There were twelve baskets of fragments left over —sufficient for each of the disciples who had been our Lord's assistants.

This remarkable event rightly reminded the people of Moses, who had supernaturally provided bread for Israel in the wilderness (cf. also 6:31). Moses had also said: "The Lord thy God will raise up unto thee a Prophet from the midst of thee, of thy brethren, like unto me" (Deut. 18:15). Therefore, many who saw the miracle saw the connection between that prophecy and Jesus, and identified him as "that prophet" (John 6:14). This was

---

[2]The five loaves should be understood as barley cakes (not as large modern loaves of bread), and the two small fish (*duo opsaria*) were those commonly eaten with bread.

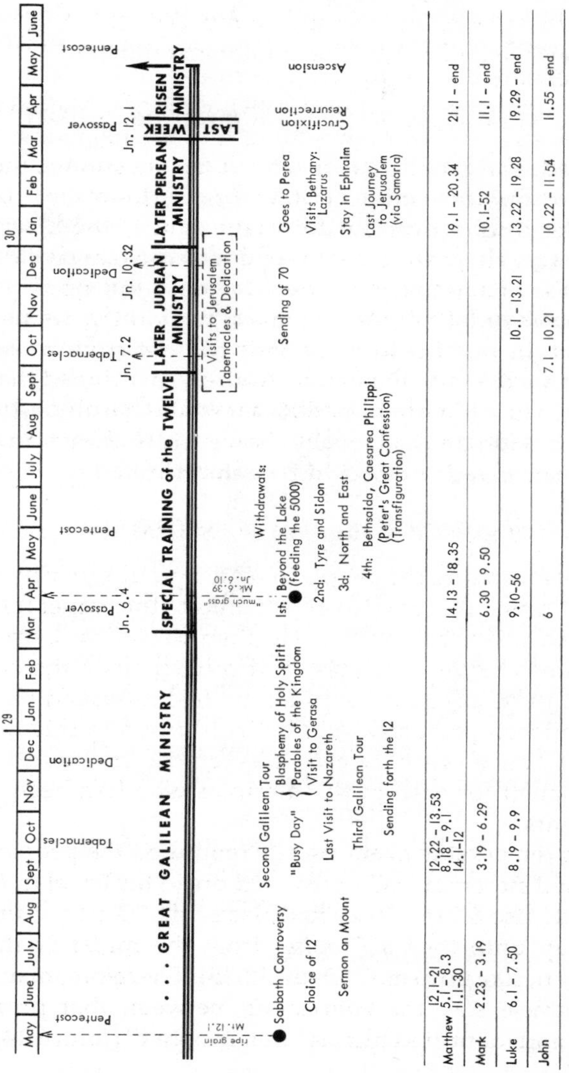
JESUS' PUBLIC MINISTRY
May June July Aug Sept Oct Nov Dec Jan Feb Mar Apr May June July Aug Sept Oct Nov Dec Jan Feb Mar Apr May June
29
30
Pentecost
Tabernacles
Dedication
Passover
Pentecost
Tabernacles
Dedication
Passover
Pentecost
Jn. 6.4
Jn. 7.2
Jn. 10.32
Jn. 12.1
. . . GREAT GALILEAN MINISTRY
SPECIAL TRAINING of the TWELVE
LATER JUDEAN MINISTRY
LATER PEREAN MINISTRY
LAST WEEK
RISEN MINISTRY
ripe grain
Mt. 12.1
"much grass"
Mk. 6.39
Jn. 6.10
Visits to Jerusalem
Tabernacles & Dedication
Sabbath Controversy
Choice of 12
Sermon on Mount
Second Galilean Tour
"Busy Day"
Blasphemy of Holy Spirit
Parables of the Kingdom
Visit to Gerasa
Last Visit to Nazareth
Third Galilean Tour
Sending forth the 12
Withdrawals:
1st: Beyond the Lake (feeding the 5000)
2nd: Tyre and Sidon
3d: North and East
4th: Bethsaida, Caesarea Philippi (Peter's Great Confession) (Transfiguration)
Sending of 70
Goes to Perea
Visits Bethany: Lazarus
Stay in Ephraim
Last Journey to Jerusalem (via Samaria)
Crucifixion
Resurrection
Ascension
Matthew
12.1-21
5.1 - 8.3
11.1-30
12.22 - 13.53
8.18 - 9.1
14.1-12
14.13 - 18.35
19.1 - 20.34
21.1 - end
Mark
2.23 - 3.19
3.19 - 6.29
6.30 - 9.50
10.1-52
11.1 - end
Luke
6.1 - 7.50
8.19 - 9.9
9.10-56
10.1 - 13.21
13.22 - 19.28
19.29 - end
John
6
7.1 - 10.21
10.22 - 11.54
11.55 - end

Fig. 14.

the proper identification (cf. Acts 3:20-22; 7:37). However, those who related Jesus to that prophecy apparently saw only the material aspects, and the spiritual implications of the prophecy were either ignored or else totally misunderstood.

II. The Miraculous Walking on the Water (6:15-21)

Those who saw in the miracle of the bread only a freely supplied meal wanted more of the same. They were willing to accept Jesus as king on such a platform and were prepared to force this if necessary. They wanted to use him for their own ends, and their goals were temporal and materialistic. Doubtless they desired to take Jesus to Jerusalem, foment a great national uprising, and install him as a political messiah. Our Lord, however, was not proclaiming a kingdom which had such a materialistic character. Although the Messianic Kingdom would be a literal kingdom, its basis was a spiritual revolution in which men's hearts would first be changed and in which perfect righteousness would prevail (cf. 3:3).

Refusing to yield to this sort of political pressure, Jesus withdrew from the crowd. The parallel accounts indicate that he sent the disciples across the lake to the area of Gennesaret on the northwest (Matt. 14:22, 34; Mark 6:45, 53).[3] As the disciples were rowing their boat, they encountered a rising sea and by the time they had reached the middle[4] of the lake a gale had developed (Matt. 14:24). The Sea of Galilee lies nearly 700 feet below sea level, and the surrounding mountains are cut by deep valleys which in the afternoons and evenings serve as funnels for strong winds from the Mediterranean.

The statement that Jesus "had not yet come to them" (6:17, ASV) does not mean that the disciples were expecting a miraculous arrival. Rather, it implies either that Jesus had told them that

[3] According to Mark 6:45, their destination was to be Bethsaida, apparently the one in Galilee (cf. John 12:21) and distinguished from Bethsaida Julias in Gaulanitis.

[4] Twenty-five or thirty stadia (*stadious,* 6:19) was a distance of approximately three and one-half miles (one *stadion* equaled 607 English feet). Thus the boat was in the middle of the lake, whose widest dimensions are roughly 7 miles wide by 12 miles long. Although they were presumably not crossing at the widest point, the wind and rough sea may have driven them off course.

he would meet them at some announced spot, or else that the author, who was a participant, is writing after the fact and knows (as well as do many of his readers from the Synoptic accounts) that Jesus did meet them eventually.[5]

The miraculous walking of Jesus on the water and the stilling of the storm were events witnessed only by the disciples. This action was meant to reassure them that their acceptance of Jesus as Messiah was not mistaken. The fact that he had refused to be made king by the crowd did not mean he was not the Messiah, nor that his power was in any way deficient. Thus Jesus showed the disciples that he was sovereign in the material realm, even though he had refused the misguided zeal of the populace. (It was on this occasion that Peter walked on the water to Jesus [Matt. 14:28-31]. John did not include the incident, nor did Mark, probably because it was extraneous to the purpose each had in mind in selecting the particular material for his Gospel.)

An additional miracle may be indicated in 6:21. Whether "immediately" is intended to describe an instantaneous (and hence miraculous) transporting of the boat to shore, or merely a speedy arrival without further hindrance is debatable, but the possibility of the former is certainly open.

III. The Discourse on the Bread (6:22-40)

A. The Setting (6:22-25)

On the next day the people recognized that something strange had occurred. There had been[6] only one boat the day before—the one in which the Twelve had left. They had noticed that Jesus had not gone with the Twelve (6:22); yet in the morning he was nowhere to be found. By that time perhaps some enterprising boatmen from Tiberias had learned that a large throng of people were on the east shore of the lake and might be persuaded to hire transportation, or else the storm had forced the boats to come to

---

[5]The latter explanation is given by William Hendriksen, *The Gospel According to John* (Grand Rapids, 1953), pp. 224, 225.

[6]The verb *ēn* is in the imperfect tense but is part of a statement of indirect discourse, and should be rendered in English as the past perfect "had been." The reference is to the presence of a single boat on the previous day.

shore at this point. Whatever the cause, the crowds left for
Capernaum in these boats which had arrived from Tiberias
(6:23-24). In the town of Capernaum they soon located Jesus and
asked him when (and presumably how) he had gotten there
(6:25). Our Lord grasped the opportunity to teach spiritual truth,
based upon the miracle of the day before. This discourse took
place in the synagogue at Capernaum (6:59).

B. The Work of God (6:26-29)

The people had experienced the gift of physical bread on the
day before, and they were eager to be with Jesus once again. Yet
Jesus said that their eagerness was not due to their seeing in the
miracle a sign of his Messiahship with all of its spiritual implications. Rather, what they had seen was a meal and very little else
(6:26). He challenged them to give their attention to (*ergazesthe*,
"work for") spiritual nourishment which was available from him
(6:27). Jesus had been sent as God's gift to man, and he would
freely supply this spiritual food which would bring eternal life.

When the people wanted to know how they might "work" so
as to obtain eternal life (6:28), they were undoubtedly thinking
in terms of performing some meritorious deed or deeds so as to
merit divine approval and ultimate salvation. The Pharisees
especially, but also Jews generally, had reduced the Old Testament to a series of rabbinical interpretations by performance of
which they expected to achieve the righteousness which God
requires. Their question to Jesus reflects this understanding.

Our Lord explained by his answer that this "work" which men
need to perform is not really a work at all (6:29). Instead of doing
something which will merit God's verdict of righteousness, men
are asked to believe in God's work. The "work of God" was to
provide full salvation by the merits of his Son, and to offer this
finished work of God to men freely for the taking. Man's faith is
not a "work" in the sense that implies effort which achieves
some earned result, but is man's response to the work which God
has performed through Christ, his unique and divine Son.

C. Contrast of the Mosaic Manna with the Bread of God (6:30-33)

The Jews demanded a Messianic miracle before they would
accept Jesus as Messiah in any divine sense (6:30). It seems

incredible that those who had experienced the miraculous feeding the day before should act as if it had never occurred. They were apparently minimizing that miracle, and comparing it unfavorably with Moses and the manna (6:31). It was as if they said: Moses provided manna during forty years, but Jesus did so only once. Furthermore, Moses supplied "bread from heaven" (*arton ek tou ouranou*), but Jesus had produced only earthly loaves, the same sort they were accustomed to having. Thus Jesus could hardly be as great as Moses.

Christ affirmed, however, that it was not actually Moses who had provided the manna, but God (6:32). Moses was God's agent, but it was God who sent it for the Israelites in the wilderness, as Moses himself stated (Exod. 16:15). It was also the case that, miraculous though it was, the wilderness manna was itself perishable and merely sustained physical life. It served as a symbol of the spiritual bread from heaven which is life-giving, not merely life-sustaining (6:33). Just as Jesus had used the term "work" in a twofold sense to capture the interest of his hearers (6:27, 29), so his statement "the bread of God is he which cometh down from heaven" (6:33, KJV) could also be rendered "the bread of God is that which[7] cometh down out of heaven" (ASV, NASB). Should his audience understand the reference to be to "bread" or to the person who here claimed to be from heaven? The bare statement does not settle the matter, and perhaps it was purposely enigmatic in the fashion of a Hebrew *mashal* or dark saying to insure their continued attention for the riddle to be unraveled.

D. *Identification of the Bread of Life* (6:34-40)

Just as Jesus had whetted the appetite of the woman of Samaria by his description of living water (4:10), so he aroused the desire of the multitude for the bread of life. They eagerly requested it for themselves, but by their asking they revealed that they did not understand that he was really offering himself to them (6:34). Therefore, Jesus explicitly stated: "I am the bread of life" (6:35).

---

[7]The Greek participle *katabainōn* (cometh down) is masculine, in grammatical agreement with the masculine noun *artos* (bread). English, however, treats "bread" as neuter.

Receiving him by faith as the Redeemer from sin and the giver of eternal life would result in spiritual satisfaction that would never cease.

Nevertheless, Jesus recognized that the bulk of the crowd had not come to him with that sort of faith (6:36). He then pointed out the inestimable blessing which comes to those who do respond in faith (6:37-38). Such are in the protective care of Christ, and this is in harmony with the Father's will because Jesus perfectly carried out that will. Believers are not only secure in their status with God, but have been granted a new kind of life which insures eventual resurrection and everlasting existence in the presence of God (6:39-40). Jesus himself promised it, and he will perform the raising of believers. Thus men were challenged to put their trust in what he said and receive these incomparable blessings.

IV. The Murmuring Against the Bread (6:41-71)

A. *Murmuring of the Jews* (6:41-59)

The unbelieving Jews objected to seeing in Jesus anything more than just an ordinary man (6:41-42). They completely rejected his claim of a heavenly origin, for they thought they knew all about his family connections. This is another instance which demonstrated the truth of Jesus' proverbial statement: "A prophet hath no honor in his own country" (4:44).

The mention of "the Jews" is another of John's many uses of this expression in the specialized sense of "Jewish leaders."[8] Here the reference is to Jewish religious authorities in Galilee (specifically Capernaum), who showed the same resistance to Jesus as their counterparts in Jerusalem.

Our Lord explained their skeptical attitude in a way which should have sobered every unbeliever present (6:43-46). Belief in Christ was shown to be not a casual response which one could off-handedly make or not, depending on his whim of the moment. No one could genuinely come to Christ unless the Father should draw him. There may be a superficial coming to Christ, but there must be a work of God performed in the heart before

[8]See Chapter 2, footnote 1.

one's coming to Christ is spiritually valid. How does God "draw" men to Christ? Jesus cited Isaiah 54:13, "They shall all be taught of God." The true believer, therefore, is one who hears the Word of God and that Word is interpreted to his heart by the Holy Spirit. In this way God acts upon men's hearts and creates that spiritual attraction toward Christ that draws men to him. It must not be imagined, however, that this "drawing" is a mere influence which may be wholesome and beneficial if followed, but is not always successful. The verb employed is a strong one,[9] and is used of the actual dragging of a net (John 21:6, 11), dragging someone from the temple (Acts 21:30), and haling someone into court (James 2:6). In none of the uses where material objects are involved is there any suggestion that the "drawing" was not accomplished. This concept must not be overlooked when the word is found in the figurative sense of the divine pull on man's spirit as here and in 12:32. Those who come to God by responding to the gospel must still give *all* the glory to God who first loved them and has drawn them to himself. It was God who sent his Son, and only through the Son can we truly comprehend the Father (6:46).

Again Jesus asserted his claim to be the Bread of life (6:47-50). To counter the previous objection that Jesus was not as great as Moses (6:31), Christ pointed out that the manna furnished through the leadership of Moses did not grant eternal life to its eaters. But Jesus, the Bread of Life, provides life forevermore.

He then explained that the bread is his flesh which men must eat in order to live (6:51-59). This startling statement created a stir among the listeners, as Jesus intended. He spoke of giving his flesh for the life of the world, and the need of men to eat his flesh and drink his blood. What did he mean? It is not likely that he was referring to the Christian observance of Holy Communion, for this had not yet been announced, nor is the partaking of the communion symbols a necessity for salvation. However, he was referring to the same truths which the eucharistic elements symbolize. In order to have eternal life, men must become united with Christ so that the merits of his matchless life and atoning death become efficacious to them. The giving of his flesh refers

---

[9]*Helkō* or *helkuō*, to draw, drag.

to Christ's bodily sacrifice, and his blood pictures the atoning value of his death. These values must be partaken of by men in order for them to be saved.

How does one "eat" Christ's flesh and "drink" his blood? To state it another way, how does a person take to himself and assimilate the effects of Christ's sacrifice on his behalf? The answer is seen when two very similar statements in this passage are compared.

Everyone that beholdeth the Son, and believeth on him   should have eternal life: I will raise him up at the last day. (6:40, ASV)

He that eateth my flesh and drinketh my blood   hath eternal life; and I will raise him up at the last day. (6:54, ASV)

It seems clear that the promises of eternal life and resurrection made to those who are described in 6:40 are repeated in 6:54, with the only difference being in the way the beneficiaries are described. Even the literary style shows parallelism, and thus one concludes that the recipients of these promises are the same. "Beholdeth" and "believeth" (6:40) are parallel to "eateth" and "drinketh" (6:54). Further parallelism is seen by comparing 6:33-36 with 6:51-56. Jesus, therefore, is not talking about a ritualistic act, but about believing in his atoning death on man's behalf.

B. Murmuring of the Disciples (6:60-71)

As John has been describing the development of unbelief, he has traced this sad circumstance among the Jewish leaders in Jerusalem and now in Galilee. But the problem had proportions even beyond this. There were defections also among those who had become followers of Jesus (6:60). Many of the disciples found these teachings of Jesus too difficult to accept. "Hard" in this passage (6:60) means "hard to take," not "hard to understand." The clear implications of this discourse demanded much more than intellectual commitment to a gifted teacher. One must either make the tremendous leap of faith and receive Jesus as the Divine Son of God, equal with the Father, and the One on whom men must depend for eternal life, or else he would regard Jesus as a blasphemer. It would be hard to find any middle ground.

Fig. 15. *Remains of a third-century synagogue at Capernaum.*

The word *disciple* means "learner" and does not always denote a true believer.[10] Sometimes it merely refers to those who were temporary adherents of Christ. If their initial attraction to Jesus did not develop into settled faith, they eventually lost interest and followed no more. On this occasion many were offended at his statements regarding the eating and drinking of his flesh and blood. Jesus declared that his ascension would clearly prove the truth of his claim of a heavenly origin (6:61-62). Nevertheless, their unbelief was no surprise to Jesus. He was well aware of their attitude and repeated his early comment that no superficial loyalty was sufficient (6:63-65). Unless one came to

[10] "Disciple" (*mathetes*) in general usage denoted a pupil or learner, one who received instruction from a teacher. The vast majority of the 264 NT occurrences of the term refer to persons who were disciples of Jesus. However, three distinct uses of the term appear: (1) The Twelve (Matt. 10:1; 11:1; 26:20), who were Christ's closest companions. (2) All true believers (Luke 6:17; 19:37; Matt. 10:37; Luke 14:26, 27, 33). (3) Temporary followers (John 6:66), or those with very imperfect faith (Acts 19:1).

Christ as a result of the action of the Holy Spirit energizing the words of Jesus, no merely human enthusiasm ("flesh," 6:63) would bring the new life which God requires. Once again the initiative is traced to God (6:65), just as in 6:44.

When many of these casual followers dropped away, Jesus put the question to the twelve,[11] "Will ye also go away?" (6:66-67). Was it possible that there might be unbelief even here? Peter spoke for the group and asserted their firm faith that Jesus was the Messiah, the Divine Son of God (6:68-69). There was no other teacher who was on a plane with Jesus. No one else had the message of eternal life. The title "Holy One of God"[12] (6:69) is the same description used of Jesus by a demon-possessed man in this same synagogue at Capernaum much earlier in his ministry (Mark 1:24; Luke 4:34). It reminds us of the Old Testament name "The Holy One of Israel" (Isa. 1:4), and was understood as a Messianic title by the early church (Acts 3:14, cf. Ps. 16:10; I John 2:20).

Yet even within this smaller company, there was one not in sympathy with Peter's confession. And once again Jesus was not caught unawares (6:70-71). Though Judas did not outwardly object to Peter's statement, our Lord knew the condition of his heart. Judas was partaking of the nature of Satan,[13] turning good into evil, and failing to receive Christ with true spiritual understanding. By this statement and others, Jesus gave Judas opportunity to face up to himself and make his heart right before God. Judas's personal tragedy was that he never did.

---

[11]The Gospel of John does not record the appointment of the twelve, and 6:67 is the first mention of the apostolic group by this designation in John.

[12]This reading (*ho hagios tou theou*) has the strong support of P[75] Aleph B C D L W, and is adopted by ASV and NASB.

[13]"Devil" (*diabolos*, 6:70) means slanderous, devilish, partaking of the nature and quality of Satan. The term appears in 6:70 without the article, thus emphasizing the qualitative sense. Jesus did not mean that Judas was the devil incarnate and thus not a true human, any more than he meant that Peter was actually Satan on one occasion (Matt. 16:23). In both instances the striking personification pointed to the source of their wrong thinking.

Questions for Discussion

1. Why did Jesus refuse to let the crowd make him a king?
2. What is the one "work" which God wants men to do? Is it really a work in the usual sense?
3. Why do you think the Jews minimized the miraculous feeding by Jesus in comparison to Moses and the manna?
4. How does the Father draw men to Christ?
5. How does one eat Christ's flesh and drink his blood?
6. What did Jesus mean by saying, "One of you is a devil"?

Chapter 7

At the Feast of Tabernacles

(John 7-8)

Chapters 7-10 of John's Gospel are a unit in which Jesus is seen in Jerusalem at the annual Feast of Tabernacles. The feelings of men toward Jesus were becoming more settled by this time. Among the unprejudiced hearers, John shows the growing conviction that Jesus is the Christ (7:41). Among the rulers, however, was hostility that was deepening into murderous hatred (7:1, 44; 8:40, 59). These events took place about six months after the feeding of the five thousand in chapter 6.

I. The Situation Before the Feast (7:1-13)

A. The Time (7:1-2)

During the previous months Jesus had been avoiding the province of Judea (i.e., "Jewry," KJV) because of the intense opposition of the Jews in Jerusalem (5:18). He had much more freedom in Galilee to preach to crowds without such hindrances. At this time, however, the Jewish Feast of Tabernacles drew near. This feast occurred annually in the fall and commemorated the wilderness experiences of Israel and God's provision for the nation at that time. Instructions for the celebration are found in Leviticus 23:33-43 and Deuteronomy 16:13-15. It consisted of a seven-day festival beginning on the fifteenth day of the seventh month, followed by an eighth day observed as a sabbath. The people constructed temporary huts (i.e., "tabernacles") of leafy branches on their rooftops or along the roads, and lived in them during the festival.

Approximately six months remained until the crucifixion of Jesus.

B. The Advice of Jesus' Brothers (7:3-5)

There was a lack of appreciation of Jesus even within his family circle. His brothers urged him to make an appearance before his adherents in Jerusalem and capitalize on his political opportunity. These brothers were most likely the younger half-brothers of Jesus, children of Joseph and Mary. There were four of them: James, Joseph, Simon, and Judas (Matt. 13:55; Mark 6:3). In all probability Jesus had not visited Jerusalem for a year and a half (not since the feast of 5:1). Their argument was that Jesus needed to be seen in the limelight of Jerusalem, not in out-of-the-way Galilee, if he seriously hoped to be accepted as the national Messiah. Although this advice seems to contain a degree of practical wisdom, John tells us that it was really the product of unbelief. These brothers failed to see in their own family one who was the Divine Messiah. Perhaps there was a touch of sarcasm in their urging.

C. The Purpose of Jesus (7:6-9)

Our Lord's intentions were not precisely the same as those his brothers had in mind. He was observing a timetable of which they had no knowledge. As the perfect Servant of Jehovah, Jesus was always led by the Spirit. His actions were not determined by human political procedures. Thus it was not yet the time for him to announce himself in a great public way as the Messiah in the historic capital city. That time would come at Passover the next spring. It was proper for his brothers to visit Jerusalem, how-ever, for they had no Messianic schedule to observe nor any revelations to make. As unbelievers still, these brothers would encounter no opposition at Jerusalem, for they were not at var-iance with their world as epitomized by the religious au-thorities.

The ancient manuscripts vary at 7:8 between "not yet" (*oupō*)[1] and "not" (*ouk*)[2] in the statement of Jesus, "I go not up (yet?) unto this feast." The evidence is early for both readings. The understanding is simpler if "not yet" is regarded as original, in view of the fact that Jesus did go to the feast a bit later. However, this very factor causes some to suspect "not yet" as being an alteration of the more difficult "not" so as to make the passage

[1]Supported by P66, 75 B L T W X, as well as the Byzantine sources. This reading is adopted by KJV and ASV.

[2]Supported by Aleph D K, and adopted by RSV, NEB, and NASB.

easier. If "not" is then regarded as the true reading, one must suppose that Jesus changed his mind about not going (most unlikely), or else that the statement refers not to attendance at the feast per se, but to the showing of himself to the world at the feast as his brothers were urging. He did intend to go to Jerusalem a few days later, but it was not as a regular worshiper (he arrived when it was half over), and he did not produce the display his brothers had suggested. This explanation is supported by Jesus' words, "for my time is not yet full come."

D. The Arrival of Jesus in Jerusalem (7:10-13)

Since he went to the feast late, rather than with the caravan of pilgrims who went for the full round of festivities, his arrival in the city midway through the week was somewhat unexpected. ("In secret" does not mean that he was hiding in the city, for he taught publicly in the temple when he arrived [7:14]. The sense is, "he arrived quietly.") When he did not arrive at the beginning, the Jews[3] were on the lookout for him. They felt that he would certainly appear at this great national gathering so as to arouse more popular support for his claims. The general populace remained divided in their opinion of Jesus, but fear of the Jewish authorities made them cautious in expressing themselves.

II. The Discussion During the Feast (7:14-36)

A. Discussion with the Jewish Authorities (7:14-24)

As Jesus began teaching in the temple after his arrival, he entered into a discussion with the Jewish authorities. His teaching was performed with such professional skill that the Jewish leaders were amazed (7:14-15). They knew that Jesus had not received rabbinical training. To this amazed reaction Jesus explained that his teaching was derived from the Father, and that recognition of this divine Source would come to anyone who was really submitted to God's will (7:16-17). The person who sin-

[3]Again John speaks of "the Jews" in the technical sense of the religious authorities in 7:11, 13, 15. This is especially clear in 7:13, where the people who feared "the Jews" were themselves Jews nationally. See 1:19 (chapter 2, footnote 1).

cerely wants to know God's will and is genuinely submitted to the doing of it will intuitively recognize that Christ's words are true and divine (see 8:47 and I John 4:6 for similar statements). The Holy Spirit will impart to the understanding a sensitivity to God's Word. It is a matter of willingness on man's part. Unbelief is not basically lack of information but a will in rebellion against God. Of course, if one is promoting himself, then his words may well be unreliable; but Jesus was conveying the message of his Father and seeking to glorify him (7:18; the similar thought as expressed in 5:41-44).

Jesus also pointed out to these authorities that mere outward acquaintance with God's will was not proof of subjection to it (7:19-24). These men gave lip service to the Law of Moses, and yet they found a variety of ways to avoid submitting with the heart to this particular expression of God's will. Their inconsistency in trying to kill[4] Jesus for healing a man on the sabbath (the impotent man of 5:1-16)[5] was shown by Jesus to involve a failure to subject themselves to the intent of God's revealed will. The Jews themselves "violated" their sabbath in order to circumcise a male child. They should not have accused Jesus for employing the sabbath as an occasion to restore a man to physical soundness.

B. Discussion with the People of Jerusalem (7:25-31)

These are distinguished from the rulers (7:26) and also from the crowds which included visitors to the feast. They were the permanent residents of Jerusalem, who had a superficial knowledge of messianic truth and also an awareness of the political intrigues being carried on by their leaders, but the shallowness of their understanding of Jesus is very evident. They were surprised that Jesus spoke so courageously when it was well known that the leaders were plotting his death (7:25-26). They ruled out

---

[4]The crowd which interjected their denial of attempting to kill Jesus (7:20) could have been unaware of the fact that the leaders had already discussed this possibility (5:18).

[5]The "one work" to which Jesus referred (7:21), although occurring 1½ years earlier, is clearly the healing of the impotent man of 5:1-16, as shown by Jesus' further statement in 7:23.

the possibility that the authorities had changed their minds,[6] and also revealed their own thinking that Jesus was not the Messiah (7:27). These people reflected a current tradition (not based on Scripture) that Messiah's origin would be unknown. Although the religious leaders seem well-informed about Messiah's predicted birthplace in Bethlehem (Matt. 2:4-7) and this was known also by many ordinary people (7:41-42), there was a belief that Messiah would be unknown until Elijah came to anoint him. Trypho the Jew argued with Justin: "Christ, if he has indeed been born and exists anywhere, is unknown."[7] Because the dwellers at Jerusalem thought they knew all about Jesus, they were sure he could not be the Christ.

Jesus acknowledged that the people of Jerusalem had a superficial knowledge of him, and yet they knew not his true origin from the Father (7:28-29). The tragedy was that they were rejecting the one who was the revealer of the Father, and the only one who could fully explain the real nature of his origin. Once again a division of opinion occurred, with many impressed because of the undeniable miracles they had seen or heard about, but others being even more resolute in their unbelief (7:30-31). The unbelievers, however, were divinely restrained from seizing Jesus.

C. Discussion with the Officers (7:32-36)

Legal steps were taken by the authorities, and the order was issued to have Jesus arrested (7:32). This may have been a general order to the officers to find some pretext if possible to take him into custody. Jesus' words, while heard by the crowds standing by, were also spoken in the hearing of the officers (as 7:46 makes clear). He announced his coming departure to his sender, and the inability of his enemies to find him (7:33-34). He was referring, of course, to his ascension about six months away. The Jews, however, sneered at the statement and interpreted it geographically as a possible trip outside of Palestine to the

---

[6]Their phrasing of the question implies a negative answer: "The rulers do not really know that this is the Christ, do they?" (7:26, NASB).

[7]Justin Martyr, *Dialogue with Trypho*, Chapter VIII. *The Ante-Nicene Fathers*, ed. Alexander Roberts and James Donaldson (Grand Rapids, reprinted 1950), I, 199.

Diaspora[8] where he might actually confront not only Jews but Greeks as well (7:35-36). Because they could not conceive of the Messiah as teaching Greeks,[9] they found in this statement one more reason to reject him.

III. Events on the Last Day of the Feast (7:37-52)

A. The Invitation by Jesus (7:37-39)

This occurred on the "last day, the great one, of the feast." It is debated whether this was the seventh (which ended most of the ritual) or the eighth day (which was observed as a sabbath).[10] In addition to the ritual prescribed in Leviticus 23:40, the custom had developed of having the priests bring a vessel of water daily during the festival from the Pool of Siloam (see Fig. 18), and come with it in procession to the temple.[11] Here the water would be poured on the altar of burnt offering as a reminder of how God supplied Israel's need in the wilderness. On the eighth day the ceremony was omitted, signifying Israel's presence in the land. If this event occurred on the eighth day, Christ's invitation to men to come to him for living water was especially dramatic, as he claimed to be the fulfillment of the typology carried out at the feast. He was the supplier of the spiritual living water (4:10; I Cor. 10:4).

At least two major problems confront the interpreter of 7:37-38. The first has to do with the punctuation of the words "he that

[8]Diaspora was the designation given to the thousands of Jews who lived outside of Palestine in the Greek world. The term comes from the verb *diaspeirō* (sow, scatter) and the concept is based upon such passages as Deut. 4:27 and 28:64-68. Originally the scattering was due to conquest, but later the term was applied to all who lived away from the Jewish homeland, regardless of reason. The term appears in the NT also in I Peter 1:1 and James 1:1.

[9]*Hellēnas* (7:35, KJV "gentiles") refers not to Greek-speaking Jews, but to ethnic Greeks. Although Jesus did not do this, this was precisely the method of evangelism employed by the apostle Paul who went to the Jewish synagogues in the Greek world and used them as a base of operations to reach the Gentiles.

[10]See William Hendriksen, *The Gospel According to John* (Grand Rapids, 1953), pp. 21-22, for a summary of the arguments for the two views.

[11]Alfred Edersheim, *The Temple, Its Ministry and Services as They Were at the Time of Jesus Christ* (Grand Rapids, reprinted 1950), pp. 277-281.

believeth on me." Should they be placed with the preceding clause, or with what follows? If they are attached to the previous words, they form a further description of the subject "anyone," and enable the interpreter to explain the living water as flowing from Christ rather than from the believer.[12] This explanation faces the difficulty, however, of identifying the one who thirsts (i.e., his thirst still unquenched) with the one believing (presumably already receiving satisfaction). Furthermore, the employment of *ho pisteuōn* ("the one believing") is a common pattern in John to introduce a construction, but not to be tacked on to some preceding clause.[13] It is more likely, therefore, that the words in question should be regarded as introducing the next statement.[14]

The second problem concerns the identity of the Old Testament quotation. No one passage is being cited precisely, and it is best to regard the reference as being the gist of many passages such as the following, which speak of Messianic blessings:

> Behold, God is my salvation; I will trust, and not be afraid: for the Lord Jehovah is my strength and my song; he also is become my salvation. Therefore with joy shall ye draw water out of the wells of salvation (Isa. 12:2-3).

> For I will pour water upon him that is thirsty, and floods upon the dry ground: I will pour my spirit upon thy seed, and my blessing upon thine offspring: and they shall spring up as among the grass, as willows by the water courses (Isa. 44:3-4).

> And the Lord shall guide thee continually, and satisfy thy soul in drought, and make fat thy bones: and thou shalt be like a watered garden, and like a spring of water, whose waters fail not (Isa. 58:11).

The thought that from believers there would issue spiritual blessings upon others may be implicit in 4:14 where the living water given to the believer becomes a spring which bubbles up. John interprets for us that Jesus was speaking of the blessings that would come when the Holy Spirit would be given in a new way to bless believers and empower them after the return of Christ to heaven (7:39).

---

[12]This is the view of R. E. Brown, *The Gospel According to John* in The Anchor Bible Series (Garden City, 1966), pp. 320-321.

[13]Brown admits this, but minimizes its importance. *Ibid.*

[14]This conclusion is reflected in KJV, ASV, RSV, and NASB.

B. Reaction of the People (7:40-44)

As a result of this dramatic pronouncement, many were ready
to acknowledge Jesus as the Messiah. Some related him to the
"prophet" whom Moses had predicted (Deut. 18:15), and others
categorically pronounced him to be the Christ, but these meant
essentially the same thing (7:40-41a). Some, however, refused to
believe because of their misunderstanding about Jesus' birthplace (7:41b-42). They assumed that because he had been reared
in Nazareth of Galilee, this disqualified him from fulfilling the
prophecy of Micah 5:2. Others were more hostile, and would
actually have seized him for prosecution or bodily harm, but no
concerted effort materialized at this time (7:44).

C. Reaction of the Sanhedrin (7:45-52)

The officers who had been sent by the Sanhedrin to arrest
Jesus (7:32) returned without accomplishing their mission
(7:45-46). This meeting with the Sanhedrin supports the conclusion that their orders had not been for a simple arrest, but to
watch for some incident which could be exploited for seizing
Jesus. The officers expressed amazement at Jesus' teaching, with
particular wonder at the manner by which he taught. His authoritative pronouncements, coupled with his gracious invitation, impressed these police as being far different from the usual
rabbinic discourse they had heard.

The Pharisees in the Sanhedrin retorted with great spiritual
arrogance (7:47-49). Such men had little respect for the 'am hā'
āres, "the people of the land" or ordinary folk whom they regarded as religiously illiterate. Their opinions could hardly be
considered in the light of the great learning of the Pharisees, or
so they thought. Hence any viewpoint which ran counter to the
opinions of the Pharisees was automatically treated with dis-
dain.

The one moderate voice in the council was that of Nicodemus,
to whom the readers have already been introduced in chapter 3.
Inasmuch as this was a private meeting, Nicodemus must have
later become a Christian and reported the proceedings to John.
On this occasion, however, he made a plea for justice (7:50-51).
The council was itself guilty of prejudice if it condemned Jesus

without even giving him a hearing. Nicodemus has been blamed for failing to take a bold stand for Christ in this meeting. However, it could well be that Nicodemus had not yet become a believer. Furthermore, it did take considerable courage for a Pharisee to say even as much as he did, when all the rest of his party was in violent opposition. His carefully worded reminder may have been the most effective witness at this point.

The others were convinced that Jesus' origins were in Galilee, and they sarcastically inferred that only local pride could account for Nicodemus's mild defense (7:52). Their claim that "no prophet" comes from Galilee is at best a generalization, for there were some prophets from that area, Jonah (II Kings 14:25) and Nahum (Capernaum?) being two examples. It is of special interest that Papyrus 66 contains the article so that the expression is

Fig. 16. *The city of Bethlehem, nestled among the Judean hills south of Jerusalem. Bethlehem was the family home of David, and the prophesied birthplace of Christ.*

"the prophet." If this be the original reading, then the statement asserts that the Prophet (i.e., Messiah) would not arise out of Galilee. The whole argument of the Sanhedrin, however, betrays their ignorance of Jesus' birthplace, which was in Bethlehem of Judea.

IV. The Woman Taken in Adultery (7:53—8:11)

This paragraph has had the strangest history of any portion of the New Testament. It does not appear at all in the major manuscripts Aleph A B C W Theta, nor in P[66] or P[75]. The most important early document to include it at this place in John is codex D. Many later manuscripts which do include it have it marked with asterisks or obeli to indicate some question about it. What is even more strange is its unstable position. It occurs at the end of the Gospel in some manuscripts, after John 7:36 in one, and after 7:44 in some Georgian version copies. In one group of manuscripts it even occurs in the Gospel of Luke after 21:38.

Nevertheless, the passage was known early,[15] and the general conservative opinion of this portion is that it records an authentic incident in the life of Christ, although there is serious doubt whether John wrote it as part of his Gospel. Westcott stated: ". . . it is beyond doubt an authentic fragment of apostolic tradition."[16] Barrett notes: ". . . (1) it closely resembles in form and style the synoptic narratives (especially the style of Luke . . .); and (2) it represents the character and method of Jesus as they are revealed elsewhere.[17]" Morris writes: "But if we cannot feel that this is part of John's Gospel we can feel that the story is true to the character of Jesus. Throughout the history of the church it has been held that, whoever wrote it, this little story is authentic . . . It rings true."[18]

[15]Ambrose, Augustine, and Jerome were acquainted with the passage, and Papias may have known it (although there are some uncertainties about the statement attributed to Papias by Eusebius). C. K. Barrett, *The Gospel According to St. John* (London, 1967), pp. 490-491.

[16]B. F. Westcott, *The Gospel According to St. John* (Grand Rapids, reprinted 1950), p. 125.

[17]Barrett, *John*, p. 491.

[18]Leon Morris, *The Gospel According to John* in the New International Commentary on the New Testament Series (Grand Rapids, 1971), p. 883.

Fig. 17. *The Mount of Olives, viewed from the south. Jesus often spent the night here when he was in Jerusalem.*

A. The Accusation (7:53—8:6a)

After Jesus had spent the night on the Mount of Olives (cf. Luke 21:37-38), he came back to Jerusalem and taught in one of the open courts of the temple. Some scribes and Pharisees brought to him a woman caught in the act of adultery. Since no mention is made of the man, who was equally guilty under Mosaic Law and who could presumably have been seized at the same time, it is strongly suggested that this was a case contrived for the express purpose of placing Jesus in a difficult position. The accusers thought Jesus could not extricate himself from the dilemma. If he contradicted the command of the Mosaic Law (Lev. 20:10)[19] and did not advocate stoning, then he would

---

[19]Lev. 20:10 prescribed death for both parties guilty of adultery, but the method was not mentioned. Stoning, however, was the usual form of Jewish execution. Deut. 22:23-24 specifies stoning for a betrothed woman, leading to the possibility that this woman was not a wife but betrothed. However, Ezek. 16:38-40 indicates that stoning was the practice for all cases of adultery.

surely be disqualified as Messiah (a prophet like unto Moses, Deut. 18:15). On the other hand, if he urged her execution, he would lose popular favor, endanger his image as a friend of publicans and sinners, and perhaps be accused of promoting a policy contrary to Rome (only Rome could execute death sentences).

B. The Answer of Jesus (8:6b-8)

Jesus, however, raised the issue from legal to spiritual ground. He was not a civil judge, but a private citizen. Therefore, he discussed not the problem of witnesses and points of law, but sinfulness in relation to God. He did not mean that only sinless persons could ever perform judicial acts, for this would make all human courts impossible. But as Calvin said: "He reproves hypocrites, who gently flatter themselves and their own vices, but are excessively severe and even savage judges of others. . . . Every man should begin by interrogating his own conscience and being both witness and judge against himself before he comes to others."[20]

C. The Outcome (8:8-11)

By writing on the ground (perhaps naming the sins of the onlookers, as one manuscript suggests),[21] Jesus convicted the accusers and they left the scene. We must not conclude that Jesus took a lenient view of sin, for he told the woman to "sin no more." But the reason for Christ's action may go deeper than this. We note that the woman addressed him as "Lord" (8:11). If she had recognized in this encounter the truth regarding this amazing person about whom she must have previously heard, then her calling him "Lord" takes on new meaning (cf. Rom. 10:13; 8:1). Jesus may have seen in this sinful woman a newborn child of God and thus spoke words of release and comfort that are inherent in the gospel.

[20]John Calvin, The Gospel According to St . John, 1-10, in Calvin's Commentaries Series, ed. David W. Torrance and Thomas F. Torrance, trans. T. H. L. Parker (Grand Rapids, 1959), p. 208.

[21]One should refrain, however, from dogmatism in deciding exactly what Jesus wrote on the ground. Apparently the content of that writing was not material to the incident; otherwise the narrator would have included it.

V. Resumption of the Discussion After the Feast (8:12-59)

The remainder of chapter 8 contains our Lord's further discussion while at Jerusalem for the feast. He makes a series of claims regarding himself which reveals more about his person.

A. Jesus Claimed to Be the Light of the World. (8:12-20)

In the temple's Court of the Women (also called the treasury, 8:20; see Fig. 5) were golden candelabra which had been ceremonially lighted during the observance of the feast as reminders of the pillar of fire which had guided Israel in the wilderness.[22] Thus a second time Jesus applied to himself the spiritual reality of the symbolism of the Feast of Tabernacles (8:12, cf. 7:37-38).

To the Pharisees' objection that self-testimony is inadmissible, Jesus replied that the Father endorsed him. Furthermore, Jesus himself had perfect knowledge of his origin and function, and to these things regarding Jesus no ordinary human could possibly give testimony. Yet though they regarded his words with sneering contempt, no effort at this point was made to arrest him (8:13-20).

The Pharisees' sneering question, "Where is your Father?" could have been a slur against the manner of Jesus' birth (cf. 8:41). More likely, however, it was a demand that Jesus produce the testimony from his Father which he had just mentioned (8:18).

B. Jesus Claimed a Heavenly Origin. (8:21-23)

The arrival of Jesus' "hour" (8:20) would accomplish the purpose of his coming, and this would culminate in his return to the Father. His pronouncement was completely misunderstood by the Jews, whose only explanation was that he must be contemplating suicide, although they doubted it.[23] Jesus pointed out that their problem was the difference between their origin and his. They were spiritually dead in sins, limited to this world, and thus insensitive to spiritual truth. Jesus, on the other hand, had a heavenly origin and would soon return to the Father.

[22]Edersheim, *The Temple*, pp. 282-285.

[23]The Jews' question with *mēti* expects a negative answer.

C. *Jesus Claimed to Be the I AM of His People.* (8:24-29)

This claim, made in 8:24 and 8:28 (also 8:58) was an assertion of deity (Exod. 3:14; Deut. 32:39; Isa. 43:10). By demanding, "Who art thou?" the Jews insisted that Jesus complete the statement by adding a predicate, "I am. . . ."[24] This, he refused to do, leaving the impressive "I am" to arouse their imaginations. (Our translators have usually supplied "he" as the predicate, but the Greek text does not.) His coming crucifixion ("when ye have lifted up the Son of man") would vindicate his claim, for it would be followed by resurrection, exaltation, and the Spirit's new ministry to the world.

D. *Jesus Claimed to Be the Truth Which Sets Men Free from Sin.* (8:30-36)

As a result of Jesus' teaching, many of his hearers "believed on him" (*episteusan eis auton*, 8:30). This raises the question of whether it was true saving faith inasmuch as the following discussion was also addressed to those who "believed on him" (*tous pepisteukotas autōi*, 8:31), and Jesus accuses them of seeking to kill him (8:37). No clear transition can be seen here between different groups of Jews, and this makes it questionable whether the slight difference in grammatical construction following the words for "believe" is significant in the interpretation.[25] Apparently the sense is that these who believed in Jesus had come to a sort of mental acceptance, but not to any personal trust or surrender.[26] True discipleship would mean a full acceptance of his revelation, and would be demonstrated by continuance therein. Only this could accomplish the freedom from sin which was the essential aspect of Messiah's ministry (8:31-32).

Many Jews, however, felt that their physical relationship to Abraham secured for them the highest standing with God (8:33). Because this was their heritage, they denied that they had ever

---

[24]Greek: *egō eimi.*

[25]In 8:30 the verb is followed by *eis* with the accusative; in 8:31 the participle is followed by a simple dative.

[26]A helpful resumé of views is given in Hendriksen, *John,* pp. 50-52.

been in any sort of spiritual slavery.[27] Jesus showed that sin causes enslavement, and this is not a racial but a spiritual problem (8:34-36). As a slave has no rights in the master's house comparable to those of a son, so Israel as a slave to sin did not have the access to the Father's house which she imagined. (An illustration is the case of Ishmael and Isaac, both of whom were physically descended from Abraham, but one was a slave.) Christ alone, the embodiment of the truth (14:6), can change men from slaves to sons (cf. Gal. 4:4-7).

E. Jesus Claimed for Himself a Sinless Character. (8:37-50)

For Abraham to be the Jews' father in the all-important spiritual sense demanded a display of Abraham-like faith and conduct. Since this was not visible with these Jews, their spiritual paternity lay elsewhere (8:37-41a).

"We be not born of fornication" (8:41b) may perhaps be a slur on Jesus' birth, but it is more likely a reference to spiritual parenthood, in which they claimed God as their Father. They thought they were not "illegitimate," or religiously perverted as the Samaritans.

Jesus explained that their response proved their spiritual condition (8:42-44). God's spiritual children would love the One whom God had sent. The reason why they could not understand Jesus' audible words (*lalian*) was that they were unable to grasp the basic message (*logon*) he was bringing (8:43). They were not "tuned in" to him. They were more attuned to the devil, the one who from the beginning of man's history[28] has opposed God's truth and deluded men. Jesus, on the other hand, always spoke the truth of God, and if the Jews had possessed the nature of sons of God, they would have recognized the voice of God speaking in Jesus (8:45-47). He hurled the challenge to them to find any sin in him, and except for the charge of demon-possession, they could not. Yet their spiritual blindness prevented their drawing the

[27]This is more likely their meaning than to suppose they were denying any experience of political or social slavery, both of which they had known more than once in their history.

[28]The "beginning" (*archēs*) must here be related to human history inasmuch as the devil would hardly be termed a "mankiller" (*anthrōpoktonos*) before man's creation.

right conclusion from the sinlessness of his person (8:48-50). "Thou art a Samaritan" is taken by some as a reflection on Christ's paternity, but it is more likely an insult to denote one who was regarded as religiously impure.[29]

F. Jesus Claimed the Power to Bestow Spiritual Life. (8:51-55)

Faith in the message proclaimed by Jesus results in spiritual life, which means that the believer will never experience death in the sense of final separation from God (8:51). Even physical death will ultimately be overthrown by resurrection and glorification for believers. Such a pronouncement only confirmed the Jews in their opinion that Jesus was speaking wildly by demon possession (8:52-53). They thought only of the physical deaths of Abraham and the prophets, and failed to grasp the grand sweep of God's plan of redemption in Christ which has made provision for both spiritual life and physical resurrection. Jesus, however, did not back away from this declaration, but insisted that he must remain true to his Father whom he knows and who was the source of his message (8:54-55).

G. Jesus Claimed an Eternal Existence. (8:56-59)

In spite of the Jews' veneration of Abraham, Jesus showed that most of them did not share his faith, for Abraham "rejoiced to see my day" (8:56). With the eye of faith Abraham saw the truth of resurrection when he offered Isaac on the altar (Heb. 11:17-19). Christ's statement, however, may refer to the visions given to Abraham whereby he could have been made aware of more Messianic truth than the Old Testament specifically states (Gen. 12:7; 15:1-21).

The Jews were incredulous at such a statement (8:57). That Jesus was less than fifty years old was obvious.[30] How could he have seen Abraham? Jesus then made the stupendous claim, "Before Abraham was, I AM" (8:58). By using the timeless "I

[29]See comments on 4:4-5.

[30]This statement is not sufficient warrant to conclude that Jesus was nearly fifty, in the light of Luke 3:23. It should be regarded as a round number denoting the contrast between the great antiquity of Abraham and the period of one short lifetime.

am" rather than "I was," Jesus conveyed not only the idea of existence prior to Abraham, but timelessness—the very nature of God himself (Exod. 3:14). Rushing to unfinished parts of the temple where stones could be found, the Jews wanted to pelt Jesus for this latest claim (8:59). Our Lord, however, hid himself from them and departed from the temple unmolested.

Questions for Discussion

1. Was Jesus trying to deceive his brothers concerning his trip to the feast?
2. Was the action of Nicodemus commendable or should he have said much more?
3. Why did Jesus not condemn the woman taken in adultery?
4. In what ways does Jesus make men "free"?
5. Why did the Jews call Jesus a Samaritan?
6. Why did Jesus say, "Before Abraham was, I am," rather than "I was"?

Chapter 8

A Blind Man and the Shepherd
(John 9-10)

Our Lord's discourse on the Good Shepherd has provided Christians with one of the most graphic and best-loved symbols of their faith. The quiet scenes of rural life and the tender care of a Palestinian shepherd for his little flock have long been recognized as particularly appropriate in picturing Christ's concern for his followers, and the peace which is so characteristic of the soul at rest with God.

The Old Testament employs the figure of the shepherd to describe God's relation to his people. "The Lord is my shepherd," said David (Ps. 23:1). Isaiah wrote: "He shall feed his flock like a shepherd: he shall gather the lambs with his arm, and carry them in his bosom, and shall gently lead those that are with young" (Isa. 40:11). In the New Testament, Jesus applied the shepherd figure to himself. Those who rejected him were likened to "sheep having no shepherd" (Matt. 9:36; Mark 6:34). He compared his ministry to a seeking of the sheep that was lost (Luke 15:3-7). When he comes again, he will separate men "as a shepherd divideth his sheep from the goats" (Matt. 25:32).

Christ's most extended use of the metaphor was in the discourse of John 10. What is often overlooked, however, is that the discourse arose out of a most pertinent situation. Only by properly understanding the setting in John 9 can one fully appreciate the import of this discourse.

I. The Healing of a Blind Man (9:1-41)

A. *The Miracle* (9:1-7)

The incident occurred on a sabbath (9:14) while Jesus was still in Jerusalem. No major break from the previous material is indicated, and therefore it is assumed that these events took place shortly after the Feast of Tabernacles. At this time Jesus and his disciples encountered a blind man (9:1). Such are still all too frequently seen in the Middle East. The blind man may have been well known inasmuch as the disciples knew that he was blind from birth.

The disciples used the occasion to raise the question of the relation between sin and misfortune (9:2). They were sure that such calamities as blindness were caused by sin, but whose sin caused congenital blindness? Were the sins of the parents being exacted from their offspring (Exod. 20:5), or was it really possible for the soul to sin in the womb or in a previous existence as some rabbis suggested?

Our Lord's answer had two parts (9:3-5). First, he declared that no particular sin had produced this case of blindness. He did not discuss the fact that ultimately sin is the cause of all misfortune because of the Fall, nor that some ailments may be traceable to certain sins of the individual or his parents (e.g., syphilis). The error of their thinking was in supposing that every misfortune must be due to a specific sin.

Jesus then explained that the presence of this misfortune was an opportunity for the work of God to be demonstrated. God must not be held morally responsible for the evils in the world, but nevertheless he often incorporates such situations into his plan to accomplish the ends he desires. The emphasis in Jesus' words was not, however, upon the theological explanation of the origin of evil, but upon his ability to deal with it. During the brief "day" of his earthly ministry, he must perform the tasks given him by the Father who sent him. One of those tasks was to reveal himself as "the light of the world" by granting sight to this blind man.

The anointing of the man's eyes with clay formed from spittle (9:6) was a means similar to that used previously upon a deaf and dumb man (Mark 7:33) and another blind man (Mark 8:23). Inasmuch as Jesus usually healed without material means, it is clear that he attributed no medicinal properties to the clay. It was the divine will and power which healed, with or without physical means. Touch and hearing were the blind man's chief avenues of contact with the outside world, and the employment of the clay gave the man added reason for obeying Christ's instruction to wash at the pool.

The command to wash in the Pool of Siloam (9:7) was regarded as especially significant by John, as he calls attention to the meaning of the name, "the pool of the Sent One."[1] This pool is located in the southeast part of the city where the Tyropoean Valley joins the Kidron (see Fig. 18). Its waters come from the Gihon Spring by way of the tunnel built by Hezekiah (II Kings 20:20; II Chron. 32:30). At the Feast of Tabernacles the waters of Siloam were used to symbolize the blessings of God upon the people, and Jesus had related the symbolism to himself (7:37-38). John wants his readers to see that the blessing which the man was to experience really came from Messiah, the Sent One. In Isaiah 8:6 these same waters were used to symbolize God's provision for his people.

The man's obedient response brought restoration of sight. Apparently the man went directly home inasmuch as the neigh-

[1]From the Hebrew šalaḥ, send. The pool may have been so named because its waters were sent from Gihon Spring via the tunnel.

Fig. 18. *The Pool of Siloam. The water flows from Gihon Spring through Hezekiah's Tunnel to fill the pool.*

bors appear next in the narrative. He did not need to undergo any process of ocular education as infants do, but was fully developed in sight at the moment of healing.

B. The Reaction (9:8-34)

1. The Neighbors (9:8-13)

Such an event would not go unnoticed, especially since the man was an adult and had been blind since birth. The neighbors who had known him responded with much surprise (9:8-9). One group was sure he was the blind beggar they had known,[2] but others refused to commit themselves. Perhaps they suspected that a straightforward admission of a miracle would involve them in difficulties they would rather avoid. Having ascertained that Jesus was involved, the neighbors finally decided that an official investigation was warranted, so they took him to the Pharisees (9:10-13). They were doubtless aware of the officials' displeasure with Jesus and his following (9:22).

2. The Pharisees (9:14-17)

Why was the man brought to the Pharisees? It may have been known that they were leading the opposition to Jesus because of his alleged violations of rabbinical traditions. However, in view of the apparently official nature of the investigation which followed (and its results in 9:34), it seems better to regard the Pharisees as duly authorized by the Sanhedrin to deal with this matter.[3] On one previous occasion John has mentioned Pharisees as composing a delegation from the Sanhedrin (1:19, 24).

The Pharisees, no friends of Jesus, were placed in a dilemma. Some were so prejudiced against him and so firmly committed to their traditions regarding sabbath observance that all they could see was a supposed sabbath violation.[4] Others, however, recog-

---

[2]Their question with *ouch* expected an affirmative answer.

[3]William Hendriksen marshals convincing reasons for so understanding this reference. *Exposition of the Gospel According to John* (Grand Rapids, 1953), pp. 79-80.

[4]Scrupulous Pharisees would have called making clay on the sabbath an act of kneading which was expressly forbidden by rabbinical regulation. "Tract Sabbath," *Babylonian Talmud,* ed. Michael L. Rodkinson (Boston, 1918), I, 135-136.

nized that a genuine miracle had been done, and they were unable to explain it away. None of them wished to acknowledge the supernatural power of Jesus; yet they could hardly deny the miracle for the healed man was standing before them. As for the man himself, he was quite ready to announce that in his opinion Jesus was a prophet.

3. The Parents (9:18-23)

The parents of the blind man, when questioned by the authorities, assented to the facts of the miracle (9:18-20). Even so, they were very careful how they answered, and refused to offer any interpretation of these facts (9:21). In a court of law they would be justified as witnesses in stating no more than this, for anything additional would be opinion and hearsay.

John, however, indicated a more basic reason for their reticence. The parents feared excommunication from the synagogue (9:22-23). Expulsion from the religious community of Israel, whether permanently or for a shorter period,[5] would involve forfeiture of social and business relations, to say nothing of religious privileges, and was a penalty to be dreaded by any Jew.

4. The Man Himself (9:24-34)

For the second time the Pharisees called in the man and questioned him. Their statement, "Give God the praise" (9:24), can be understood in several ways. They could have meant that the man should give the credit to God, not Jesus. If so, it would have been a tacit acknowledgment on their part that a miracle had indeed occurred. Sometimes, however, these words meant "Confess your sin" or "Tell the truth" (see Josh. 7:19). With this meaning, the Pharisees would be demanding that he admit to some fraud.

The man refused to disavow his previous statement (9:15), and affirmed that a miracle had been done (9:25). At first he did not feel qualified to debate with the learned Pharisees as to whether Jesus was a sinner, but he could testify that his blindness was

---

[5]Information on the various degrees of excommunication come from Jewish records of a later time, and thus it is not certain what the exact character of this ban was. It was obviously serious enough to strike fear into the hearts of these parents.

now gone. When they kept pressing him, hoping no doubt to find some discrepancy in his retelling of the incident, the man resorted to sarcasm (9:26-27). The Pharisees then accused him of being a follower of Jesus, while they piously claimed adherence to Moses and professed their ignorance of Jesus' origin (9:28-29). Of course, it was quite true that they did not know that Jesus was from above (8:23).

By this time the man had warmed to the challenge and offered the Pharisees some theology of his own (9:30-33). Building upon their premise that a sinner could not do such miracles (9:16, 24), he concluded that Jesus, who was obviously Godfearing and whom he had already called a prophet (9:17), must be from God and thus must not have been performing a sinful act.

The Pharisees were not about to be lectured by this lowly beggar, so they expelled him (9:34). Although many have argued that this was no more than dismissal from the meeting, there are good reasons for understanding that the Pharisees were acting with authority for the entire Sanhedrin, and were carrying out the threat previously announced.[6] John had already prepared his readers to expect this by explaining that disciples of Jesus were candidates for excommunication (9:22), and the man has now been accused of this very thing (9:28). The restatement that he had been cast out (9:35) suggests that it was more important than merely an abrupt ending of the meeting. It also gives a clear understanding to Jesus' teaching on the shepherd which followed immediately, as we shall see.

C. The Outcome (9:35-41)

Jesus did not abandon the man whom he had healed. When he learned what the leaders had done, Jesus found the man and challenged him to put his faith in the divine Son of man (9:35-38).[7] This was the first time the man had actually seen

---

[6]Others holding the view that excommunication is meant are: George Reith, *The Gospel According to St. John* (Edinburgh, reprinted 1948), II, 32; Merrill C. Tenney, *John, The Gospel of Belief* (Grand Rapids, 1951), p. 159; William Hendriksen, *John*, pp. 79-80; C. K. Barrett, *The Gospel According to St. John* (London, 1967), p. 302.

[7]The preferred reading in 9:35 is "Son of Man" (*ton huion tou anthrōpou*) as found in P[66], [75] Aleph B D W. Although this is the only NT instance where *pisteuein* is used with "Son of man," it would seem to indicate clearly that this title is in no sense a denial of deity.

Jesus, and his knowledge was still meager. Our Lord then identified himself to him as the one who should be the object of his faith, and the response was immediate and complete. Though he had been expelled from Judaism, he had been brought to a saving faith in Jesus Christ.

Our Lord then explained that his coming into the world made possible not only physical sight for blind men, but also spiritual sight for those who would trust him (9:39-41). Judgment was not the primary purpose of Christ's coming (3:17), but it was an inevitable result, for men were forced to make a decision either for or against, and this in turn would determine their destiny. His enigmatic statement that "they which see might be made blind" made the Pharisees suspect that they were in view. And truly they were, for Jesus indicated that he was taking them at their own estimate of themselves.[8] If they would have acknowledged their spiritual darkness, they would have come to Jesus for forgiveness of their sin. But by claiming to possess spiritual sight, they were blind to their true condition and thus they remained in their sinful state. It was to this group that Jesus proceeded to give his teaching about the Good Shepherd, in order to place in true perspective the relationship between Jewish religion and his own ministry.

II. The Discourse on the Good Shepherd (10:1-21)

The shepherd's life was a common pursuit in Palestine. This fact, coupled with the frequent Old Testament use of this figure, made the following discourse most graphic and arresting. The movement of thought proceeds through a typical day of a shepherd from morning to night, presenting the picture in three separate scenes.

A. The Shepherd Forms His Flock. (10:1-6)

Palestinian sheepfolds were usually walled enclosures near the village (see Fig. 19). Numerous shepherds would place their flocks in the fold at night, and then each would gather his own

---

[8]Jesus did this on other occasions, as for example when he said that he did not come to call "the righteous" to repentance (Matt. 9:13).

Fig. 19. *A fold used for sheep, cows, or donkeys.*

sheep in the morning and lead them out to pasture for the day. It is this morning activity of forming the flock around the shepherd that is the theme of the first part of the discourse.

The shepherd in the story represents Christ, and the fold is a picture of Judaism, the religious system in which God's people were kept until Christ came. This seems clear from 10:16, where Jesus called the Gentiles "other sheep I have, which are not of this fold." It must also be remembered that Jesus was talking to the representatives of Judaism who had just seen the blind man removed from its communion. Thus he was explaining how Judaism is related to Messiah and his followers. The fold does not picture heaven, for there can be no thieves or robbers there (Matt. 6:20). Nor is it a picture of salvation or the church, for the shepherd found his sheep already in this fold and then led them out of it (10:3).

1. *He Comes the Proper Way.* (10:1-2)

The shepherd who has a right to the sheep does not need to sneak into the fold or climb over the wall. He can enter through the door. So Christ could come to his people because he had the right. The Old Testament prophecies pointed to him (and to no one else). He was born of a virgin, as Isaiah had foretold (Isa. 7:14). He had the title to the throne of David from Joseph, his legal father (Matt. 1:1-16).

2. He Is Received by the Porter. (10:3a)

The porter or doorkeeper was the person who was in charge of the fold until the shepherd came, and then admitted him to the sheep. This seems to picture John the Baptist, the one who officially introduced this Shepherd to the nation (1:26-34).

3. He Calls His Sheep by Name. (10:3b)

Many flocks were kept in a Palestinian fold but would be separated by their own shepherds, who gave their special call. So when Christ came to the nation of Israel, not every Jew recognized him as Messiah. Though most gave allegiance to the religious system of Judaism, they were not all the true spiritual flock of God. Some, however, were his true flock. There were some who were truly waiting for the redemption of Israel (e.g., Zacharias, Elisabeth, Simeon, Anna, Mary, and Joseph) and received with joy the Savior who came. The blind man in the context was one. When the true Shepherd came, he recognized his voice.

4. He Leads His Sheep Out of the Fold. (10:3c-6)

As Jesus presented himself to his nation, the leaders rejected him. Eventually they persecuted not only him, but also all who followed him. This is our Lord's explanation of his relation to the blind man. He had been removed from Judaism because he had responded to Christ. The fold of Judaism had fulfilled its function. It had kept the nation under the protection of the Mosaic Law and separate from the idolatrous nations of the world. But now that Christ had come, a new order was beginning (cf. Gal. 3:24-25). The Pharisees might object that Jesus did not lead the man out, but that they had cast him out. However, God in his sovereignty often uses the acts of men to accomplish his purposes. Messiah was forming his flock in fulfillment of the ancient prophecies. It is of interest that the passage nowhere states that the flock is led back into this fold again.

The audience of Jesus was composed largely of unbelieving Pharisees (9:40), and they failed to grasp the truth embodied in this figure (10:6)[9]

B. *The Shepherd Feeds His Flock* (10:7-10)

Jesus proceeded to describe a second scene which gave additional instruction. The scene is midday, with the sheep having been led away from the village fold and out to the grassy slopes and running brook for pasture and drink. Jesus called himself the "door" to teach the truth about his provision for his own. We should not think of him as the door of the fold, however (for he has already been differentiated from the fold door by being called the Shepherd who entered through the door, 10:2). Rather, we must understand the door as representing the entrance perhaps to a wooded thicket where a sheep would enter to find shade and water and from which it would pass to find pasturage.

1. *He Is the Door to Salvation.* (10:7-9a)

Perfect safety for the sheep lay in being near the shepherd. So with Christ spiritual salvation is provided by one's union with him. By faith in him as Lord and Savior, the believer is introduced to the realm of salvation. Christ becomes our Shepherd and assumes the responsibility for supplying all our needs.

2. *He Is the Door to Nourishment.* (10:9b)

Shepherds took the responsibility for locating pasture for their flocks, a task not always easy in that largely arid land. So Christ is the nourisher of believers, and their spiritual growth occurs as they "feed" upon him by hearing his word and following it (Acts 20:32; I Tim. 4:6; II Peter 3:18). To "go in and out" is a common Biblical idiom to depict the idea of living and carrying on one's affairs (Deut. 31:2; II Chron. 1:10; Acts 1:21).

3. *He Is the Door to Abundant Life.* (10:10)

The life the believer receives from Christ is eternal. It is not merely an extension of mortal life, but a far richer life than he has

---

[9]"Parable" (KJV, ASV) or "figure of speech" (NASB) is the term *paroimia*, "proverb," which may also have the sense of "hidden, obscure speech," akin to the Hebrew *māšāl*. Friedrich Hauck, "Paroimia," *Theological Dictionary of the New Testament*, ed. Gerhard Friedrich, trans. Geoffrey W. Bromiley (Grand Rapids, 1967), V, 854-856.

ever known before. And he begins to experience it the moment he puts his faith in Christ. Access to God in prayer, knowledge of full pardon for sin, possession of God's Spirit to illuminate God's Word and guide him in daily life—all these and many more give abundance to the Christian life.

C. The Shepherd Protects His Flock. (10:11-18)

The scene now shifts to evening. Often Palestinian shepherds took their flocks so far from the village in search of pasture and water, especially in the dry season, that they could not get back to the fold at night. Thus they spent the night outdoors. But this was the time when danger lurked and when the shepherd's protection was most needed.

1. He Dies for His Sheep. (10:11-13)

Many shepherds died while defending their flocks. There were knives and clubs of robbers to be faced, as well as the attacks of wild animals. In their cases, however, death was always unintended. Christ, on the other hand, was also going to die for his sheep in order to save them, but he was going to do so voluntarily. He would "give his life." His sheep were in danger of the greatest kind. "All we like sheep have gone astray" (Isa. 53:6). Jesus was thus predicting his own death which would occur the following spring.

Such sacrificial action of the shepherd is in stark contrast to the hireling, whose only real interest was his personal gain. Hired hands may have watched over the sheep when it was to their advantage, but they would not risk their lives for someone else's property. The reference would seem to be to the religious leaders who profited from their professional labors but had no real concern for the "sheep."

2. He Knows His Sheep. (10:14-15)

This Shepherd protects his sheep because he has perfect knowledge of them. He knows their proneness to wander and their infirmities. Thus he can preserve them as members of his flock. None of them can wander away and be lost because he knows all about them. "Those that thou gavest me I have kept, and none of them is lost" (17:12). This knowledge of his sheep is as complete as the knowledge of Christ and the Father about each other.[10]

3. He Gathers His Sheep. (10:16-18)

As the Good Shepherd, Christ also has an interest in gathering "other sheep" which were never a part of the "fold" of Judaism. The reference seems clearly to be to Gentiles whom the Shepherd would be gathering from all parts of the world wherever the gospel would be proclaimed. When his sheep respond to his voice in the gospel, they become "one flock"[11] with "one shepherd." Following Christ's death and the establishment of the New Testament Church at Pentecost, all who respond to Christ, whether Jew or Gentile, are members of one flock with Christ as the Shepherd. The apostle Paul wrote of it as one body, with both Jew and Gentile a part of it (Eph. 3:6; Col. 3:11).

D. The Response (10:19-21)

The immediate response to this teaching of Jesus was divided. Some heard nothing of significance in his words, and discounted him as demon-possessed or insane. They failed to recognize the Shepherd's call. Others, however, found the outright rejection that some expressed inadequate to account for the person and work of Jesus.

III. Renewed Discussion at the Feast of Dedication (10:22-42)

A. The Setting (10:22-23)

The time was December, and the Feast of Dedication, a few months after the Feast of Tabernacles (7:1). This feast was not of Mosaic origin, but was instituted to commemorate the cleansing and rededication of the temple under Judas Maccabaeus in 164 B.C., after its defilement by Antiochus Epiphanes (I Macc. 4: 52–59; II Macc. 10:5). It was also called the Feast of Lights and is

---

[10]The translation of 10:14-15 in the ASV and NASB is preferable to KJV, and clearly states this mutual knowledge: "I know my own and my own know me, even as the Father knows me and I know the Father."

[11]The unfortunate KJV rendering "one fold" is based upon a poor translation in the Vulgate. The Greek text uses *poimnē* (flock), not *aulē* (fold).

observed by Jews today as Hanukah. Because winter can be cold, windy, and rainy in Jerusalem, Solomon's Porch (the covered colonnade along the east side of the temple area) offered some protection from the elements. Later this spot became a meeting place for Jerusalem Christians (Acts 3:11; 5:12).

Some scholars hold that this time note refers to the preceding portion of Scripture thus separating the discourse on the Good Shepherd from the events associated with the Feast of Tabernacles. The reading *egeneto tote*[12] ("at that time was . . . ," 10:22 ASV marg.) is often pointed to as supporting this. On the other hand, there has been no clear indication of any time break since 7:1 until 10:22 is reached. Furthermore, the alternate reading at 10:22 is *egeneto de*[13] ("and there came. . . ."). No strong reason exists for not placing the break at 10:22. The fact that a similar discussion occurred as on a previous occasion is not unusual.

B. The Question of Messiahship (10:24-31)

While Jesus was in the temple precincts, the Jews questioned him about his claim of Messiahship, and he repeated some of his earlier statements about himself and his sheep. When they demanded a clear pronouncement, Jesus explained that he had already answered their question by his words and his works. It was not more information they needed, but a change of nature. Their unbelief branded them as not the sheep of his flock. They still belonged to the old fold with the false shepherds. They did not have the bliss of eternal life and the knowledge that this new life was secure because it was in the safety of the Father's[14]

[12]This is the reading of P[75] and a corrector of P[66] as well as B L W.

[13]The original reading of P[66], and in Aleph A D K X Delta Theta.

[14]Textual variation occurs at 10:29 which alters the sense considerably. If the reading is followed which contains the relative pronoun in the nominative, the sense is, "My Father *who* has given . . . is greater than all" (so A K Theta P[66]). Although anti-Trinitarians have sometimes used this verse, the sense must clearly be conditioned by verse 30, and thus the reference must be to the divine economy in the Trinity in which the Father is the "First Person." There is strong support, however, for the neuter pronoun, thus *"That which* my Father has given . . . is greater than all" (so B Aleph D). This reading yields the sense that Christ's sheep are more valuable than any opposing force, and thus are certain of God's protection.

powerful hand as well as Christ's. Jesus then emphasized that he and the Father are "one." This was a claim of oneness not only in purpose, but also in nature. The Jews understood this perfectly well, and once again went to nearby construction areas and "carried" (*ebastasan*) stones to Solomon's Porch to use against Jesus.

C. *The Charge of Blasphemy* (10:32-38)

These enemies of Jesus recognized nothing but blasphemy in the statements he made. "Thou being a man makest thyself God" (10:33). This was the basic charge which eventually brought the demand for his crucifixion (19:7). Jesus based his answer on such passages as Psalm 82:6 and Exodus 4:16 and 7:1, where God's spokesmen who minister his word are called "gods." His point was that if Scripture can term such men "gods" because they were the agents to interpret divine revelation, how could Christ be a blasphemer by claiming the title "Son of God" when he was sent from heaven as the very revelation of God himself?

D. *The Results* (10:39-42)

Hostility became so great that Jesus withdrew across the Jordan.[15] Yet even in the face of such opposition many new believers were made.

Questions for Discussion

1. Is there any relation between sin and physical misfortune?
2. Why do you think Jesus sent the blind man to the pool to be healed, rather than healing him immediately?
3. In what sense did Jesus make blind those who see (9:39-41)?
4. In the discourse on the Good Shepherd, what do you think the fold represents? Why?
5. What is the meaning of the quotation, "Ye are gods" (10:34), and why did Jesus use it?
6. What statements in John 10 teach that the believer's eternal life is secure?

---

[15]The place was apparently the same as mentioned in 1:28, but not 3:23.

Chapter 9

The Raising of Lazarus and the Close of Public Ministry

(John 11-12)

The incident of Lazarus recorded in John 11 is certainly one of the most amazing performances in the career of Jesus. It served to set Jesus apart from all other miracle workers who ever lived. In Old Testament times prophets had wrought miraculous deeds, and some had even raised dead persons (cf. Elijah: I Kings 17:17-24; Elisha: II Kings 4:1-37; 13:20-21). However, in no case had death occurred as much as four days previously. None of our modern "healers" make such claims. To raise a man dead four days was an act unparalleled in human history before or since.

Even our Lord did not raise many from the dead during his ministry. On only three occasions did he do so, of which the raising of Lazarus was the most dramatic. He raised the daughter of Jairus, who had been dead a short time (Luke 8:41-56). He raised a widow's son who must have been dead no longer than one day (Luke 7:11-16). This apparent reluctance by Jesus may have been due to the fact that these raisings brought a mere return to this present mortal life. They were not final resurrections which would bring glorified bodies and an end to human ills. Thus they were not an unmixed blessing. It seems apparent that those who were raised had all memory of their experience erased, for otherwise their return to this life would have made earthly existence neither happy nor fully normal. Nevertheless the case of Lazarus was a striking proof of Christ's power to those who are called to put their trust in him.

I. The Raising of Lazarus (11:1-57)

A. The Background (11:1-16)

1. The Sickness of Lazarus (11:1-6)

The family of Mary, Martha, and Lazarus appears three times in the Gospels. It was at this home that Mary showed her devotion by sitting at Jesus' feet to hear his words (Luke 10:38-42). Just before the crucifixion Jesus was guest at another meal where this family was prominent (John 12:1-9).[1] On the occasion of John 11, Lazarus had become gravely ill. He was perhaps a younger brother in the family, since he seems to have had no particular responsibilities in the home on any of the afore-mentioned occasions. Vhen this illness occurred, the sisters sent word from their home in Bethany, a suburb[2] of Jerusalem, to Jesus who was at that time across the Jordan River in Perea.

The response of Jesus that "this sickness is not unto death" did not mean that Lazarus would not die, nor that Jesus was mistaken about what would happen. In all probability Lazarus was already dead by the time word reached Jesus, for the two days Jesus remained where he was, plus one day for the trip to Bethany, account for only three of the four days Lazarus had been dead (11:39). It seems likely, therefore, that Lazarus had died the same day on which the messenger had left to find Jesus.[3] The statement of our Lord took all of this into account but indicated that physical death was not to be the final movement of the episode.

2. The Alarm of the Disciples (11:7-10)

The suggestion of Jesus that he and the disciples return from Perea to the area of Judea (in which Bethany was located) filled his followers with fear for his safety. The reason he had left Judea some weeks before was the murderous hostility of the Jewish leaders (10:39-40). An attempt to stone him had been unsuccessful, but there was no guarantee that it would not be tried again (10:31).

Jesus replied that he could walk in safety while it was day. In the Father's calendar for him it was still day (cf. 9:4). The night,

[1]John's identification of Mary by reference to an event he has not yet described assumes that the incident of Mary's anointing Jesus' feet was already known to his readers from the earlier Synoptic accounts.

[2]The village of Bethany was on the far side (i.e., east) of the Mount of Olives in relation to Jerusalem. The distance from Jerusalem was a little less than two miles (11:18; a furlong or *stadion* equaled about one-eighth of a mile).

[3]Of course, it is possible that the journey of the messenger may have taken more than one day, inasmuch as the exact location of Jesus at this moment is not certain.

though not far off, had not yet arrived. As he put it on other occasions, his "hour" had not yet come (2:4; 7:30). There is a principle here that all do well to remember. As long as one is fulfilling God's specific plan and until that plan is accomplished, there is nothing that God's servant need fear. He can rely upon God's protection, for angels are deployed to give strength and preservation (cf. Ps. 91).

3. The Purpose of Jesus (11:11-16)

Jesus announced his intentions regarding Lazarus as a waking of him out of sleep. This was a figure of speech in their day, even as it is today. Yet it was misunderstood by the disciples. They thought Lazarus had passed the crisis in his illness and was now on the road to recovery.

It required the plain statement, "Lazarus died,"[4] before the disciples understood the true situation. Note that Jesus knew clearly that Lazarus was dead, and thus his remark in 11:4 cannot be an indication of inadequate information. Jesus purposed to turn this incident from one of sorrow and loss to one of strengthening for the disciples. Their faith needed bolstering at this time when they had been forced to flee for their lives.

The response of Thomas, "Let us also go, that we may die with him," may be taken in two ways. It is possible he meant that they should die with Lazarus. If so, it was an exclamation of utter despair, revealing an attitude of hopelessness so far as Jesus and his program were concerned. More probably Thomas referred to dying with Jesus, which he assumed to be a virtual certainty if they should venture into Judea again (11:8). Thus he expressed a reckless courage by suggesting that if Jesus were going to expose himself to death, he and the others would join him. (As it turned out, it would not be on this visit to Judea but the next that the death of Jesus would occur.)

B. The Miracle (11:17-44)

In this section Jesus is depicted with each member of the family separately, meeting each particular need and showing himself to be keenly sensitive to individual problems.

---

[4]The aorist tense is employed: *apethanen.*

1. Jesus and Martha (11:17-27)

By the time Jesus arrived at Bethany, Lazarus had been in the grave four days. Many mourners were at the home, bringing what comfort they could in the traditional Jewish manner. Martha, the energetic sister, went out to meet Jesus as he approached. When they met, she made a statement which implied a most remarkable request.

"If thou hadst been here, my brother had not died." Here was an exclamation of strong faith in Jesus' power to heal the sick. Martha was not blaming Jesus for not hurrying (11:6) because she knew that Lazarus was probably dead by the time Jesus received the message. She had implicit faith that the one who had healed so many would certainly have healed her brother.

Martha, however, did not stop with this affirmation. She went on to say: "I know that even now, whatsoever thou wilt ask of God, God will give it thee." What did she want Jesus to ask from God? These words can mean only one thing. Martha was asking Jesus for the raising of her brother. This was a stupendous request. No one else ever asked Jesus to do such a thing. He was often asked to heal the sick, but no one except Martha ever had the faith to expect him to raise the dead. She knew that he had raised two others (both the widow's son and the daughter of Jairus were raised prior to this). She might possibly have received a report of Jesus words of 11:4. She asked, therefore, not from blind and irresponsible optimism, but on the basis of Christ's revelation about himself. Her faith may have been limited in that she felt he would need to "ask" God (she employed a term which sometimes meant "beg," one which Jesus never used in his asking of the Father),[5] and she wavered later at the tomb, but the important thing is that she dared to ask at all.

Jesus then gave her some instruction. He wanted her to make sure that her faith really understood who he was, whether or not this particular miracle were performed. When Jesus assured her that Lazarus would rise again, Martha affirmed her belief in the final resurrection of believers. This had not been doubted by her, and it was not what she was asking for now. Jesus then pointed out to her that resurrection power, whether at the last

---

[5]Martha used *aiteō*; Jesus always used *erōtaō*.

day or at the present moment, resided in him. He stated that believers who die physically (like Lazarus) will someday be resurrected (11:25). And at that time those still alive on earth will never need to die at all.[6] To all of this Martha gave her sincere confession, "I believe." Having put her trust completely in him as the God-man and the Savior, she could repose full confidence in him for whatever he might choose to do.

2. Jesus and Mary (11:28-37)

During this time Mary had remained in the house with friends and mourners. In personality she differed from her sister. She needed sympathy rather than persuasion. Therefore Jesus dealt with her differently than with Martha. To Martha he gave explanation and challenge. To Mary he brought tears of genuine compassion.

[6]Another view of 11:26 interprets the living and dying as spiritual, understanding the reference to be present possessors of spiritual life who will never have it broken off.

Fig. 20. *The traditional tomb of Lazarus at Bethany.*

Two things are said of Jesus: he groaned and wept. The groaning actually is indicated by a word which expresses indignation.[7] He was indignant at what he saw. The miseries and bereavement caused by sin, perhaps the too-professional type of mourners who really were not comforting—such matters would be sufficient to cause Jesus to be indignant at what sin has wrought in human life.

Jesus also wept. This was not the loud wailing of mourners. It was the shedding of tears of sympathy. He was moved by human sorrow. Even though we have God's word that all things work together for the good of the Christian in God's will, and this means that even our sorrows will ultimately work for our benefit, we also have the assurance that Christ's knowledge of our ultimate benefit does not prevent him from being our compassionate Friend in the time of trial.

Some of the Jews standing by recognized the sympathetic nature of Jesus and his genuine concern for this lovely family. But others suspected him of hypocrisy. They suspected either that his power was lacking or else that his friendship with Lazarus was false.

3. Jesus and Lazarus (11:38-44)

The command of Jesus to roll away the large stone which closed the entrance to the tomb brought certain qualms to Martha. She had asked for this raising, but her faith in Christ's power was almost engulfed by her awareness of conditions inside the sepulcher. Embalming was not practiced in first-century Palestine. Burial usually occurred, therefore, on the day of death. Bodies were wrapped in strips of cloth, with spices sprinkled among the bindings to dispel the odor. Jesus encouraged Martha by pointing her away from the corruption in the tomb to the glory which he had promised.

Our Lord then prayed to the Father. The communion between the Son and the Father was complete and harmonious. He did not pray at the tomb in order to ascertain God's will or to direct it, for this was already known (11:4), and now he publicly thanked

---

[7]Greek: *embrimaomai* (11:33, 38). The word commonly denotes an expression of anger. Such meanings as "scold," "censure," and "warn sternly" are frequent. Because of the difficulty of seeing anger in Johannine context, some have suggested the sense of "be deeply moved" for this passage.

Fig. 21. *A rolling stone, used to close a first-century tomb. Herod's Cave, Jerusalem.*

him for what was about to happen. This public thanksgiving would enable the people to see that he was truly the One whom the Father had sent to do his will.

Calling with a loud voice so that the crowds would know what was happening, Jesus brought Lazarus alive from the tomb. If the legs were wrapped separately in the burial cloths, as was sometimes done, walking would have been possible though awkward. It is difficult even to imagine the amazement which must have gripped the witnesses of this miracle. Surely it was one of the most dramatic in Jesus' ministry.

C. The Consequences (11:45-57)

1. To the Eyewitnesses (11:45-46)

Many having seen this remarkable miracle of raising put their faith in Jesus. That this number must have been sufficiently large is indicated by the fact that the Jewish leaders feared a full-scale uprising by his followers (11:47-48). There were other persons who had seen the miracle but did not become believers. On the contrary, they reported the incident to the Pharisees, for they knew that they would be greatly disturbed over any new wave of popularity around Jesus. This response of unbelief in the face of the clearest proof is confirmation of Christ's teaching in Luke 16:31: "If they hear not Moses and the prophets, neither will they be persuaded, though one rose from the dead." The chief cause of unbelief is not inadequate information, but a heart in rebellion against the authority of God and his word.

2. *To the Sanhedrin* (11:47-53)

When the leaders of the nation received the report of Jesus' latest miracle, they called a meeting of the Sanhedrin. This was the highest ruling body among the Jews, subject only to the Roman governor. They expressed the fear that if Jesus continued to increase in popularity, it would diminish their own authority in the eyes of the people, and there might even be an attempt by Jesus and his followers to seize political power. The leaders knew that Rome would not sit idly by while such events were in the making. Thus there was the possibility that Rome would step in, remove the present Jewish leaders, and rule the nation with a firmer hand.

Caiaphas, the high priest[8] and president of the Sanhedrin, was a shrewd politician. The answer he proposed was viciously simple. They need not fear wholesale Roman intervention with much loss of life. All that would be required was the sacrifice of one life. If they would do away with Jesus, the problem would disappear. As a result the group passed a resolution to bring about the execution of Jesus. When John wrote this Gospel many years later, he noted that the words of Caiaphas had a far wider fulfillment than the crafty politician had intended. For by the death of Jesus for the nation there was brought about spiritual deliverance for all men who trust him.

---

[8]The mention of Caiaphas as high priest "that year" (11:49) does not imply that the author mistakenly thought this was an annual office, but that Caiaphas was high priest "in that fateful year" of Christ's death.

3. To Jesus (11:54)

The Sanhedrin's hatred caused Jesus to withdraw from Judea for a time. Knowing that his death had already been agreed upon by the authorities and awaited only the opportune moment, he retired to a city near the desert, called Ephraim.[9]

4. To the Passover Pilgrims (11:55-57)

An interval of unspecified length has passed, and the spring feast of Passover was approaching. Many Jews made the pilgrimage to Jerusalem and were curious as to the whereabouts of Jesus. They knew the extreme antipathy of the authorities to him, which his miraculous works had not dispelled but only made worse, and wondered whether he would appear at all.

II. The Supper at Bethany (12:1-11)

A. The Setting (12:1-3)

Six days before Passover, Jesus made his way toward Jerusalem and arrived at Bethany. That evening[10] a meal was provided for Jesus, at which were also present the twelve, Martha, Mary, Lazarus, and a man named Simon the Leper.[11] The event of particular interest was the action of Mary, who took a pound of costly ointment[12] and anointed the feet of Jesus, wiping them with her hair. Matthew and Mark indicate that she anointed his head also (Matt. 26:7; Mark 14:3).

---

[9]This city is often identified with Et-Taiyibeh, a few miles northeast of Bethel and about fourteen miles north of Jerusalem.

[10]Some harmonists place this meal several days later (i.e., two days before Passover, Matt. 26:2-6; Mark 14:1-3), but John seems to place it on the same day as the arrival. On the assumption that John's order is chronological, the Markan account of the dinner must be understood as retrospective, in which Mark has mentioned the betrayal and then taken his readers back to the origins of it at the dinner several days before.

[11]Simon is not mentioned in John, but is named as the owner of the house in Matt. 26:6 and Mark 14:3. He was apparently one of many lepers who had been healed by Jesus.

[12]The Greek term *murou nardou pistikēs* is difficult because of the uncertain use of *pistikēs*. The tendency today is to regard it as derived from *pistos*, "faithful," hence "genuine," thus yielding the sense: ointment of genuine nard.

B. The Objection (12:4-6)

Judas[13] voiced the objection that the ointment should have been sold and the proceeds given to the poor. Because Jesus and the disciples were poor, the act may at first have seemed wasteful to men who had sacrificed all to follow Christ. Three hundred denarii represented almost a year's wages for a laboring man.[14] However, the basis for this criticism was not a genuine concern about the wise use of funds. It started with Judas, the one who would ultimately be unmasked as the betrayer and who is also called a thief—this last being a fact that must have come to light later. Judas was the custodian of the common purse, and the verb "bear" (ebastazen) can mean "bear away" in the sense of embezzle. The imperfect tense may suggest a continual pilfering during Christ's ministry. Hence Judas may have hated to see his prospects for greater enrichment dissipated in this way.

C. Christ's Answer (12:7-8)

Our Lord's answer had a dual focus. As to Mary, Jesus explained her act as an anointing for his burial.[15] It is commonly explained that Jesus invented this motive for her to relieve her embarrassment. As it turned out, this was the only anointing his body received, for the resurrection occurred before the women arrived at the tomb. What was actually in Mary's mind? Taking the text as it stands, we must assume that Mary had the stated purpose in mind, for Jesus said so (cf. Mark 14:8). She sensed the darkness of the hour, and the hostility against Jesus. Furthermore, Jesus had recently revealed his coming death, and some of these occasions were public (10:11, 17-18; cf. Matt. 20:18-19; Mark

---

[13]Judas may have started the criticism, but Matthew mentions that "the disciples" said it. Apparently they all joined in.

[14]One denarius was a laboring man's daily wage (Matt. 20:2).

[15]The aorist subjunctive tērēsēi ("keep") in 12:7 poses problems. Jesus can hardly be suggesting that she should keep the ointment for his burial, or that she should keep the residue, since she has already used it. Nor does the subjunctive form support the translation "has kept." Apparently there is a condensed expression here, and the sense is that she should not be criticized but rather permitted to utilize the ointment according to her wishes (which in fact she was now doing).

10:33-34). Even though the disciples refused to believe it, Mary's mind accepted the fact, and realized that when the tragedy came, there would be no time for the usual niceties. If Mary knew to some extent what she was doing, then the tremendous praise bestowed upon her is more readily understood (Matt. 26:13).

As to the disciples, Jesus reminded them that Mary's act did not rob the poor. There remained abundant opportunity for assisting those in need (Mark 14:7). One must grasp opportunities that will not return. Now was the time for Mary to pay homage to Jesus, for this opportunity would not come again. Furthermore, those who truly honor Jesus will share his concern for those in need.

D. The Results (12:9-11)

As a result of this dinner, many people learned of Jesus' presence in Bethany and came to see both him and Lazarus. The leaders, however, became more determined than ever to do away with Jesus and with Lazarus as well because of the impact which his miraculous return from the dead was having in the making of new converts to Jesus.

III. The Entrance into Jerusalem (12:12-19)

A. The Scene (12:12-13)

On the day following the supper at Bethany, Jesus went with his disciples to Jerusalem. Crowds from the city heard that he was coming, and met him waving palm branches and shouting, "Hosanna." They quoted Psalm 118:25-26. What did the multitudes mean by this cry? The passage was generally regarded as messianic, as rabbinical quotations indicate. ("The coming one" was a title of Messiah.) On this occasion it seems to have been sung spontaneously, and was more or less consciously done. The expectations of many were kindled, and his followers hoped that he would make good his claims to the kingdom.

B. The Prophecy (12:14-15)

Jesus rode on a young ass—a dramatic act because he usually walked. (The details about the procuring of the animal were well known from the Synoptics and John does not repeat them.) The ass was a humble animal. It is doubtful if any king since Solomon had ridden one. Thus was fulfilled to the letter the prophecy of Zechariah 9:9. Jesus was publicly claiming Messianic homage.

C. The Reaction (12:16-19)

These dramatic events could not escape notice. That was why Jesus had made careful preparation for them. Yet some of the reaction was not what one might have expected. The disciples, for instance, did not understand the significance of what was happening until much later (12:16). What Jesus did seemed to be occurring in the normal course of events. There was no mechanical fulfilling of prophetic details.

The crowd which accompanied Jesus from Bethany was still greatly impressed with the raising of Lazarus, and gave their testimony to that astounding miracle (12:17). Another crowd, composed of those from Jerusalem who had learned Jesus was in Bethany, came to meet him (12:18). They had also heard of the miracle of Lazarus, and had not seen Jesus in Jerusalem since then. The Pharisees, who had already plotted his death (11:47-53), expressed helpless rage that none of their efforts to diminish Jesus' influence seemed to be doing any good (12:19).

IV. The Request of Certain Greeks (12:20-36)

A. The Wish of the Greeks (12:20-22)

These men were not Greek-speaking Jews, but Gentiles (Hellēnes). Apparently they were "proselytes of the gate"—Gentiles who had forsaken pagan gods and worshiped the God of Israel, but who stopped short of adopting circumcision and the Mosaic food laws. Such men could worship in synagogues and at the temple in Jerusalem, but could enter only as far as the Court of the Gentiles (see Figs. 5, 6). The men under discussion requested a private interview with Jesus, and the request was conveyed by Philip and Andrew. They may have been unsure of his attitude, for Jesus had previously stated that he was sent only to "the lost sheep of the house of Israel" (Matt. 15:24).

B. The Response of Jesus (12:23-36)

1. The Parable (12:23-26)

Even though these Greeks may not have received a private interview with Jesus, they were probably present at the following public discussion. The parable was given to explain the program of Jesus and its purpose. It doubtless was meant to show that his restriction of activities at present to Israel did not mean that he had no world-wide concern. Rather, it was to bring about the salvation of others. Just as grain must be planted and the original kernel must actually disintegrate before the new plant can come, so Christ must die if his ministry was to have the widest fruitage.

2. The Prayer (12:27-28a)

This prayer was voiced as Christ contemplated his approaching death. As he spoke, he seemed to suggest two alternatives.[16] The first one (12:27) he rejects; the second he voices as an indication of his faith and commitment to the Father's will.

3. The Voice from Heaven. (12:28b-33)

The voice from heaven brought the Father's reassurance. It was primarily intended for the crowds, whose faith would be severely tried in the next few days. This was the third occurrence of the divine voice during Christ's ministry (baptism, transfiguration, passion). Those who were not spiritually discerning interpreted the sound as thunder; others, as an angel.

The coming crisis of the cross would draw all men to Christ (12:32). This is commonly explained as a drawing of men to Christ in salvation because of Calvary. This view has a weakness in that John elsewhere uses the concept of "drawing" as a divine act which accomplishes its goal (6:44). Yet we must weaken this concept considerably if we apply it to "all men," for some effectively resist salvation. Others explain this as the drawing of all men to the crucified Christ in judgment. Judgment is clearly the subject of the immediate context (12:31). Every man must stand before the crucified Christ, either as a penitent sinner to receive

[16]For a summary of other views see William Hendriksen, *Exposition of the Gospel According to John* (Grand Rapids, 1953), pp. 198-201.

judicial pardon, or else to face him as the judge to hear his doom pronounced (5:22).

4. *The Final Appeal* (12:34-36)

The audience understood that Jesus was speaking of his death, and they could not reconcile this with their ideas of Messiah. Jesus appealed once again to them to receive by faith the light which he alone could give. Only then would they be able to see the truth. Otherwise their state would remain one of spiritual blindness.

V. Summary of Christ's Public Ministry (12:37-50)

This section is a clearly indicated close of a major division of John's Gospel. It consists of two summarizations—one by John and one in the words of Jesus.

A. *Summarized by John* (12:37-43)

John notes the two diametrically opposed results of Christ's ministry: unbelief among the vast majority, but faith on the part of many, including even some timid belief among Jewish leaders. The unbelief was accounted for in the words of Isaiah 53:1 and 6:10. Scripture had foretold long before that many would disbelieve God's Messiah, and that this would itself be a judgment upon them for their sin. As Morris puts it: "God's purposes are not frustrated by the opposition of evil men. They are accomplished."[17]

The many believing rulers are not known to us. Probably Nicodemus and Joseph of Arimathea reported the fact to John. Later it is known that a large company of priests identified themselves with the Christian movement (Acts 6:7).

B. *Summarized by Jesus* (12:44-50)

Here John has selected certain statements of Jesus which are indefinite as to the time and place, but which serve well as a summation. Most of these subjects have been previously incor-

---

[17]Leon Morris, *The Gospel According to John* in the New International Commentary Series (Grand Rapids, 1971), pp. 604-605.

porated in this Gospel. The results of belief in Christ are shown to be a removal from darkness into light (12:44-46). The reason is that Jesus is the one sent from the Father and is actually one with the Father. Unbelief, however, leaves one to face certain judgment, and it leaves him without excuse (12:47-50). The revelation of God in Christ which has been rejected will serve to judge him in the last day.

Questions for Discussion

1. What is the meaning of Jesus' words about Lazarus, "This sickness is not unto death"?
2. For what was Martha asking Jesus in 11:22?
3. What was Mary's purpose in anointing Jesus?
4. Do you think Jesus granted an interview to the Greeks? Why?
5. In what sense does Jesus "draw all men" unto him?

The
Private
Instruction
(John 13-17)

Chapter 10

Christ's Final Discourse
Part One: In the Upper Room
(John 13-14)

The first twelve chapters of John cover a period of approximately three years in the ministry of Christ. These were the great public actions of Jesus, when he moved among the people working miracles and preaching his message. The second division of the Gospel, chapters 13-17, is restricted to one evening in Christ's life. The audience also is limited, for only the twelve were present with Jesus. This one evening was the last night before the Crucifixion, and as Jesus met with his closest associates in the upper room, he gave them his final instructions before his passion.

Of the many incidents that occurred on that final evening, John alone records the washing of the disciples' feet and provides the fullness of detail regarding our Lord's subsequent discourse. A harmony of the Gospels should be consulted for the complete description of all that transpired. The dramatic character of Jesus' act in washing their feet, the spiritual application which he made of it, and the obligation which he then placed upon the disciples caused John to devote the opening portion of this narrative to this action.

I. The Washing of the Disciples' Feet (13:1-17)

A. *The Setting* (13:1-3)

It was Passover season and great throngs were gathering in Jerusalem to observe this ancient feast. Passover commemorated the deliverance of Israel from death in Egypt, when the blood of a slain lamb sprinkled on the door had spared the occupants from the angel of death. The Passover lamb pictured redemption of sinners by the sacrifice of a substitute. The fact that Isaiah pictured the Messiah as a "lamb" (Isa. 53:7), and John the Baptist referred to Jesus as "the lamb of God" (1:29, 36) led the early church to associate the symbolism of the Passover with Christ. Paul called Christ "our Passover" (I Cor. 5:7). The Passover festival was initiated by the eating of the lamb, which was followed immediately by the week-long Feast of Unleavened Bread. John places this upper room incident *before* the Passover. This is made clear also by comparing 13:29, 18:28, and 19:14, where even the events early the next morning were said to be on the day of preparation; that is, the day on which the lambs were slain and other preparations made for observing the feast. The Last Supper, therefore, was one full day before the Passover meal.[1]

Furthermore, Jesus fully realized that his "hour" had arrived. Thus there is particular significance in his acts in view of his awareness of the time. We note also that love for his disciples governed his actions toward them.

The evening meal was actually in progress when Jesus rose from the table.[2] It must have been shortly after they had gathered, since the main part of the eating is mentioned subsequent to the feet-washing (13:26). By this time the plans of Judas had already been laid. The word "now" (*ēdē*) in 13:1 should be translated "already." Several days before, Judas had made an agreement with the chief priests to deliver Jesus to them at the first opportunity (Matt. 26:14-16).

The authority of Jesus at this time is also an important factor mentioned by John. Jesus knew that he had the full authority from the Father to win the victory of the cross and also to institute the symbols for his followers on that evening. Thus the action of Christ was introduced in John's record with the greatest of solemnity.

[1]This is a chronological problem of long standing. It is commonly assumed that the Synoptic Gospels treat the Last Supper as Passover. Some, therefore, attempt to interpret John in a way that allows this Gospel to be describing the Passover, in spite of the difficulties noted above. Others assert a discrepancy between John and the Synoptics. It is the view of this commentator that there is no discrepancy, and that the statements regarding this meal in the Synoptics can be interpreted in harmony with John as referring to a meal one full day before Passover.

[2]The KJV translation "being ended" is based upon the aorist reading *genomenou*, found in A D K and a corrector of Aleph, as well as the Byzantine text, and in a slightly variant form in P66. The present tense form *ginomenou* is supported by Aleph B L W, and is adopted by ASV, NASB, and RSV. The translation "during supper" or "as supper was occurring" best represents this.

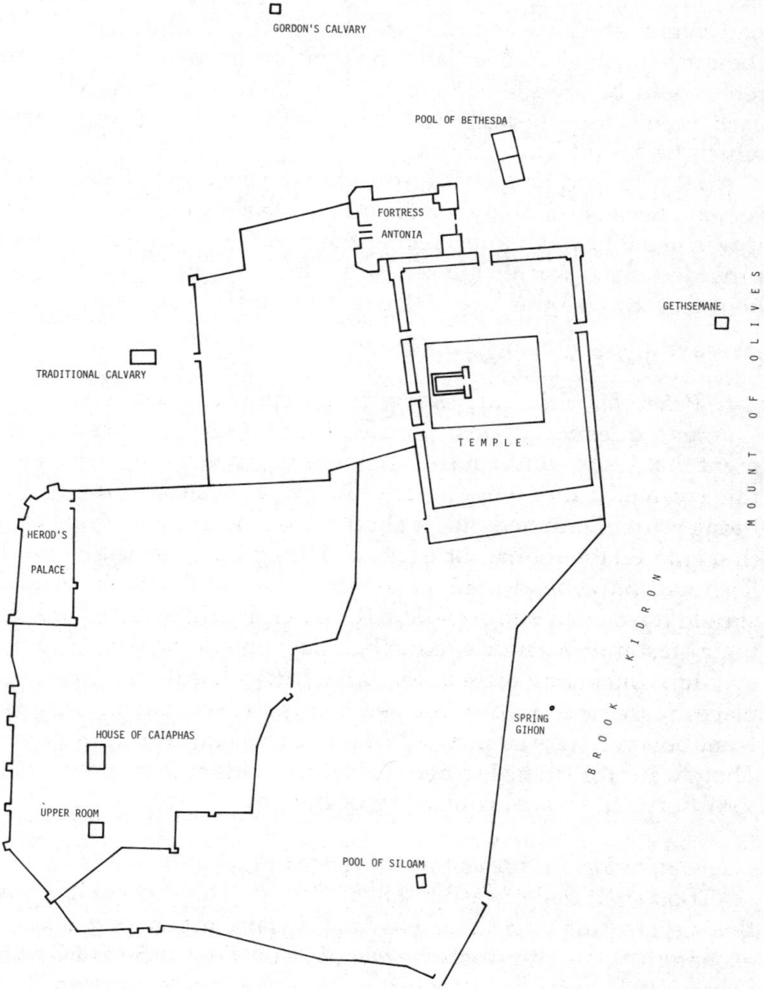

Fig. 22. *New Testament Jerusalem.*

B. The Action (13:4-5)

After the group had gathered at the table, Jesus got up, took off his outer robe, and girded himself with a towel. The disciples had begun stocking the room with provisions and utensils for their use during Passover, and the items he needed to wash their feet would be readily available. Jesus then proceeded to wash each man's feet, Judas's included, with the water and basin which he found in the room.

What Jesus did had a background in the custom of Palestinian society. Because of dusty roads and the wearing of open sandals, it was usual to wash one's feet at the door. At a dinner the host provided water for his guests, and either the guest washed his own feet, or else the host delegated the task to servants.

C. The Objections (13:6-11)

1. Peter objected to the change in the custom. (13:6-7)

Peter's question, "Dost thou wash my feet?" shows amazement that Jesus would at this moment begin washing the feet of the Twelve. If this were merely the social custom, then it was being wrongly carried out. It should have been done when they first entered the room, not after a considerable time had elapsed. It should have been done at the door, not at the table. And it should have been performed by the disciples themselves, not by their Master. Even if this action had been overlooked early in the evening, once they were at the table it was hardly the time and place to care for it. Jesus indicated by his answer that his purpose went beyond mere custom. "What I do thou knowest not now." There was more to be learned from this incident than a reminder to observe the social courtesies of the day.

2. Peter objected to such humility. (13:8)

"Thou shalt never wash my feet." What Peter did not like was this reversal of positions. He would have much preferred to exchange places and wash the feet of Jesus. For the Son of God to assume the servant's place was certainly a condescension. It is consistent with the Biblical descriptions of Christ found elsewhere which speak of his becoming poor (II Cor. 8:9), taking the "form of a servant" (Phil. 2:7), and being "meek and lowly"

(Matt. 11:29). Yet if all we see in this incident is a lesson in humility, we miss most of what Jesus was endeavoring to teach.

Jesus answered by saying: "If I wash thee not, thou hast no part with me." Now, humility is a virtue which primarily blesses its possessor (although secondarily others are benefited thereby). But Jesus did not tell Peter that if he did not wash his feet, he would be lacking in some virtue. Rather, Jesus said that if he did not wash Peter's feet, Peter would be the loser. The act symbolized some blessing to the person whose feet were washed, not primarily the humility of the one who washed them.

The blessing being depicted by this washing has to do with a "part with me." It speaks of participation in fellowship with Christ, and is further explained in the following verses.

3. Peter objected to a partial washing. (13:9-11)

If this washing by Jesus had something to do with one's having a "part with Christ," then Peter was willing to forget all his previous reluctance and have the fullest bath possible. He was beginning to see that spiritual cleansing and spiritual fellowship were involved, and he wanted all he could obtain.

The answer of Jesus pointed out Peter's confusion and confirmed the truth Christ was trying to convey. In 13:10 the English word "wash" occurs twice, but these are the translations of two different terms in the original text. The first one (louō) denotes a full bath; the second (niptō), a washing of parts of the body. Hence Jesus actually said: "He that has been bathed has no need to wash, except for his feet." The person just returned from the bath would find that his sandaled feet had become dusty from the path. These would need washing upon arrival at the home, but he would not need to repeat the complete bath.

The statement, "Ye are clean, but not all," proves that spiritual defilement and spiritual cleansing are what is being illustrated. The unclean one was Judas, and the uncleanness was sin. The particular aspect of cleansing being illustrated is not the initial experience of salvation (i.e., the full bath, symbolized by baptism), but the subsequent cleansing from defilement which the true believer may contract as he walks in a sinful world.

This repeated cleansing of the believer's defilement from sin is the present work of Christ. He cleansed us from sin's guilt at Calvary when he shed his blood in our stead. This did away with the guilt of all our sin—past, present, and future. The present cleansing of believers is performed by Christ through the Word. Ephesians 5:25-27 speaks of this: "Christ also loved the church, and gave himself for it; that he might sanctify and cleanse it with the washing of water by the word, that he might present it to himself a glorious church, not having spot, or wrinkle, or any such thing; but that it should be holy and without blemish." As one studies the Word of God, he sees God's holy standards, and his sin is called to his attention. The believer then can be led to repentance and receive forgiveness, with the full joy of fellowship restored. It is Christ's particular function to bring this about for his church. It was this concern that led him to pray for believers: "Sanctify them through thy truth: thy word is truth" (17:17).[3]

D. The Explanation (13:12-17)

Jesus revealed that his action was intended as an example to be followed (13:12-15). The disciples were obligated (*opheilete*) to do so because their Lord and Master had commanded. The word "example" (*hupodeigma*) was commonly used for a model to be copied. Of course, the act of washing one another's feet does not obtain any spiritual privilege for the participants, but it does serve as an objective memorial of what Christ provides for believers.

He reminded them of his right to lay this obligation upon them (13:16). They had freely acknowledged him as Lord. This implied that their own position was that of servants. Since Christ set the

---

[3]This explanation is well put by the note on this passage in the Scofield Bible: "The underlying imagery is of an oriental returning from the public baths to his house. His feet would acquire defilement and require cleansing, but not his body. So the believer is cleansed as before the law from all sin 'once for all' (Heb. 10:1-12), but needs throughout his earthly life to bring his daily sins to the Father in confession, so that he may abide in unbroken fellowship with the Father and with the Son (I Jn. 1:1-10). The blood of Christ answers forever to all the law could say as to the believer's guilt, but he needs constant cleansing from the defilement of sin. . . ." *The New Scofield Reference Bible*, rev. ed. (New York, 1967), p. 1145.

example and then told them to do likewise, they owed him their obedience if they were truly willing to accept his lordship.

He then pointed out that obedience ("if ye do them") to the example is an evidence of spiritual blessedness (13:17). "Happy" (*makarioi*) is the word usually translated "blessed" in the New Testament (e.g., the Beatitudes, Matt. 5). It refers to one's inner spiritual condition. In Biblical terminology, the "blessed man" is the saved man (cf. Psalm 1 for an Old Testament description of the blessed man). Conduct demonstrates nature, and obedience to the commands of Jesus demonstrates the new nature. Obedience to this particular command is especially revealing, for it displays a comprehension of a precious spiritual truth, and it asks the individual to exert himself toward that which may be inconvenient and a bit humbling. The early church also thought that washing the saints' feet was indicative of a godly life, for it was made a factor to be considered when widows were evaluated as recipients of aid (I Tim. 5:10).

II. The Identification of the Betrayer (13:18-30)

A. The Prediction (13:18-21)

In contrast to those who show their blessedness by obeying his commands, Jesus stated that the forthcoming action of one of the twelve would demonstrate his evil nature (13:18). He referred to the betrayal that was soon to occur, and explained it as fulfilling Psalm 41:9. The psalmist is thought to have had immediate reference to Ahithophel, the trusted counselor of King David, who turned against him in the rebellion of Absalom (II Sam. 15:12, 31). Sometimes, however, an event which occurred to God's anointed king in the Old Testament was regarded in the New Testament as predictive (i.e., a type) of a more significant happening to the final Anointed One, Jesus. By his statement Christ revealed that he knew exactly what would occur (13:19), and he also let Judas know that he had been detected. Nevertheless, as an encouragement to his true disciples, Jesus showed that servants who do what he asks are acknowledged by him as sharers of his ministry (13:20). These words were followed by a direct prediction that one of the twelve would be his betrayer (13:21).

B. The Questioning (13:22-26)

A general questioning immediately followed the prediction (13:22). The eleven innocent disciples knew individually they had made no plans to betray Jesus. Of course, the prediction did not say how *soon* it would occur, and they may have interpreted it in a vague fashion. Matthew states that even Judas joined the questioning (Matt. 26:25). To have been the only silent one would have been incriminating.

A more specific question was put to Jesus by Peter through John (13:23-25).[4] It was customary at meals for the participants to recline on couches, resting on their left elbow with the right arm free for eating. The head would be nearest the table, with the feet extending away from it. The person on one's right would have his head nearest the chest of the person to his left. This was the position of John in relation to Jesus. Hence the way in which the question was relayed to Jesus makes it evident that most of those at the table did not hear the question nor its answer.

The direct answer from Jesus indicated Judas as the betrayer (13:26). The morsel[5] of bread dipped in the common dish of broth and then handed to the guilty one was the indicated sign. As Jesus offered it to Judas, one more appeal was being made to his conscience. Yet Christ knew what the outcome would be, and he chose this method to answer the question from John and Peter.

C. The Command (13:27-30)

It was after the morsel had been given to Judas that Satan "entered into him" (13:27). Judas once more had rejected our Lord's overture to him, and this seems to have been the final surrender of his will to Satan. The entry of Satan into Judas did

---

[4]For the identity of the "disciple whom Jesus loved," see Introduction (Canonicity and Authorship).

[5]Whether the offering of the *psōmion* ("sop," KJV) was a traditional sign of special friendship cannot clearly be established, but it was surely a friendly act. See Ruth 2:14 and Prov. 17:1 for other Biblical references to the morsel.

not mean that he became demon-possessed,[6] but that Judas yielded totally to the temptation of Satan and became obedient to his leading. Then our Lord dismissed him. John is careful to show that Jesus was still the Son of God, sovereign in a situation that was otherwise humiliating.

Christ's command for Judas to depart was variously interpreted among the disciples (13:28-29). Some thought Judas left to purchase provisions for the Passover. Others supposed he was on some mission of benevolence as the treasurer of the group. Even John and Peter who had been told he was the betrayer did not understand that the deed would be done that very night. Judas, however, left at once. (Where he went may be learned from 18:2-3.) It was clear to John that Jesus was still in control. His timetable, not Judas's, was being followed.

III. The New Commandment (13:31-38)

With the departure of Judas, Jesus could speak more intimately with the disciples. He first announced that the glorification of God in his Son was about to take place (13:31-32). This was "the hour" for which he had come. It would require, however, a separation of Jesus from his followers (13:33). This separation had been announced previously to the Jews (7:33-34). It would be caused by his death and return to the Father, and they would not be able to join him immediately.

In anticipation of his departure, Jesus announced a new commandment, in which they were enjoined to love one another (13:34-35). This was hardly a new idea (cf. Lev. 19:18), but its distinctive feature was that they should love "as I have loved you." The disciples would shortly have the greatest illustration of this love in the actions of Jesus himself, a love which always sought the good of its objects and was willing to sacrifice life itself to achieve that good. As they would demonstrate such love in their lives, it would provide a great proof to others of their discipleship with Christ.

[6]According to the NT, demon-possession is the actual occupancy of an individual by a separate entity known as an evil spirit. In some cases the victim may be responsible for allowing the demon to enter, but he is not directly responsible for what the demon proceeds to do. In the case of Judas, however, he is always held responsible in the NT for his heinous deed. He was not a victim to be pitied as the demon-possessed usually were.

The self-confident Peter was certain he was ready to follow
Jesus anywhere, and would offer his own life if necessary. He
failed to understand the enormous implications of Jesus' words,
and to recognize how inadequate his own capabilities really
were. Christ's words to him pointed out that before a cock[7]
should crow again, Peter would not only fail to do what he
claimed, but would deny his Lord three times. The fulfillment of
this prediction is recorded in 18:15-27.

IV. The Departure of the Lord (14:1-15)

A. The Statement of Jesus (14:1-4)

The previous announcement that he would soon depart produced a spirit of gloom and uncertainty among the disciples.
Therefore Jesus said, "Stop letting your heart be troubled."[8]
Coupled with this negative command was the positive challenge, "Believe in me." Grammatically there are four possible
ways to translate this statement,[9] but regardless of the rendering
adopted, Christ's equality with God is strongly implied, and was
thus a reassuring fact for their troubled hearts.

Jesus announced that he was going to the Father's house (a
reference to heaven, Matt. 6:9). This departure would climax at
the ascension, but would actually begin in a few hours with the
events of Calvary. The purpose of his going was to secure access
to heaven for men (Heb. 6:20). It would be accomplished by the
expiation of sin which Christ was about to make at the cross.
"Mansions" (KJV)[10] is the rendering of the same word which is

[7] Although the name "cock-crowing" seems to be used sometimes as a designation for the third watch of the night (Mark 13:35), the form of the expression
here more likely denotes the actual crowing of a rooster.

[8] The negative with a present imperative (*mē tarassesthō*) often denotes an order
to desist from what has already been in operation.

[9] The Greek form *pisteuete* (believe) occurs twice, and may be either imperative
("believe ye") or indicative ("ye believe"). Hence both forms could be treated
as imperatives (ASV, RSV, NASB), or as indicatives, or the first one imperative
and the second indicative, or vice versa (KJV). The previous verb "be (not)
troubled" is imperative and this may offer some evidence that imperatives are
more probable throughout the verse.

[10] Greek: *monai.*

translated "abode" (KJV) in 14:23. It emphasizes not the idea of palatial residences, but of places for wandering pilgrims finally to dwell. The fact that there are "many" reveals that there will be room for all who qualify.

Just as certain as his departure would be his return. The sad disciples thus were challenged to look beyond the present with its immediate disappointments to the glorious future which was just as certain of fulfillment.

B. Thomas's Problem Concerning the Way (14:5-7)

Thomas questioned the accuracy of Jesus' statement in 14:4 and also picked up the question asked previously by Peter in 13:36. He was not looking beyond the temporal and physical scene. He seemed to think Jesus was referring to a departure for some geographical location. To him it didn't appear important to discuss the "way" until he first knew the destination.

The answer of Jesus was, "I am the way," and he also made it clear that the destination was the Father. He did not say that he came to show the way, but that he himself was the actual means for bringing men to God. An illustration might be a flowing river whose current actually conveys the boat to its destination, or the modern escalator which is not only the route but is also the conveyor from one level to another.

C. Philip's Problem Concerning the Father (14:8-11)

Christ's concluding words to Thomas indicated that not only is Christ the way to the Father, but also that this was not just a future prospect but could be a present reality (14:7). Philip, however, was no more spiritually perceptive than Thomas, and so he asked, "Show us the Father." This is the problem lying at the heart of all idolatry. Philip asserted that if he could see the Father in clear and unmistakable form, then he and the others would be content to be left alone.

The response of Jesus pointed the disciples to himself. "He who hath seen me hath seen the Father." This is one of the profoundest assertions in the New Testament. Everyone who comes in faith to Christ is thus brought to God (cf. 10:38). It is the function of the Son as the image of the invisible God (Col. 1:15) to be the revealer of the Father to finite men (1:18). He alone is so qualified, and to him we look as the highest and final revelation of God (Heb. 1:1-4).

D. Privileges of the Disciples (14:12-15)

In the light of Christ's departure, two privileges are explained as encouragements for the disciples. First, they are granted the privilege of performing greater works (14:12). This certainly did not mean that believers would perform more amazing physical miracles than Jesus did (e.g., stilling the storm, feeding 5,000). The answer is indicated by the fact that Christ's return to the Father is said to be the cause. Hence these greater works would be spiritual ones, in which the good news of Christ's death and resurrection would be proclaimed as the transforming power for sinful men. As a consequence, Gentiles as well as Jews would be reached, and a new spiritual body, the New Testament church, would be created.

The second privilege is prayer in Jesus' name (14:13-15). Christ lent his name to believers to use in their petitions to the Father.[11] We may ask on his merits, with all of his personal influence as our great High Priest at our disposal (Heb. 4:14-16). Of course, prayer in Christ's name must be consistent with Christ's character. "In Jesus' name" is not a ritualistic formula which automatically insures a favorable response. Rather, prayer will be honored when it is made in the atmosphere of obedience to our Lord's commandments (14:15).

V. The Promise of the Spirit (14:16-26)

A. The Description of the Spirit (14:16-17)

The Holy Spirit is promised by Jesus as about to be given by the Father at the request of the Son. Two names designate the Spirit in this passage. He is called "another Helper" (NASB). The term "Helper" (*paraklētos*) is used of Jesus in I John 2:1. It conveys the ideas of strengthener, encourager, advocate, or helper.

[11] An interesting variant in 14:14 has the strong support of P66 Aleph B W Theta, and may well be original. It reads: "If you ask me anything in my name, I will do it." Thus prayer can be directed to both the Father and to Christ.

The other name is "the Spirit of truth." "Truth" was likewise a designation of Christ (14:6). Thus the Spirit who was promised by Jesus as the one to take his place is called by two names used elsewhere of Jesus himself. The Spirit would be the helper who would implant the truth in human hearts and illuminate its meaning for believers.

When the Spirit would be given (at Pentecost, Acts 1:4-5; 2:1-4), he would come to be with the disciples forever. He had been with them (*par' humin*) previously, bringing spiritual understanding and causing them to recognize Jesus as Lord (I Cor. 12:3). But when the Spirit would be given in this new way, he would be in them (*en humin*) in an individual and permanent indwelling that would constitute them as members of a new spiritual unity, the church (I Cor. 12:13).[12]

B. The Significance of the Spirit (14:18-21)

Christ's return to the Father would not leave his disciples as orphans (*orphanous*) because the Holy Spirit would take his place. In this sense Jesus said, "I will come to you." Perhaps the statement is broad enough to include Christ's coming to them at his resurrection, later at Pentecost when the Spirit would be given, and finally in the consummation at the Second Coming. The emphasis in the context, however, would point particularly to the giving of the Spirit, who would come as the representative of Christ.

C. The Question of Judas Not Iscariot (14:22-24)

This Judas was apparently the man known elsewhere as Judas the brother of James, and also called Thaddeus or Lebbaeus.[13] He asked, "What has happened (*ti gegonen*) that to us you are going

---

[12]The interpreter must beware, however, of downgrading the relationship of the Spirit to men expressed by "with you" (*par' humin*), and suppose that this relation would be replaced by that of being "in you" (*en humin*). It must be noted that the same preposition "with" (*para*) is used to describe the present relation of the Father and the Son to believers when the Holy Spirit comes upon them (14:23). One must avoid making too sharp a distinction between these prepositions, and at the same time not minimize the importance of Pentecost.

[13]This conclusion is based upon a comparison of the four NT lists of the Twelve: Matt. 10:2 ff; Mark 3:16 ff; Luke 6:14 ff.; Acts 1:13 ff.

to disclose yourself and not to the world?" He was thinking in terms of the outward manifestations of the Messianic kingdom which would certainly have world-wide effects. Christ answered that the manifestation to the disciples would be a spiritual one in which he and the Father would make their abode in the hearts of all believers. During Christ's bodily absence the coming of the Spirit to believers would mean that the Triune God was present with them. He did not deny that the world would eventually be confronted with the returning Son of God, but that must await the divine timetable.

D. The Ministry of the Spirit (14:25-26)

Among the Spirit's ministries would be the supplying of remembrance and true interpretation of Christ's words. Many things the disciples did not presently understand would be made clear. Implicit in this statement was the authorization of the apostles as the witnesses who would be qualified to give the New Testament record to the church.

VI. The Bequest of Peace (14:27-31)

Before leaving the disciples, Jesus bequeathed the priceless gift of peace. This is not the objective peace with God which was accomplished through the expiation of sin at Calvary, although it is based upon it. Emphasis here is upon the inner peace which calms the troubled heart. This is different from "peace" which the world offers, for that is dependent upon circumstances which are constantly changing. Christ's peace is based upon his own unchanging person and work.

The crisis which was about to occur would be the first of many occasions when this peace would be sorely needed. It would sustain them during his departure, and enable them to see that he as the Messianic Son was returning to his Father.[14] In the crisis of the next few hours, Satan[15] would attack with full power.

[14]The assertion that the Father is greater than Jesus refers to Jesus in his Messianic office, not to the essential nature of the Godhead.

[15]Satan is termed in this passage *ho tou kosmou archōn*, "the ruler of the world" (cf. 16:11). This, of course, is only with the present permission of God while the world is under curse, and is not permanent. He is called "the prince of the power of the air" in Eph. 2:2.

However, there was nothing in Christ which Satan could claim as his property. He could not accuse Jesus before God as deserving of death because of sin (cf. Job 1:6 ff.). Christ's death would be voluntary and would occur because he delighted to do the Father's will. Satan had no voice in it.

The statement "Arise, let us go hence" (14:31) causes problems at this point because of the supposed difficulties involved in placing the next three chapters outside the upper room. Of the proposed solutions, the following are the most commonly suggested. (1) There has been a dislocation of the text, and this statement belongs to the close of the entire discourse. However, no manuscripts support this hypothesis. (2) The statement was made at this time, but the group did not actually leave until after chapter 17. However, it is puzzling why John writing more than sixty years after the event would think it important to include this statement if it had turned out to be almost meaningless. (3) The statement should be interpreted spiritually, not physically.

Fig. 23. *The excavation of first-century steps near the Church of Saint Peter in Gallicantu. Jesus and the disciples may have descended these steps en route to the garden from the upper room.*

Jesus meant that they should boldly prepare to meet the Satanic attack of 14:30. It is hardly the most natural way to interpret the words, however. (4) The words indicate an immediate departure from the upper room. This is the most obvious meaning, and there is nothing impossible about the remaining instruction being given en route to the garden.

Questions for Discussion

1. What was Jesus symbolizing by washing the disciples' feet?
2. What did Jesus mean by saying, "If I wash thee not, thou hast no part with me"?
3. Why didn't the disciples suspect that Judas was the betrayer, even after Jesus told John?
4. What "greater works" did the disciples do than Jesus?
5. What did Jesus mean by his statement, "My Father is greater than I"?

Chapter 11

Christ's Final Discourse
Part Two: En route to the Garden
(John 15-17)

As Jesus and eleven of his disciples left the upper room (14:31), they made their way toward the Kidron Valley and the Mount of Olives. If the traditional site of the upper room is reasonably correct (Fig. 22), the little group may have gone down the steps which have been excavated beside the present church of St. Peter in Gallicantu (Fig. 23). Along the way the remainder of Christ's final discourse was given.

I. The Vital Union of Jesus and the Disciples (15:1-11)

Jesus taught this truth by employing the figure of a vine and its branches. Whether some immediate circumstance prompted the use of this illustration is not certain. Suggestions such as a real vine growing nearby, the vine-pruning fires along the brook Kidron, the golden vine engraved on the temple gateposts,[1] or the use of the wine at the supper, have been made. It is better, however, to regard the statement of Jesus, "I am the true vine,"[2] as a contrast to certain Old Testament passages in which Israel was called a vine (Isa. 5:1-7; Jer. 2:21; Ps. 80:8 ff.; Hos. 10:1). Israel was intended by God to be faithful and spiritually fruitful, but instead she had proved to be sadly deficient. Jesus, however, would be all that God wanted, and by a life-sharing union with him, believers may have lives of fruitfulness.

---

[1]Josephus *The Jewish War*, Book V, Sec. 210 (V. 5. 4).

[2]The word "true" (*alēthinē*) means genuine or real, in contrast to counterfeit, illegitimate, or a mere copy.

Fig. 24. *The Kidron Valley, looking south. The Arab village of Silwan is on the left.*

The significant details of the allegory were interpreted by Jesus. He himself is the vine; the Father is the vinedresser who cares for the vine with its branches that fruit might be produced. The branches are persons who have professed faith in Christ. These are of two types: (1) Fruit-bearing branches, representing true believers who by their vital union with the vine exhibit the fruit which is the evidence of life. (2) Fruitless branches, representing persons attached in some superficial way to the vine, but without the vital life flowing through them to produce fruit. The purging instrument is Christ's word which cleanses the branches from all hindrances to proper life and growth (cf. 13:8, 10 for the same truth). The fruit is the development of the spiritual life as the result of being a sharer of eternal life.[3] In this

[3]"Fruit" is popularly restricted to soulwinning, but this was by no means the prevailing idea in this term as used by NT writers. The noun *karpos* occurs sixty-six times in the NT, and only once does it mean soulwinning *per se* (John 4:36). A more Biblical understanding of the term sees it as the production and manifestation of Christian virtues through the action of the Holy Spirit. Of course, if these are what they should be, there will be an effective witness to the lost.

context some of the fruit is named: successful prayer (15:7); joy (15:11); love (15:12). Other passages describing the fruit which the Christian bears through the action of the Holy Spirit within him are Galatians 5:22-23 and II Peter 1:5-8. In this allegory of the vine, every true believer bears fruit, and the normal progression is fruit, more fruit (15:2), much fruit (15:5).[4]

The greatest problem of interpretation has to do with the fruitless branches. Three views are worthy of mention. (1) These branches represent true Christians who finally perish. This Arminian explanation runs counter to the consistent Biblical teaching that "eternal" life is unending, and that Christ and the Father keep believers secure (10:28-29). (2) The fruitless branches are true Christians who are "taken up"[5] to heaven by physical death as a discipline. The burning represents the burning of their unfruitful works at the judgment seat of Christ (I Cor. 3:12-15). However, the figure clearly depicts a removal from the vine, whereas physical death does not sever a true believer's connection with Christ. Furthermore, it is the branches themselves (i.e., the persons) that are burned, not just their works. A comparison with Psalm 80:15-16 shows that the burning is clearly the judgment of unbelievers. (3) The fruitless branches represent the mere professed believer who is finally severed from his superficial connection with Christ. This had actually happened earlier in the evening with the removal of Judas from the group. The difficulty posed by the phrase "in me" (15:2) is caused by interpreting it in the same sense as the phrase "in Christ" used by Paul especially in the Prison Epistles. However, when Jesus spoke these words, the phrase would probably have been understood in a sense similar to the expression "in the kingdom," and that concept included both false and true believers (Matt. 13:41,

---

[4]Although the expression "fruitless Christians" is sometimes heard, such terminology must be understood as relative, not absolute, in the light of this allegory. In the absolute sense every true believer has borne some fruit (for instance, love for Christ, joy), but he may not have borne as much as he could. Any "Christian" who is absolutely fruitless is clearly stated to be devoid of the life of the vine.

[5]The precise sense of $air\bar{o}$ (take up, take away) must be determined by the context. Its general meaning denotes a removal.

47-50).[6] The phrase should be understood here as meaning "united to me by profession only." The last view has been adopted in this study.

Jesus taught that this life-sharing relationship which is essential for bearing fruit is accomplished if one "abides" in him. How does one "abide" in Christ? A comparison of other passages in John's writings suggests the answer.

> Whoever confesses that Jesus is the Son of God, God abides in him, and he in God. (I John 4:15, NASB)

> And this is His commandment, that we believe in the name of His Son Jesus Christ, and love one another, just as He commanded us. And the one who keeps His commandments abides in Him, and He in him. (I John 3:23-24a, NASB)

> As for you, let that abide in you which you heard from the beginning. If what you heard from the beginning abides in you, you also will abide in the Son and in the Father. (I John 2:24, NASB)

[6]It must be remembered that these words were spoken prior to Pentecost, the time when believers would be baptized by the Spirit into the body of Christ. See Charles R. Smith, "The Unfruitful Branches in John 15," *Grace Journal*, Vol 9, No. 2 (Spring 1968), pp. 10-12.

Fig. 25 . *A vineyard in Palestine with its watchtower.*

These passages show that confessing Jesus as the Son of God (i.e., believing in Jesus) establishes the relation of abiding. Thus to abide in Christ is equivalent to believing in Christ. This relationship of abiding is initiated at the moment of faith, and is continued as we walk by faith. Obeying Christ's commandments results in the believer's continuing to abide in Christ's love, and brings a participation in his joy. Christ's joy came from his perfect obedience to his Father's will and hence his consciousness of the Father's love. Likewise believers who obey the commands of their Master experience the joy of knowing that no shadow has marred the full enjoyment of Christ's love for them.

II. The Love of the Disciples for Each Other (15:12-17)

Jesus repeated to his disciples the new commandment he had given earlier in the evening (13:34) that they should love one another just as he had loved them. This time he enlarged upon it and showed how limitless his love really was. The greatest possible sacrifice one can make for a friend is to give up life itself. Jesus was about to do this for believers, whom he calls his "friends."[7] He did not adopt this terminology lightly, for he explained the difference between a friend and a slave. Friends are those who share each other's confidences. So it was that Christ had not held back from the disciples anything of the revelation of God that he had been commissioned to bring. He had revealed the Father's plans for the future, and was even now engaged in laying out before them the purposes of his departure to the Father and his plans for them during the interval until his return.

Nevertheless, he also reminded them that their status as friends was not of their making. Rather, his love for them had been so great that he had taken all the initiative. He had chosen them to be his friends, had appointed them as his emissaries, and had made provision for the successful accomplishment of their ministries.

Being a "friend" entails mutual obligations. A one-sided

---

[7]Jesus died also for his enemies (Rom. 5:10), but that is not the point here. He was speaking to the disciples who had already believed in him.

"friendship" is no friendship at all. Hence Jesus explained that his friends will carry out his directives (15:14), and the particular command emphasized here was to love one another (15:17). By letting their Christian love for one another flourish unhindered, they would be producing the spiritual fruit which the Holy Spirit was being sent to accomplish among them (Gal. 5:22), and would be offering a clear testimony to the world of their identification with Christ (13:35).

III. The Hatred of the World Against the Disciples (15:18—16:4)

A. The Description of the World's Hatred (15:18-20)

Although the relation of the disciples to Christ would produce in them a love for one another of a most sublime sort, the world of unbelievers would not understand nor appreciate them. In fact, the world would react with the same hatred which it meted out to Christ. They would be regarded as servants of Christ, and servants cannot expect better treatment than their masters. The picture was not totally black, however, for Jesus did win some individuals out of the world, and the disciples could expect this result also. But the mass of the world would remain unconverted.

B. The Reason for the World's Hatred (15:21-25)

It would help the disciples to bear the hatred of the world if they understood its causes. It would not really be directed against them, even though they would personally have to suffer. The true reason for this hostility was the world's hatred of Jesus and its ignorance of the Father who had sent him. The tragedy was (and still is) that men who are without knowledge of God blindly reject the only One who can fully reveal him. Of course, there are moral reasons for this. The coming of Jesus revealed in a clearer way the enormity of man's sin, and men resented him for it. But because he came, men are without excuse and are guilty of the greatest of sins—rejecting God's own Son.

C. The Answer to the World's Hatred (15:26-27)

Christ made provision for his disciples to stand against the oppressive forces that loomed ahead. His sending of the Holy

Spirit would supply the Helper *(paraklētos)*. Because he is the Spirit of Truth, he would enable them to see clearly the world's false position and would strengthen the disciples for their task and their ordeal of suffering. Through this spiritual strengthening of the disciples themselves, it would be possible for them to give a strong witness to the world. They would be qualified, not only because they would possess the Spirit's power, but also because of their personal knowledge of Christ gained during their association with him during his ministry.

D. A Warning Against the World's Hatred (16:1-4)

Even though Christ had repeatedly told the disciples what the future would hold, another warning was in order for they would still be disturbed when they became the direct objects of the world's attack. Christ did not want them to "stumble."[8] Furthermore, Jesus himself had been the object of attack as long as he was with them (Luke 4:28-29; John 5:16, 18; 7:1; 18:7-8), and the disciples had been spared. This situation was about to change.

The hostility that would soon erupt against them would be of a religious nature. Instead of seeing all their families, friends, and fellow countrymen in the synagogues respond to Jesus as the Messiah, the believers themselves would be cast outside by their fellow Jews. Yet their Jewish persecutors would justify their actions as a religious duty. An outstanding example was Saul of Tarsus who persecuted Christians on the assumption that they were blasphemers of God when they worshiped Jesus (Acts 26:9-11). The real cause of the problem was the complete failure of the world to know the Father or the Son. In spite of Jewish claims to be devout worshipers of Jehovah (and the present Gentile boast of believing in God but not in Jesus), the world really is ignorant of the true nature of Jesus and thus has no final means of knowing God.

---

[8]The Greek verb *skandalizō* is one of a word group that developed out of the concept of a trigger stick which caused a trap to spring shut. The translations "be offended" (KJV), "caused to stumble" (ASV), or "falling away" (RSV), should be understood in the severe sense of serious entrapment. See G. Stählin, "Skandalon, skandalizō," *Theological Dictionary of the New Testament,* ed. Gerhard Friedrich, trans. Geoffrey W. Bromiley (Grand Rapids, 1971), VII, 339-358.

IV. The Work of the Holy Spirit (16:5-15)

A. *The Need for the Holy Spirit* (16:5-7)

Jesus next discussed the Holy Spirit who would take his place when he departed. This subject had been introduced earlier that evening (14:16-18; 15:26), and is now elaborated. The previous announcements by Jesus regarding his departure had raised the question as to where he was going (13:36; 14:5), but it had not been pursued and now they were too confused and discouraged to press it further. They had need for spiritual encouragement if they were to be the witnesses Christ had authorized (15:27).

When Jesus said, "It is expedient for you [i.e., to your advantage] that I go away," the disciples probably found the idea difficult to accept. They would have preferred that Jesus remain with them. Yet Jesus was looking beyond the immediate sorrow of separation to the ultimate accomplishment of his program. He must die and be resurrected in order to accomplish redemption. Only then could he in conjunction with the Father send the Spirit to dwell in believers and to empower them as witnesses to announce the finished work of Christ. Furthermore, Christ's earthly ministry limited his physical presence to one location at a time, but the Spirit indwelling each believer simultaneously would multiply Christ's presence.

Caiaphas the high priest had also stated that it was "expedient" for Jesus to be removed (11:50), but for a far less worthy reason. Yet God was about to take the wicked scheming of vicious men and use it to accomplish the divine will.

B. *The Ministry of the Holy Spirit Toward the World* (16:8-11)

The Spirit would come to the disciples at Pentecost (16:7), and would use them to perform a ministry toward the world. Through the disciples as they preached the gospel, the Spirit would "convict" the world. This verb *(elengchō)* had a number of meanings, such as expose, convict, convince, and blame, but the New Testament usage is with the sense of showing someone his sin and summoning him to repentance.[9] Here Jesus meant that

---

[9]Friedrich Büchsel, "Elengchō," *TDNT*, II, 474.

the ministry of the Spirit would clearly establish the world's guilt before God. In some cases this exposure would result in confession by the sinner and subsequent conversion, but in all instances the world's guilt would be amply demonstrated.

This convicting ministry of the Spirit deals with sin, righteousness, and judgment—the three basic issues in determining a person's spiritual state. The world's guilt is established because of its sin of unbelief. The basic issue is not *sins* (the symptoms) but *sin* (the disease), and the greatest demonstration of sin against God is the rejection of his Son. The Spirit also convicts the world because of its failure to accept the standard of righteousness which God approves. The world has been all too ready to devise its own standards and then measure itself by them (Rom. 10:3). In Christ was the exhibition of perfect righteousness, and the proof that this righteousness was acceptable to God would be his return to the Father through resurrection, ascension, and exaltation.

Finally, the Spirit convicts the world of its liability for judgment. Satan, the archenemy of God, was defeated at the cross (12:31) when Christ's death satisfied the demand of God's righteousness and provided the grounds for reconciliation of sinners to God. Hence Satan is a defeated foe, and all who follow him may expect to share his fate (Matt. 25:41).

C. *The Ministry of the Holy Spirit in the Disciples* (16:12-15)

In relation to the disciples, the Spirit would guide them into all the truth which they were presently unable to receive. These men would be Christ's authorized interpreters, and the Spirit would operate within them and bring remembrance of Christ's words and deeds and the meaning of them (14:26). He would also reveal prophetic truths to them. All of these truths are embodied in the New Testament, which was received by the church on the authority of the apostles.

Another function of the Spirit would be to glorify the absent Christ. Occasionally the criticism is heard that the Holy Spirit is not honored sufficiently by present-day Christians. However, if Christ is given the proper emphasis, then the Spirit's basic ministry among believers is being responded to. Any movement supposedly led by the Spirit which focuses most of the interest on the phenomena of the Spirit is contrary to this statement of Jesus. The Holy Spirit is honored when Christ is glorified in our lives.

V. The Coming Separation (16:16-24)

Jesus brought the discussion back to the immediate situation. In just a few hours the storm would break. The old relationship would be changed (16:16-18). They would not be able to see him with their physical eyes because he would be killed and placed in the grave. After a little while, they would see[10] him again, but there would be differences. Though he would be resurrected bodily, their relationship to him would be basically a spiritual one, and his bodily presence with them would be only temporary.

This coming separation would bring great sorrow to his followers. The unbelieving world would rejoice at the accomplishment of its purpose regarding Jesus, while the disciples would have a brief interval of grief. But their grief would not merely be replaced by joy at the resurrection; the grief itself would be turned into joy as they came to understand the full significance of Christ's death (16:19-22).

When once the tragic hour would be over, there would be some resultant privileges for his followers (16:23-24). They would have no further need to ask questions[11] about this puzzling prospect of his death. Its purpose would be clear to them, and their questions would be resolved. The questioning of ignorance would be replaced by definite prayer[12] to the Father on the merits of the name[13] of the divine Son. By faith in him believers

---

[10]The first Greek verb in 16:10 is *theōreite*, a term used by John of an actual physical beholding (2:23; et al.). The second verb is *opsesthe*, which often in John denotes a mental or spiritual vision or understanding (1:51, et al.).

[11]Greek: *erōtēsete*, to ask a question.

[12]Greek: *aitēsete*, to make a request of.

[13]The phrase "in my name" is attached, however, not with "ask" but with "give" in certain important manuscripts, including P5 Aleph B C L X, and this reading is adopted by ASV, RSV, and NASB. If this reading is original, it indicates that the Father's answers to believers' prayers are also on the basis of Christ's person and work.

become sharers of Christ's life, and he grants the use of his own name in their prayers to the Father for the needs of life.

VI. The Hour of Victory (16:25-33)

Lest the emphasis upon the dark days ahead prove too depressing to the apprehensive disciples, our Lord encouraged their faith by lifting their thoughts to the time of victory after Calvary.

He explained that when the victory of the cross had been won, there would be no further need for obscure sayings (16:25). The use of parables and other figures, and the employment of enigmatic statements would be replaced after the resurrection by the plain teaching of Jesus himself during a forty-day ministry, and after that by the indwelling and illuminating Spirit who would grant direct understanding of spiritual truth. A comparison of the apostles' frequent confusion in the Gospels with their confident understanding in Acts demonstrates the truth of Jesus' statement.

In the future the disciples would not need to ask Jesus to make request to the Father for them, for they were assured of the Father's love for them and the availability of direct access to him (16:26-28). The next few days, however, would bring a great testing of their faith (16:29-32). Nevertheless, the victory of Christ was certain, and thus they could have spiritual peace even in tribulation (16:33).

VII. The Prayer of Jesus (17:1-26)

The precise moment and location in which Christ uttered this prayer cannot be ascertained. It must have occurred somewhere on the way to Gethsemane, after they had left the upper room (14:31) but before they reached the garden (18:1). How the apostle John came into possession of the words is not indicated. Perhaps the prayer was made in the hearing of the apostles, or if it was uttered in private, perhaps Jesus informed them later of its content.

A. The Prayer for Himself (17:1-5)

Christ's motive in prayer was the glorification of the Father

(17:1). The significant "hour" which had been in his consciousness from the beginning of his ministry (2:4; 7:30) had now arrived, and Jesus desired to set forth God's perfect wisdom and righteousness by accomplishing the divine plan of redemption. The Father would be glorified when his plan was effected for bringing lost men to God. At this crucial time it was understandable that Christ should pray for himself, but even then he was primarily concerned with the Father's glory.

The ministry of Jesus on earth had been devoted to the glorifying of the Father, and thus the present concern was no afterthought (17:2-4). Christ had been exercising his authority from the Father to grant eternal life to men. He had brought many to trust him, and as they had come to know Christ, they had been brought into a relationship with God (8:19; 14:7, 9). This knowledge of God through Jesus Christ is the essence of eternal life, for Jesus is "the life" (14:6). But now the earthly phase of this ministry was coming to its close. He had done all he could prior to the cross. More work for men would be done in heaven as he would intercede for his own (Heb. 7:25), but that would require the cross, resurrection, and ascension.

Christ's request was for the resumption of his own eternal glory (17:5). He had voluntarily laid aside many of his eternal glories when he became man. He did not lay aside his deity, but he did put off some of the glories of his deity. This has been described as the refraining from the independent exercise of his divine attributes.[14] Submitting himself completely to the Father's will (Phil. 2:5-8), he used his divine attributes, not independently, but only when the Father indicated that it was his will (8:28; 12:49). Thus he used his omnipotence to still a storm or multiply the loaves; yet at other times he became physically weary (4:6). Now Jesus was facing the close of this period of humiliation and was asking for the resumption of the full glories which he had laid aside.

---

[14]An excellent discussion of this subject is found in Alva J. McClain, "The Doctrine of the Kenosis in Philippians 2:5-8," *Grace Journal*, Vol 8, No. 2 (Spring 1967), pp. 3-13. Reprinted from *The Biblical Review Quarterly*, Vol. XIII, No. 4 (October 1928).

B. *The Prayer for the Disciples* (17:6-19)

As Jesus presented the needs of his disciples to the Father, he described their present status (17:6-10). He had revealed God[15] to them by the words which he had spoken. His teaching about sin, righteousness, judgment, salvation, and God himself, were the very words of God (7:16; 12:48-49), and Jesus himself, was the personal Word of God (1:1). The disciples had responded with faith in Jesus and his words, and thus evidenced the fact that they had been chosen by the sovereign love of God and had been given to Jesus.

When Jesus said, "I pray not for the world" (17:9), he was not indicating lack of interest in lost men. On other occasions he showed his compassion for the lost (Luke 13:34). But just now he was praying specifically for his disciples who would be his messengers to reach the lost world after he had left it.

Jesus made three petitions for the disciples (17:11-19). The first request was; "Keep them in Thy name . . . that they may be one, even as We are" (17:11, NASB). This unity for which he prayed was not organizational but spiritual, and is likened to the very unity of God in which the Father and the Son share a spiritual oneness of nature. Believers experience this through the Holy Spirit as they are made sharers of God's life. Of course, spiritual unity will manifest itself in peaceable relations, but mere organizational unification is no substitute for spiritual oneness, nor was it the intent of Jesus.

The second request was: "Keep them from the evil one" (17:15, NASB). Christ himself had been the chief object of satanic attack and had served as a buffer for the disciples (17:12). Consequently, all of them who had been given to him had been preserved. Of the twelve, only Judas was lost, and he was not one of those who had been given to Christ by God's election,[16] for his defection had been predicted long before (13:18; Ps. 41:9). Now

---

[15]To manifest God's "name" to the disciples implied much more than simply telling men that God's name was Jehovah. "Name" stands for the whole person, and thus the statement in 17:6 means that Jesus had revealed God to them.

[16]The case of Judas is not stated as an exception, for *ei mē* ("but," 17:12) can denote a contrasting illustration that is not an exception to what has just been stated. See Luke 4:26 for another instance.

the disciples were being left in the world to perform a task for Christ. It was a world which hated Christ and would also hate them. Jesus, therefore, prayed that they would be preserved from the clutches of Satan.

The third request was: "Sanctify them in Thy truth" (17:17, NASB). It would be accomplished by the word of God. As the disciples lived for God day by day, the application of God's truth to their lives would have a purifying effect as it would call sin to their attention, and cause confession and restoration to follow. By this means they would be set apart from sin and consecrated to the ministry to which Christ had called them. This sanctification[17] was what Jesus had illustrated by washing their feet (13:1-17), and was also stated by Paul in Ephesians 5:25-26.

C. *The Prayer for the Church* (17:20-26)

The final movement of thought in the prayer widens the scope from the little band of disciples who had been personally collected by Christ prior to the cross to those who would believe in succeeding days. For these subsequent believers (and this includes all present-day Christians) Jesus prayed that they might have spiritual unity with each other and with God (17:20-23).

On the basis of the parallelism with 17:8, the glory which Christ gave to the disciples could be interpreted as God's word which he faithfully conveyed to men. Perhaps a better explanation relates it to 17:5 where Christ's glory from the Father is specifically mentioned. The resumption of Christ's glory through his presence with the Father in heaven is shared with believers who are seated with him in heavenly places (Eph. 2:6). Through their union with Christ, believers have Christ in them and the Father is in them also—to a limited extent analogous to the relation between Christ and the Father. This idea seems more consistent with the immediate context.

[17]Sanctification has several phases in Scripture. There is a past aspect which is based upon Christ's blood shed at the cross. In this aspect, which occurs at the moment of faith, every believer is constituted a saint (i.e., "sanctified one") and is positionally invested with Christ's perfect holiness. There is also a future aspect to sanctification, which will be realized when Christ comes again and we see him face to face (I John 3:2; I Thess. 5:23). The present aspect of sanctification is accomplished by the word of God. It is progressive and enables believers to increase in personal holiness. Present sanctification is in view in 17:17.

Christ next prayed that believers might be with him and behold his glory (17:24). This looks ahead to the great consummation of redemption, in which believers have been resurrected or raptured and will see Jesus in the full glory of his deity. The answer to the request of 17:5 will be displayed to the gaze of Christ's church. This beholding of Christ's glory will transform Christians into his likeness (I John 3:2). Here is Christ's own prayer that believers will not fall short of that final salvation and entrance into the world to come.

The final request was that believers might share the Father's love (17:25-26). The Father's love for the Son was a source of incomparable satisfaction to Christ. Our Lord desired that the strength and blessing which this love provided might be fully realized by men. It was God's love which sent Christ to die for them. And for those who respond in faith to that love, the warmth of the Father's heart is entered into by the believer in the deepest sort of spiritual communion (I John 3:1).

Questions for Discussion

1. What does it mean to "abide" in Christ?
2. What is the "fruit" which believers should produce?
3. Do all believers suffer persecution? What forms may persecution take?
4. Why was it expedient for Jesus to go away and for the Spirit to come, rather than for Jesus to remain and not need to be replaced?
5. According to the Bible, how are believers sanctified?
6. What was the glory which Jesus gave to his disciples?
7. Are the prayers of Jesus always answered?

The
Passion
Victory
(John 18-21)

Chapter 12

The Crucifixion
(John 18-19)

The final portion of John's Gospel describes the momentous events of Calvary and its aftermath. This was the "hour" for which Jesus had come, and it would bring into collision the great redemptive program of God and the powers of darkness led by Satan. Because Calvary was followed by the resurrection, we understand that Christ's suffering and death produced the greatest of all victories.

I. The Arrest of Jesus (18:1-11)

After the events in the upper room, Jesus and his disciples had made their way toward the east side of Jerusalem. Going outside the city they crossed the brook Kidron (Fig. 24) to the Mount of Olives on whose slopes was a garden known as Gethsemane (Matt. 26:36).[1] It had been frequently used as a place of meeting by Jesus and the twelve, and probably had served as their lodging site on the preceding nights (Luke 21:37). Jesus was obviously not attempting to escape from his enemies, for Judas knew exactly where to find him.

The arresting party consisted of Judas, a band of Roman soldiers,[2] and some temple militia from the Sanhedrin. There was also a group of priests and elders, probably Sanhedrin members (Luke 22:52). The party came with lanterns and torches in case Jesus should try to hide in the garden, and with weapons to overpower any resistance.

As the group approached, Jesus stepped forth from the

[1]The name means "oil press," suggesting that it was located in a grove of olive trees. Such trees are still prevalent in the area.

[2]The term *speira* ("band," KJV) denoted a Roman cohort under the command of a tribune (*chiliarch*, 18:12). This Roman detachment must have been secured from Pilate (Matt. 27:65 implies that Pilate had made soldiers available to the chief priests at some time previous to the burial). The KJV is not as clear in 18:3 as ASV or NASB.

Fig. 26. *An ancient olive tree in the Garden of Gethsemane.*

shadows and presented himself. The kiss of Judas presumably occurred at this time (Matt. 26:48-49). John does not mention it because he was emphasizing the majesty of Jesus. He thus makes it clear that Jesus was not "caught" but surrendered himself (even though the kiss from the betrayer did occur).

When Jesus identified himself as the one whom they sought, the crowd fell backward and to the ground. This appears to be involuntary and to some degree supernatural. It was hardly mere awe followed by respectful obeisance. On another occasion officers had also been completely unnerved by Jesus (7:46). This startling effect showed clearly to the disciples that Christ's death was wholly voluntary, for he could not have been seized if he had willed otherwise.

Our Lord revealed his majestic control over this situation by his actions to safeguard the disciples from arrest or injury. By making the soldiers state twice that it was Jesus they were told to seize, he made it clear that doing any harm to the disciples would be going beyond their orders. As the apostolic writer looked back upon the event, he saw this physical protection of the disciples as contributing to their spiritual safeguarding of which Jesus had spoken in 17:12. He understood that at this time their incomplete faith would not have been able to endure this sort of persecution.

The power of Christ's word and the reaction of the soldiers gave Peter courage, and he struck out violently with his dagger-like sword.[3] John is not depreciating Peter by relating this incident, for Peter is not depicted as lacking in courage, faith, or love. Peter's action, however, could have seriously compromised Christ's reply to Pilate (18:36), and thus Christ performed the miracle of healing upon Malchus (Luke 22:51). This healing was doubtless the reason why Peter was not also arrested. (Luke alone mentions the healing, but none of the Synoptic Gospels name Peter as the attacker. Perhaps this was due to the possibility of reprisals, for Peter was still alive when the Synoptics were written. He had died by the time the Gospel of John appeared.) The words of Jesus to Peter clearly indicate that whatever the purpose was for the disciples' having two swords (Luke 22:36-38), their use in aggressive attack was not Jesus' intention.

II. The Trial Before the High Priests (18:12-27)

A. The Appearance Before Annas (18:12-14)

Annas had been the high priest until he was deposed by the Roman procurator Valerius Gratus[4] in A.D. 14 or 15. Five of his sons,[5] one son-in-law, and a grandson eventually occupied the high priest's office. Annas thus remained a powerful force in

---

[3]The term *machaira* was used first in the sense of knife, and later with the meaning of sword. In the LXX it was used of the knife of Abraham at the offering of Isaac (Gen. 22:6, 10) and of the dagger employed by Ehud (Judg. 3:16). W. Michaelis, "Machaira," *Theological Dictionary of the New Testament,* ed. Gerhard Kittel, trans. Geoffrey W. Bromiley (Grand Rapids, 1967), IV, 524-527.

[4]Josephus *Antiquities of the Jews,* Book XVIII, Section 33 (XVIII.2.2).

[5]*Ibid.,* Book XX, Section 198 (XX.9.1).

Jewish politics, and it is not difficult to understand why Jesus should be taken before Annas first.

Joseph Caiaphas[6] was the son-in-law of Annas, and had been the official high priest since about A.D. 18. He was removed from the office by the procurator Vitellius in A.D. 36 or 37.[7] From 11:47-53 it is obvious that he was primarily a politician rather than a spiritual leader, and very little justice could be expected from him.

Both Annas and Caiaphas probably lived in quarters at the same house. The Middle East custom of erecting large residences around a central courtyard makes such an assumption quite reasonable. The fire where Peter warmed himself seems to have been the same in each instance of denial. Furthermore, the presence of a female doorkeeper makes it probable that these events did not occur at the temple but at the high priest's residence (see also Luke 22:54).

B. *The First Denial By Peter* (18:15-18)

Peter and John[8] followed the arresting party to the high priest's quarters. All the disciples at first had fled (Matt. 26:56), but these two came back. Because of John's connections with the high priest (not otherwise explained in Scripture), he was able to gain access to the grounds for himself and Peter.

As Jesus was being interrogated in one of the rooms off the courtyard, Peter joined the servants and officers warming themselves by the fire. Nights that time of year can be chilly in half-mile-high Jerusalem, and Peter joined the group to make himself comfortable as well as less conspicuous. The servant girl who had admitted Peter was already acquainted with John, and presumably she knew he was associated with Jesus. It was natural, therefore, for her to suspect that Peter may have been a disciple also. Her question, however, was stated so as to expect a

[6]The name Joseph is given in Josephus *Antiquities*, Book XVIII, Section 95 (XVIII.4.3).

[7]Josephus *Antiquities*, Book XVIII, Section 95 (XVIII.4.3). See also S. Sandmel, "Caiaphas," *The Interpreter's Dictionary of the Bible* (New York, 1962), Vol. A-D, 481-482.

[8]It is assumed that the "other disciple" of 18:15-16 was the author John. See comments on 1:35-36.

negative answer: "You are not one of this man's disciples, are you?" Satan made it easy for Peter to sin. It was simpler to go along with his questioner, giving the answer he was expected to give.

C. The Examination By Annas (18:19-24)

It is difficult to disentangle the events here. The problem hinges upon the identification of the high priest in 18:19. Caiaphas was the official high priest, and is so identified in this context (18:13, 24). However, it is apparent that former high priests were still given this title[9] (see Luke 3:2; Acts 4:6; Josephus *The Jewish War*, Book IV, Sections 151, 160 [IV.3.7, 9]). Furthermore, 18:24 clearly states that Annas sent Jesus to Caiaphas at the conclusion of this hearing.[10] This last consideration makes it exceedingly probable that Annas was the high priest who conducted this pretrial hearing.

Annas asked Jesus about his disciples and his teaching. He wanted to get some evidence to use at the trial before the Sanhedrin. The Jews did not have much of a case, and eventually had to resort to false witnesses (Mark 14:55-59). Jesus, however, should not have been forced to testify against himself, and therefore he challenged his interrogator to ask those standing around, for it was public knowledge who his followers were and what he had taught. He had not been secretive in his ministry. Because the high priest had been out-maneuvered in argument, an officer gave Jesus an insulting blow, thinking perhaps to restore the advantage to Annas. Violence rather than solid legal evidence would mark most of the proceedings of this night.

The Gospel of John mentions the sending of Jesus from Annas to Caiaphas (18:24), but does not describe what occurred at the official Jewish trials before Caiaphas and the Sanhedrin. These events were thoroughly covered by the Synoptic accounts (Matt.

---

[9]This may have been due at least partly to the fact that the priesthood was for life, and Roman interference could not alter what the Old Testament said. Hence Annas could have been regarded as still the legitimate high priest.

[10]The verb "sent" (*apesteilen*) in 18:24 is aorist, and there is not warrant for translating it "had sent" in this passage. It most obviously states that Jesus was sent to Caiaphas after the former high priest Annas had concluded this preliminary hearing.

26:57-68; 27:1-2; Mark 14:53-65; 15:1; Luke 22:54, 63-71), and John confines himself to describing the hearing before Annas which the other accounts did not give.

D. Further Denials By Peter (18:25-27)

A careful examination of the four Gospel accounts of Peter's denials reveals some variation among the narratives, but not sufficient to necessitate the drastic measures taken by some interpreters. The accounts can be harmonized as they stand,[11] without concluding that John reports only the first and third denials,[12] or supposing that he has omitted one and divided the third into two parts.[13]

The Synoptic accounts indicate that the maid at the door (Mark 14:69) pointed out Peter to the group of bystanders and perhaps to another maidservant (Matt. 26:71) who then joined her in the accusation. A man (Luke 22:58) finally put the question directly to Peter. John merely says "they" spoke to Peter, apparently indicating that a whole chorus of accusers began harassing Peter. This second denial by Peter was again the easy response to a question so phrased as to expect a negative answer. "You are not also one of his disciples, are you?"

The third denial also was prompted by a general discussion among those in the courtyard, according to the Synoptic accounts, but John picks out the question put by Malchus (cf. 18:10). This question expected an affirmative answer: "I saw you in the garden with him, didn't I?" Now Peter could no longer go along with his questioner and mumble the expected answer, for this would contradict his previous assertions. Therefore he made a bold denial of his Lord. At this time a cock crowed, fulfilling the prediction of 13:38.[14]

---

[11]The chart and discussion by Samuel J. Andrews although old deals with the pertinent material and offers a reasonable harmonization. *The Life of Our Lord upon the Earth* (Grand Rapids, reprinted 1954), pp. 516-521.

[12]R. C. H. Lenski, *The Interpretation of St. John's Gospel* (Columbus, 1942), p. 1206.

[13]William Hendriksen, *Exposition of the Gospel According to John* (Grand Rapids, 1953), p. 339.

[14]This was the second crowing of a cock, according to Mark 14:72.

III. The Trial Before Pilate (18:28—19:16)

A. The Accusation (18:28-32)

After the Jewish trials held before Caiaphas and the Sanhedrin (see the Synoptic Gospels for the details), Jesus was taken to the Roman governor Pontius Pilate. His capital was at Caesarea, but at this festival he was in Jerusalem at a place called the Praetorium. Exact location of this spot is still questioned, but the commonest view places it at the Fortress Antonia, adjacent to the temple area on the northwest (Figs. 5, 22). The need for Roman authorities to be near the temple at feast time, the discovery of a paved courtyard at the site (cf. 19:13, *lithostrōton*), and the fact that Herod Antipas was presently in the city and would presumably have occupied Herod's palace, argue that Pilate was at the Antonia.[15] Pilate had been appointed prefect of Judea in A.D. 26. An inscription providing archaeological evidence of Pilate's appointment by the Emperor Tiberius was discovered at Caesarea in 1961.[16]

The time was very early in the morning (*prōi*). This designation was equivalent to the fourth watch, thus the period from 3:00 A.M to 6:00 A.M., according to Mark 13:35. The Sanhedrin probably had forewarned Pilate (they had already secured soldiers from him, 18:3). The Jews, however, refused to enter these Gentile precincts lest ceremonial defilement prevent them from eating the Passover meal.[17] Although bent on the killing of a man

---

[15]Some, however, locate it at Herod's palace on the western hill near the present Jaffa Gate. A discussion of the evidence for both views is found in Jack Finegan, *The Archaeology of the New Testament* (Princeton, 1969), pp. 156-158.

[16]See the article by D. H. Wheaton, "Pilate," *New Bible Dictionary*, ed. J. D. Douglas (Grand Rapids, 1962), pp. 996, 997.

[17]See comments on 13:1. The OT does not speak of Gentile dwellings as defiling, but rabbinical interpretations had apparently extended the law to this extent, perhaps based on Gentile use of leaven (cf. Exod. 12:15, 19), and perhaps on their practices regarding the dead. We do not presently know with certainty the cause of the defilement envisioned, and thus we cannot tell why it must have involved a seven-day impurity rather than one that could be cleansed at sundown. The Mishnah does state that a man or woman who has a flux suffers seven-day uncleanness, and that a Gentile is in every respect like a man who suffers a flux. Herbert Danby, *The Mishnah* (Oxford, 1933), pp. 800-801. Furthermore, Gentile dwellings were unclean because Gentiles were alleged to throw abortions down their drains. *Ibid,.* p. 675, note 10.

they knew to be legally innocent, they were religiously scrupulous. This is how men often ease their consciences.

When Pilate asked the Jews what the charges were against Jesus, they were evasive and wanted Pilate to confirm their death verdict (Matt. 27:1) without further examination. It was clear that the reason why they had brought Jesus to Pilate was their insistence upon the death penalty which they were prevented by the Romans from performing themselves. John saw in the transfer of the case to the Romans, and thus the prospect of death by crucifixion, the fulfillment of Christ's prediction about the manner of his death (3:14; 8:28; 12:32-33).

B. *The Examination* (18:33-38a)

Of the charges brought by the Jews against Jesus (Luke 23:2), Pilate concentrated on the charge that Jesus claimed to be the king of the Jews. Pilate's question with "you" in the emphatic position shows how ludicrous he regarded the whole case to be: "Are *you* the King of the Jews?" Jesus seemed to be a most unlikely prospect for a throne. Jesus answered by a question of his own. His final answer to the question must take into account what Pilate understood by the concept "king of the Jews." Ascertaining that Pilate was asking from a Roman viewpoint, Jesus replied that his kingdom was of a different sort than Pilate expected. Its source, nature, and methods were not of human origin. Although it would eventually involve an earthly domain, it would not depend on men to set it up.[18] If one had the proper understanding of Christ's kingdom, then the answer to Pilate's question would be "yes," and Jesus acknowledged that Pilate had correctly stated it. However, only those who are "of the truth" could understand what Jesus was saying. Pilate closed the examination by the cynical remark, "What is truth?" How sad that he did not wait for an answer, for the answer was standing before him (14:6).

C. *The Verdict*[19] (18:38b-40)

Pilate, after considering the case thus far, made two decisions.

---

[18]Alva J. McClain, *The Greatness of the Kingdom* (Grand Rapids, 1959), pp. 380-383.

[19]The sending of Jesus to Herod Antipas must have occurred between 18:38 and 39 (Luke 23:6-12).

He first declared the innocence of Jesus. He had found no grounds for an unfavorable verdict. However, he also decided to pacify the accusers. He hoped to accept their judgment (and thus to calm them), and then grant a pardon to the prisoner. He offered them the choice of Jesus or Barabbas, a notorious brigand and murderer (Luke 23:19). Assuming that the crowd would choose Jesus, Pilate had badly miscalculated, for the relentless Jews chose Barabbas.

D. The Violence (19:1-3)

The violence exerted against Jesus consisted of a scourging by Pilate's order and mockery by the soldiers with Pilate's permission. Scourging was such a vicious punishment that Roman citizens were exempt from it. It consisted of a beating of the prisoner with a whip made of leather thongs imbedded with metal tips. The prisoner was usually bound over a low pillar with his back exposed and then whipped until his back was a bloody pulp. The first-century historian Josephus wrote of a man whose bones were laid bare by scourging.[20] Pilate had already pronounced Jesus innocent (18:38); justice demanded that he release him. Hence these acts of violence were not performed upon a condemned man but upon one who had been acquitted. Pilate seems to have hoped to get Jesus released by this measure, and expected that the Jews would settle for this amount of blood and not continue their demand for crucifixion; but they were not to be turned aside.

The mockery by the soldiers was not only a vicious and unwarranted attack, but was also a ridiculing of Jewish Messianic ideas. The soldiers had heard of Jewish hopes for a king, and they showed their contempt for what they considered to be a laughable idea. At the site of the Antonia, a large pavement (Lithostrotos) has been excavated, where patterns for soldiers' games were inscribed on some of the stones.[21] One of them was known at the King's Game.

---

[20]Josephus The Jewish War, Book VI, Sect. 304 (VI.5.3).

[21]Finegan, Archaeology of the New Testament, pp. 160-161.

E. The Public Clamor (19:4-7)

Pilate seems greatly agitated throughout this whole episode, and he had good reason to be. He had pronounced a verdict of innocence but had failed to release the prisoner. Instead of the august demeanor expected of a Roman judge, we find Pilate passing back and forth from his chambers in the building to the Jews outside no less than seven times (18:29, 33, 38; 19:1, 4, 9, 13). While trying to make the Jews settle for release, he finds them becoming more adamant in their shouts for execution. When they tell him what to do to Jesus ("Crucify, crucify"), he reminds them who is in charge by sarcastically telling them to do it (19:6) for they both knew that this required Pilate's authorization (18:31).

This goading of the Jews brought from them the true nature of their charge against Jesus. Before this they had presented certain civil charges to Pilate which they thought would sound most serious to the governor (Luke 23:2). They now admitted that the real cause of their hatred was his claim to be the Son of God (cf. Matt. 26:63-66). This was blasphemy in their view, but they had suspected that the pagan governor would not be so greatly exercised.

F. The Renewed Questioning (19:8-11)

When this charge of claiming to be the Son of God was made, there followed some fearful questioning by Pilate. It was a superstitious fear to be sure, but he was sobered for a moment. Although Pilate was not spiritually capable of discussing the matter of Jesus' origin, our Lord took the opportunity to remind him that even a Roman governor's power was not absolute. Yet Pilate's guilt in violating justice was not as great as that of Caiaphas, who in spite of possessing Scripture had rejected Jesus and had turned to a pagan judge to carry out his evil wishes.

G. The Sentencing (19:12-16)

The decision was not made on the basis of guilt for a crime committed, but for political reasons. When it became clear that the Jews would spread the story to Caesar at Rome that Pilate was lenient toward one who had made kingly claims, the governor decided that political expediency should take precedence over justice. There is evidence that "Friend of Caesar" was an honorific title given in recognition for some special service,[22] although that is not necessarily the meaning in 19:12.

Sitting upon the tribunal at The Pavement (Greek: *lithostrōtos*), Pilate sentenced Jesus to death by crucifixion. The date was the day of preparation[23] for the Passover meal, the fourteenth of Nisan. John puts the time of day as about the sixth hour. Inasmuch as Mark 15:25 places the actual crucifixion at the third hour (9:00 A.M., Jewish time), John must be using the Roman reckoning which began counting from midnight.[24] Thus "about the sixth hour" would be around 6:00 A.M., perhaps 6:30.

The Jewish outcry, "We have no king but Caesar," was a startling one. Although it was politically true at the moment, it should have been a galling admission and was uncharacteristic of the Jews (cf. 8:33). Knowing full well that Jesus' claims of kingship were related to Old Testament prophecy, these priests seem to be saying that they rejected any messianic hope.

---

[22]*A Greek English Lexicon*, trans. W. F. Arndt and F. W. Gingrich (Chicago, 1957), p. 396; Adolph Deissmann, *Light from the Ancient East*, 4th edn. (New York, n.d.), p. 383; Raymond E. Brown, *The Gospel According to John*, XIII-XXI, in The Anchor Bible Series (Garden City, 1970), p.879.

[23]Inasmuch as the noun *paraskeuē* (preparation) was also used to describe the day of preparation for the weekly Sabbath, it came to mean Friday, and is used that way in Modern Greek. Hence many interpret "the preparation of the Passover" (19:14) to mean "Friday of Passover week," in order to protect the idea that the Passover meal had been eaten the night before. C. K. Barrett, however, thinks it cannot be so construed and must mean "eve of Passover" (*The Gospel According to St.John* [London, 1967], pp. 453-454). Certainly John has given the impression that the Passover was still future.

[24]If John were employing Jewish reckoning which began numbering the hours at dawn, the sentencing at the sixth hour would be noon and thus in obvious contradiction with Mark who has Jesus on the cross since 9:00 A.M. See the evidence for Roman reckoning presented by B. F. Westcott, *The Gospel According to St. John* (Grand Rapids, reprinted 1950), p. 282. The view that all the Gospel accounts employ Jewish reckoning is given by Morris, who treats the designations as mere approximations. Thus Mark's "third hour" means "about the middle of the morning," and John's "about the sixth hour" means "getting on towards noon." Leon Morris, *The Gospel According to John* (Grand Rapids, 1971), p. 801.

Fig. 27. *Model of the traditional Calvary. The Church of the Holy Sepulcher has been built over the traditional site of Calvary.*

IV. The Execution of Jesus (19:17-30)

A. The Crucifixion (19:17-18)

After Pilate acceded to the Jews' wishes and sentenced Jesus to crucifixion, Pilate delivered Christ to the soldiers for this purpose. John makes it clear that the procession started with Jesus carrying his own cross. (The Synoptic Gospels indicate that Simon of Cyrene was commandeered from the crowd to assist in this task, perhaps when Jesus had grown faint from the abuse he had already endured.) The usual procedure was for the prisoner to be given to the custody of a centurion who would lead him and the soldiers to the place of execution. The procession often took a lengthy route through the city so as to attract attention, humiliate the victim, and provide a gruesome entertainment for the crowd. In this instance they made their way to a place named Golgotha, a Hebrew term meaning "skull" (the Latin equivalent was "Calvary"). It may have been so named because it was a skull-shaped hill. At Golgotha Jesus was affixed to the cross, along with two other victims. Crucifixion was an excruciating way to die, for death often came slowly from thirst, sun, and bleeding.

The exact location of Golgotha is uncertain. The Church of the Holy Sepulcher in Jerusalem marks the spot which has by far the oldest tradition connected with it. It is inside the present wall of the city, but was outside the second wall at the time of Jesus (see Figs. 22, 27). Another site, known as Gordon's Calvary, has been favored by many following the suggestion first made in 1842 by

Otto Thenius. Nearby is the Garden Tomb, discovered in 1867, although most archaeologists tend to date it in the Byzantine period.[25]

B. *The Inscription on the Cross* (19:19-22)

The inscription which Pilate ordered placed on the cross was doubtless intended to be as insulting to the Jews as it was to Jesus. It was written in three languages and received wide notice. By this inscription Pilate was getting back at the Jewish leaders who had harassed him throughout the trial. He said in effect: "This unfortunate victim is the only kind of king you Jews will ever have, and he is the kind you deserve." How tragic that neither Pilate nor the nation realized that those words written so unwittingly were actually the truth. When Christ returns, his kingly status will be displayed for all to see.

The slight variations in the wording of the inscription among the four Gospels may be explained by the differences in the three languages employed, and by the fact that each Gospel has given the title in a condensed form. The full content of the inscription apparently was: "This is Jesus of Nazareth, the King of the Jews." The wording offended the Jewish authorities, and they wanted it changed so as to indicate that "King of the Jews" was merely Jesus' unwarranted claim. Pilate, however, had been badgered enough by them and ordered that the inscription should stand. Perhaps John saw in Pilate's response a deeper sense in which God had overruled to insure that the truth of Jesus' Messiahship would be publicly proclaimed.

C. *The Soldiers and the Women* (19:23-27)

Two groups of bystanders are depicted at the cross. The soldiers who had crucified Jesus distributed his clothing among themselves. There were four of them, and they portioned out the garments four ways. Sandals, girdle, outer garment, and head-dress were claimed in this manner. The seamless inner coat or tunic was a more valuable garment, and the soldiers threw dice for it. To them it seemed the most natural thing to do (far more

[25]A resumé of the historical and archaeological data is given by Finegan, *Archaeology of the New Testament*, pp. 163-174.

sensible than cutting it into four useless pieces). They had no idea that this very act had been prophesied hundreds of years before (Ps. 22:18).

The other group of bystanders was a little band of women. From John's Gospel alone it is not certain whether three or four women are mentioned. If only three are meant and thus Christ's mother's sister was Mary the wife of Cleophas, it seems strange that sisters would each be named Mary. However, by comparison with the parallel passages it seems that "his mother's sister" (19:25) is identified as Salome (Mark 15:40), who was also the wife of Zebedee and mother of James and John (Matt. 27:56). Thus four women are referred to in 19:25. This group of grieving women had been faithful to the end. To John (who by the above explanation would be a first cousin to Jesus) our Lord committed the care of his mother. In all probability Joseph was dead by this time, and Jesus' half brothers were still unbelievers and were apparently not present (7:5). Even though all the disciples had forsaken Jesus earlier (Matt. 26:56; Mark 14:50), John had come back and was now available to take the responsibility of Mary. No sufferings were sufficient to make Jesus forget the needs of others.

D. The Death of Jesus (19:28-30)

With the cry "I thirst," Jesus reflected one of the chief agonies of crucifixion. He was then given some vinegar,[26] which served to clear his throat and strengthen him for the loud cry to follow (Ps. 69:21). Earlier he had refused to drink a drugged potion, for he would not escape by any means the fullest extent of the suffering (Matt. 27:34). Now having marshaled his remaining strength, he cried out, "It is finished." By this he meant that the work which he had come to do, the securing of redemption for lost men, had been accomplished.

V. The Burial of Jesus (19:31-42)

As evening approached, preparations were made for dispos-

---

[26]This drink (oxos, vinegar, sour wine) relieved thirst more effectively than water. It was cheaper than regular wine, and was a common drink of the poorer people.

ing of the bodies. At sundown the Jewish sabbath would begin, and the presence of these bodies so close to the city would be a desecration. Furthermore, this was not the regular weekly sabbath, but the annual Passover Feast Sabbath,[27] and was therefore of special sanctity. Jewish officials requested that death might be hastened so that the gruesome spectacle might be removed. Jesus, however, was already dead, and thus was spared this added suffering of having his legs broken.[28] The spear wound in the side, which brought forth blood and water, demonstrated that death in his case had already occurred.[29]

These remarkable happenings greatly impressed the author

[27]It must be remembered that the name *sabbath* was given not only to the seventh day of the week but also to certain of the annual feast days, including Passover (see comments on 5:9). John's terming of the approaching sabbath as a "high day" indicates that it was not an ordinary weekly sabbath, and 19:14 explains that it was Passover (other references in John pointing to Passover as still future at this time are 13:1, 29; 18:28). A comparison of Luke 23:56 with Mark 16:1 indicates the possibility of two sabbaths in view with the spices being prepared by the women on the day between them. By this view the crucifixion occurred on Wednesday, the Passover Sabbath was Thursday (beginning at sundown Wednesday night), the spices were bought and prepared on Friday, the weekly sabbath was Saturday, and the resurrection occurred following sundown Saturday which was the beginning of the first day of the week. See the author's commentary, "Matthew," *Wycliffe Bible Commentary*, ed. Charles F. Pfeiffer and Everett F. Harrison (Chicago, 1962), p. 984.

[28]A modern scholar has written: "But the mechanism of crucifixion, as physicians will affirm, is such that the weight of the body fixes the rib cage; and respiration can take place only in diaphragmatic action. After a prolonged period of suspension, however, fatigue of the diaphragm will occur; and, finally, complete paralysis of this muscle will supervene. The fastening of the legs enables the victim to relieve this respiratory failure by providing a point of leverage to raise the body and thus alleviate the paralyzing tension on the thorax set up by the body weight hanging on the arms. No matter how agonizing the process, the victim may continue to surge and plunge in this way for amazingly long periods of time. When the legs are broken, however, the point of leverage is removed and the victim dies because of respiratory failure. The breaking of the legs is not to be understood, therefore, merely as an act of torture, but rather as an act of mercy, or expediency, directed to the accelerated dispatch of the victim." Gerald L. Borchert, "They Brake Not His Legs," *Christianity Today* Vol. VI, No. 12 (March 16, 1962), p. 12 (572).

[29]There is no warrant for interpreting the "blood and water" symbolically (representing baptism and communion). John is describing what he actually saw. The spear wound must have penetrated the chest cavity and allowed the clotted blood and watery serum to flow out. That the blood had separated into these two parts indicated that death had already occurred.

John[30] who was present (19:26), and he assures his readers that they are receiving a genuine eyewitness account (19:35). What was particularly impressive was the fulfillment of ancient prophecies at the death of Jesus. The fact that Jesus' legs were not broken, although those of the other two victims were, indicated to John that even this detail from the Passover ritual was being fulfilled by the Lamb of God (Exod. 12:46; Num. 9:12). The piercing of Jesus' side fulfilled another prophecy which foretold that one day the Jewish nation will mourn as they look on the One whom once they had pierced (Zech. 12:10). The piercing occurred that day at Calvary. The mourning is yet to come.

Two men, both members of the Sanhedrin which had condemned Jesus (7:50; Mark 15:43), stepped forward at no small risk to themselves to claim his body. Joseph had been a secret believer but now was willing to be identified with his dead Master. Nicodemus showed by his action that his prior contact with Jesus had borne genuine fruit (3:1 ff.).[31]

Burial preparations had to be hasty and temporary because it was nearly sundown and the beginning of the sabbath. Therefore they hurriedly wrapped the body in cloths, sprinkled spices among the folds, and laid it in Joseph's tomb which had been built nearby but never yet used. After the sabbath was over, the women planned to anoint the body (Luke 23:55-56). They were in for an astounding surprise!

---

[30] Although the use of *ekeinos* in 19:35 leads some to suppose a second person is introduced who vouches for the testimony of the eyewitness, the difficulty of identification makes this unlikely. It is better to regard one individual as in view throughout the statement.

[31] Leon Morris observes that in contrast to the disciples who had openly followed Jesus and then ran away at the end, the two secret disciples Joseph and Nicodemus affirmed their connection with Jesus when it was most dangerous to do so (*John*, p. 826). This should caution us against impatience with those whose faith may be developing more slowly.

Questions for Discussion

1. What factors contributed to Peter's denials?
2. Explain the statement of Jesus, "My kingdom is not of this world."
3. To whom was Jesus referring when he said to Pilate, "He that delivered me unto thee hath the greater sin"?
4. What are the implications of the Jews' assertion, "We have no king but Caesar"?
5. In what sense was Jesus the King of the Jews?
6. What Scriptures were fulfilled at the crucifixion of Jesus?

Chapter 13

The Resurrection
(John 20-21)

The resurrection of Jesus Christ from the dead was an event of incalculable importance. Scripture teaches that the resurrection was much more than a mere aftermath of Calvary. Paul wrote: "If Christ be not raised, your faith is vain; ye are yet in your sins" (I Cor. 15:17). If Christ were still dead, he would still be paying sin's penalty. No great High Priest would be ministering in heaven on your behalf.

It must also be remembered that Jesus always pointed to his own resurrection when he was asked for some sign to prove his claim to Messiahship (cf. 2:18-22; Matt. 12:38-40). Though others had worked miracles (Biblical prophets, Egyptian magicians in Moses' day), no one ever had predicted his own resurrection and then been able to accomplish it. This was one miracle which, if acknowledged, would authenticate all the other miracles which Jesus had performed.

The practical importance of the resurrection can be readily seen in its effect upon the original disciples. Prior to it, they were a discouraged, confused, not-too-impressive group. In spite of momentary flashes of deep faith, they were too often insensitive to the true purposes of Christ. In his darkest hour of trial they forsook him and fled. But shortly thereafter all of this confusion vanished, and they are depicted in clearest strokes as courageous, confident, and capable leaders, promoting the new faith in spite of the most forbidding obstacles. The chief factor responsible for this abrupt transformation was the resurrection of Christ. The consciousness that they served a risen and glorified Master completely revolutionized their outlook and served as the conviction that strengthened them when persecution came.

I. The Empty Tomb (20:1-10)

A. The Discovery of the Empty tomb (20:1-2)

The discovery was made by Mary Magdalene. A comparison of all four Gospels reveals the details to be very complicated at this point.[1] However, something like the following must have occurred. On the first day of the week,[2] a group of women including Mary Magdalene had set out early[3] for the tomb while it was yet dark (20:1; Luke 24:1, 10). Mary, however, must have run ahead and arrived first; when she found the tomb empty, she immediately left to tell Peter and John. Thus she did not see the angel nor hear the message he gave to the other women when they arrived after sunrise (Mark 16:2-8).

The heavy stone had been rolled away by an angel of the Lord in connection with an earthquake (Matt. 28:2). This had happened before the arrival of any visitors on the first day of the week. Its purpose was to let visitors see that the body of Jesus was truly gone. Otherwise, the presence of the soldiers and the authoritative seal on the stone would have prevented such a verification. Of course, the resurrection body of Jesus was not impeded by the stone, for it could pass through material objects without difficulty (cf. 20:26). Therefore, Jesus may have risen some hours before.[4]

B. The Examination of the Empty Tomb (20:3-7)

An examination was made by Peter and John. The "other disciple," who is also identified as the "disciple whom Jesus loved" (20:2), is assumed to be John, the author of this Gospel.

---

[1]See B. F. Westcott, *The Gospel According to St. John* (Grand Rapids, reprinted 1950), p. 288, for a detailed reconstruction with suggested times of day.

[2]The word "week" (20:1, KJV, ASV) is *sabbatōn*, which can be used in the singular or the plural with the sense either of "sabbath" or "week."

[3]"Early" (20:1, *prōi*) denotes the period from 3 A.M. to 6 A.M., equivalent to the fourth watch of the night (Mark 13:35).

[4]Those who hold to Wednesday crucifixion put the resurrection on Saturday evening, just after sundown, which was the beginning of the first day of the week by Jewish reckoning. This allows for a full three days and three nights in the tomb. See chapter 12, footnote 27.

Fig. 28. *The Church of the Holy Sepulcher, with its bell tower and two large domes, marks the traditional sites of the crucifixion and the entombment of Christ.*

He reached the open sepulcher first but stood outside looking in. Peter, who may have been older and slower of foot, arrived next and went on inside, where he was joined by John.

They noticed two peculiar features about the tomb. One was the presence of the graveclothes. If the body had been moved, why had the linen wrappings been removed and left behind? The other strange feature was the arrangement of the graveclothes. Instead of the wrappings lying about in disarray or piled in a heap in the corner, the headpiece was still in the position where the head had been. In other words, the wrappings seem to have been in the very position in which the body had lain, although they were now collapsed for there was no body within.[5] How the body of Jesus could have been removed with-

[5] Another view explains the headpiece as rolled up and placed to one side, giving evidence of its being "neatly rolled up *(entetuligmenon)*, not simply in a disordered state" (C. K. Barrett, *The Gospel According to St. John* [London, 1967], p. 468.) This fits the language well, but does not provide as clear a basis for the conclusion which John drew (20:8).

out disturbing the wrappings was a problem not answerable by normal explanations.

C. The Conclusion About the Empty Tomb (20:8-10)

Seeing the empty tomb and the graveclothes, John drew the only reasonable conclusion: there had been a supernatural removal. It cannot be maintained that the disciples merely believed what they wanted to believe, for they were not expecting a resurrection. Even though Jesus had predicted that he would rise from the dead (Matt. 20:17-19), not one of his followers really comprehended it. The Old Testament Scriptures which foretold the resurrection (e.g., Ps. 16:10) were not understood until Jesus explained them later (cf. Luke 24:44-45). John's conclusion, therefore, was based solely on what he saw in the empty tomb. Whether John shared his conviction with Peter is not stated, but it may be presumed that he did. The two men then returned to their quarters[6] in Jerusalem.

II. The Appearance of Jesus to Mary Magdalene (20:11-18)

A. The Circumstances (20:11-13)

After Mary Magdalene had reported to Peter and John the fact of the empty tomb (20:2), she went back to the spot to weep. The two apostles had preceded her but had already left by the time she arrived. Thus she knew nothing of their belief in the resurrection. Her overpowering feeling was grief, and she stood by the open sepulcher and gave way to her sorrow.

The cause of her sorrow was her personal sense of loss at the death of Jesus. This bereavement was compounded by the fact that even the body had disappeared, and thus she had lost all contact with Jesus. Looking into the tomb she saw two angels. These had the form of men, and had also been seen by the group of women whom Mary had been with earlier in the morning

[6]The phrase pros hautous (the alternate reading is pros heautous)is not the usual expression for going to one's home (eis ta idia). However, it is used in this sense in Josephus Antiquities of the Jews, Book VIII, Sect. 124 (VIII.4.6). It does not seem essential that Peter and John be understood as each owning houses in Jerusalem. Thus "their respective quarters" where they were residing while in the city is probably what is meant.

before she left them to tell Peter and John (Luke 24:4). When these angels questioned Mary, she was too overcome by her own grief to be impressed or startled by these supernatural visitors. She brokenly explained: "They have taken away my Lord." Mary had much reason to be devoted to Jesus, for he had rescued her life from demon possession (Luke 8:2).[7] The absence of Jesus was for Mary not merely the absence of "our Lord," but of "my Lord." Every Christian should examine his own relationship to Christ as to whether it is truly a personal one.

B. The Appearing of Jesus (20:14-16)

When Jesus appeared, Mary broke off her conversation with the angels and asked whether this man, who she thought might be the gardener, knew where Jesus was. She did not recognize him until he spoke her name. Although it was the same Jesus, there may have been some external differences (Mark 16:12; cf. Luke 24:16). Perhaps of more importance in the explanation is the condition of Mary herself. Grief-stricken, despairing, and completely unprepared to expect a resurrection, she was not ready in mind to accept the reality of such a circumstance. When she finally recognized Jesus by his speaking of her name, she responded with "Rabboni," the respectful form of address among the Jews used for those regarded as occupying a higher rank than the speaker.[8] This term, not materially different in sense from "Rabbi," was also used of Jesus by the blind man at Jericho (Mark 10:51). John has translated it into Greek as "Teacher."

C. The Instruction for Mary (20:17-18)

Jesus gave Mary two commands. The first was: "Stop clinging to me."[9] Apparently she had grasped his feet as if to keep him

[7]The popular notion that she had once been an immoral woman is without Biblical proof. There is no reason to identify her with the woman of Luke 7:37.

[8]Eduard Lohse, "Rabbi, Rabbouni," *Theological Dictionary of the New Testament*, ed. Gerhard Friedrich, trans. Geoffrey D. Bromiley (Grand Rapids, 1968), VI, 961-965.

[9]Greek: *Mē mou haptou*. The present imperative with *mē* is commonly used to order the ceasing of an activity already in progress.

present always. Jesus understood her thoughts, recognizing that she supposed this return to be the one which he had promised to the disciples (14:3). But this postresurrection appearance was not his second coming in which he would take believers with him. That would have to be preceded by the ascension and the sending of the Spirit. In the interim Jesus could not be retained on the earth by Mary or the others.[10] He had another function to perform in heaven, ministering on behalf of all believers.

The second command was, "Go to my brethren." She was to announce the fact of the resurrection and the coming ascension to the disciples. "My brethren" should be understood in the sense of "disciples" (cf. Matt. 12:47-50), rather than of Jesus' brothers who were as yet unbelievers. At any rate, this seems to be the way Mary interpreted the words (20:18), and there is no indication that she went specifically to the members of Jesus' family.

III. The Appearance of Jesus to the Ten[11] (20:19-23)

A. *The Circumstances* (20:19a)

The condition of the disciples as they gathered on the evening of Resurrection Day was one of fear. Thomas was absent from this meeting (20:24), and Judas was dead. The meeting was apparently a secret one, and the doors were secured because of danger from the Jewish leaders. There were good reasons for expecting trouble from the authorities. Jesus had already been executed through their efforts. His followers had been threatened with religious excommunication (9:22). Jesus himself

---

[10]This interpretation is decidely preferable to that which supposes some ceremonial reason for Jesus' command. To imagine that as the believers' priest, Jesus could not be touched until he had presented his blood to the Father (after the analogy of the OT priest) overlooks the significance of the present imperative; neither does it fit easily with Jesus' own invitation to touch his body (20:27; Matt. 28:9; Luke 24:39; cf. I John 1:1). A resumé of other views (some of them well-nigh incredible) is given by R. E. Brown, *The Gospel According to John, XIII-XXI,* in The Anchor Bible Series (Garden City, 1970), Vol. 29A, pp. 992-993.

[11]It would be unduly restrictive, however, to conclude that only ten were present. Luke 24:33 mentions "them that were with them" and they were joined by the two from Emmaus.

had taught them that if he suffered, they would have to suffer also (15:20). Already the story was being circulated by the tomb guards that disciples had stolen the body of Jesus (Matt. 28:11-15). However, as long as they were a fear-ridden group, huddled in a locked room, they would be unable to do much in carrying on the ministry of Christ.

B. The Appearing of Jesus (20:19b-20)

Even though the doors were closed, Jesus suddenly appeared in their midst. Here is indication that the resurrection body has capabilities not possessed by mortal flesh. This sudden presence of Jesus terrified the group (Luke 24:37). Although they all had heard reports of the resurrection, and Peter had probably seen Jesus already (Luke 24:34), perhaps not all of them were convinced that a true bodily resurrection had occurred. Thus Jesus spoke peace to their hearts and showed them the genuine physical nature of his resurrection body.

C. The Commission to the Disciples (20:21-23)

Jesus then gave a commission to the disciples. Their task would be to carry on the evangelizing work which he had started (cf. 17:18). This responsibility would include the announcement that Christ had died as the Lamb of God and that forgiveness was available through faith in him. Christ also gave them the power to accomplish their task. When he said, "Receive ye the Holy Ghost," he was not speaking of the coming of the Spirit on Pentecost seven weeks later, nor was this a premature Pentecost for these disciples. Rather it was an empowering by the Spirit to sustain them in their present need. At Pentecost there would occur the baptizing of the Spirit which would make them each a part of the body of Christ, the New Testament Church.

The message which Christ was commissioning the disciples to convey involved the remission of sins. It must not be thought that the absolution of sins was here committed to the disciples without restriction. Forgiveness of sins in the absolute sense is the prerogative of God alone (Mark 2:5-7). The best commentary on 20:23 is Acts 10:43, where Peter (one of those receiving these instructions from Jesus) reveals how he understood what Jesus meant. He declared to Cornelius: "To him give all the prophets witness, that through his name whosoever believeth in him shall receive remission of sins." It is by the proclamation of the gospel (not by some hierarchical authority of the apostles) that announcement of the remission or retention of sins is made. Acceptance of the gospel by faith brings remission of sins; unbelief leaves men with their guilt retained.

IV. The Appearance of Jesus to the Eleven (20:24-29)

A. The Problem of Thomas (20:24-25)

The next appearance of the risen Christ was chiefly for the benefit of Thomas, the one member of the apostolic group (except for Judas)[12] who had not been present when Jesus appeared on the evening of Resurrection Day. The condition of Thomas was such that he demanded full proof before he would believe in the bodily resurrection. The reason for his absence the previous week is not explained by John, and one should beware of misjudging his motives. It should be noted that Jesus did not rebuke him for his absence. Perhaps Thomas preferred to be alone with his grief. When the report was given to him by the other apostles, he refused belief unless he could have the same opportunity for verification which they had experienced. He seems to have suspected that the resurrection was only a vision granted to the others, not a real physical return from the dead.

B. The Appearing of Jesus (20:26-29)

The answer for Thomas came in a fresh appearing of Jesus. One week later[13] he appeared to the eleven disciples in spite of locked doors, and spoke the same greeting as before (cf. 20:19). Jesus then spoke directly to Thomas, revealing by his statement that he knew all about Thomas's previous demand. The omniscience of Jesus was a great proof to Thomas and, when coupled

---

[12]John continues to use the name "the twelve" to denote the group even though Judas was now gone (20:24). By this time it had become not just an arithmetical total, but a recognized name.

[13]By counting both termini (a common Jewish method of reckoning), "after eight days" is probably to be understood as the next Sunday evening from the previous appearance to the ten.

with the physical presence in the room, removed all his doubts. It is not stated whether or not he still felt it necessary to handle the body of Jesus, although the subsequent words of Jesus may imply that "seeing" was enough to satisfy him (20:29). But he did make to Jesus the greatest confession of any in the room: "My Lord and my God." The reality of the resurrection had satisfied the unresolved questions of the demanding Thomas.

Jesus then pronounced a blessing upon all believers (20:29). For those whose faith would need to be founded on the testimony of witnesses rather than on personal viewing, Jesus specifically said that such are blessed. Believers today must depend upon the testimony of the apostles who saw him. But this sort of faith, which does not demand immediate sight, is especially approved by Christ, for it trusts his Word.

V. The Formal Conclusion to the Book (20:30-31)

With this statement John concludes the main body of his work, and states the practical purpose of his writing. He also explains his method. A great many signs, he says, had been performed by Jesus. By the term "sign" (sēmeion) he means both miracles and other actions which served as proofs or credentials of Christ's person and authority. A miracle is a sign when its meaning is understood. For John the miracles were far more than amazing works which produced wonder among the witnesses. To him they were indicators that Jesus was who he claimed to be.

From these many signs (cf. also 21:25) John has made a selection to serve his purpose. He has described eight miracles of Jesus,[14] as well as the resurrection. Certain nonmiraculous actions, such as the cleansing of the temple and the triumphal entry into Jerusalem may also be regarded as signs. The purpose of this selection was twofold. The author first wished to convince his readers by these signs that Jesus is the Messiah, and that this concept means he is the Son of God (not just a political deliverer). Second, he wanted his readers to learn that faith in Jesus the divine Messiah imparts eternal life. Thus he has made an integral part of his narrative the fact that Jesus' ministry always produced faith in some at least, even in the midst of general unbelief. There was always some light in the darkness.

[14]See Introduction, footnote 17, for list.

Epilogue (21:1-25)

Epilogue (21:1-25)

This closing portion of the Gospel was evidently written with a somewhat different purpose in mind than the previous material. The fact that it follows the formal conclusion of 20:30-31 indicates this must not have been intended to offer proof of the resurrection, for that had been done in chapter 20. If this were merely one more postresurrection appearance, it is difficult to see why it was not placed before 20:30-31, or if it were an afterthought, why 20:30-31 was not moved to the end of chapter 21.

To regard chapter 21 as a later addition by another writer raises its own problems. There is no documentary evidence whatever that the Gospel ever circulated without chapter 21. Nor have efforts to trace a different style in this chapter been generally convincing.[15] At best a case might be made for another writer of 21:24-25, but even this is not necessary.[16] A more reasonable explanation views the chapter as Johannine, but sees it as an epilogue which balances the Prologue at the beginning (1:1-18) and sets forth the relation of the risen Christ to the society of believers. It also served to clarify the matter about John's predicted future.

I. The Miraculous Catch of Fish (21:1-14)

The disciples were now in Galilee, having gone there at Jesus' instruction (Matt. 28:10). Seven of them were together, and although they knew and believed the resurrection, they do not seem to be clear about their responsibilities. Peter's plan to go fishing was quickly adopted by the others. It did not necessarily indicate a permanent resumption of their former occupation, but it may reveal their confusion about what Christ expected them to do.

---

[15]Even Barrett, who holds to a different author for John 21, concludes: "These linguistic and stylistic considerations, when weighed against the undoubted resemblances between chs. 1-20 and ch. 21, are not in themselves sufficient to establish the belief that ch. 21 was written by a different author" (*John*, p. 480).

[16]Donald Guthrie, *New Testament Introduction, The Gospels and Acts* (Chicago, 1965), pp. 218-219.

A whole night of fishing on the Sea of Galilee[17] brought nothing into their nets. As the dawn began to break over the heights of Golan on the east, Jesus appeared on the shore but was not recognized. His words shouted out to them across the water showed his knowledge of their situation: "Lads, you don't have anything to eat, do you?" By a few simple directions to the disciples, Jesus caused a miraculous catch of fish. The miracle was so impressive that the disciples counted the fish and found the total to be one hundred fifty-three. John never forgot the number.[18]

[17] Another name for this lake was the Sea of Tiberias (6:1; 21:1), derived from the city on its west shore built by Herod Antipas around A.D. 25 and named in honor of Tiberias Caesar.

[18] Fantastic allegories have been constructed out of the total 153, more impressive for their ingenuity than for their hermeneutical soundness. Morris observes, "It is much simpler to see a fisherman's record of a fact" (*John*, p. 867).

Fig. 29. *The Sea of Galilee. On its shores Jesus prepared breakfast for the disciples after the miraculous catch of fish.*

Allowing Jesus to direct their activities, the disciples became aware of his identity. John was the first to recognize him, and Peter characteristically was the first to do something about it. Donning his outer garment,[19] he jumped out of the boat to make his way the hundred yards to shore.[20] Eventually all the disciples came to land, and Peter supervised the dragging of the net full of fish. The similiarity of this miracle to the one near the beginning of Jesus' ministry (Luke 5:1-11) could hardly have been missed by the disciples. The previous one had been used to call four of the disciples to follow Jesus, and to teach them of the need to become fishers of men. Now they saw that the risen Christ had the same power, and they could conclude that his purposes for them were unchanged.

Jesus had breakfast prepared and the disciples were invited to contribute some of the fish which they had caught. Although everyone now knew that their host was Jesus, no one ventured to ask him. The statement is puzzling, but suggests that there was something different about the appearance of Jesus (cf. 20:14; Luke 24:16). It is not mentioned that Jesus himself ate on this occasion, but he had eaten with them at least once since his resurrection (Luke 24:42-43).

This appearance of Jesus on the shore of the Sea of Galilee is called his third appearance to the disciples (21:14). Inasmuch as John has described three earlier appearances (20:14, 19, 26), and the Synoptic Gospels contain still other such occurrences (Matt. 28:9; Luke 24:15), John's calculation must have reference to appearances to the disciples as a group (even if not all were present each time). Thus the three meetings with the apostolic body would be the appearances to the ten (20:19), the eleven (20:26), and the seven by the sea.

II. Jesus' Conversation with Peter (21:15-23)

Following the meal Jesus dealt with Peter. Jesus had already

---

[19]Peter had been fishing without wearing his outer garment. His being "naked" (*gumnos*) does not necessarily mean completely bare. It can denote someone poorly dressed (James 2:15), and probably suggests here that Peter was clad only in an undergarment while at work.

[20]Greek: *pēchōn diakosiōn* (200 cubits).

met Peter privately (Luke 24:34; I Cor. 15:5) and spiritual rectification doubtless occurred at that time. This conversation in the presence of the other disciples was necessary that they also might know from Christ's own lips what Peter's status was, for his denial was common knowledge and must have been deeply resented.

In the three questions put to Peter by Jesus, two different Greek words for "love" are employed. Peter uses the same word in each of his answers (*phileō*). Jesus used another word (*agapaō*) for the first two questions, and then used Peter's word for the third question. Considerable and apparently endless debate revolves around whether there is significance in the change in verbs. The trend today is to regard the variation as merely stylistic, and thus see Jesus asking Peter essentially the same question three times.[21] On the other hand, while admitting that the two verbs have a great overlap of meaning, some see the employment of both in one context as deliberate in order to stress the distinctive connotation of each.[22] Assuming that the latter is correct, the following interpretation is given.

Jesus' first question to Peter, "Lovest (*agapāis*) thou me more than these?" probably had reference to Peter's claim of a greater loyalty to Christ than did the other disciples (Matt. 26:33; Mark 14:29).[23] It forced Peter to recognize his foolish boast and realize his weakness. Jesus' word for "love" is always the one used when love is being commanded. It seems to have more of the volitional and idealistic element in it than its companion word. This love always seeks the good of its object, even to the point of greatest personal sacrifice (13:34; I Cor. 13). In his answer Peter shrank from this term, and responded: "Thou knowest that I have affection (*philō*) for you." Peter's word was a perfectly good one.[24] However, in its distinctive sense, it refers to love within

[21] This is the view of Morris, Barrett, Brown, and Bernard.

[22] This interpretation is followed by Westcott, Lenski, Plummer, and Hendriksen. An excellent extended note is given in William Hendriksen, *Exposition of the Gospel According to John* (Grand Rapids, 1953), pp. 494-500.

[23] This view seems more likely than to interpret "more than these" as "more than you love these disciples" or "more than you love your fishing gear."

[24] *Phileō* is sometimes used of the love of the Father for Jesus (5:20), the Father's love for the disciples (16:27), and the love of Jesus for John (20:2).

the family circle, affection, fondness. Thus Peter had no wish to pursue his earlier boast, but he was confident of a genuine affection for Christ. In reply, Jesus charged Peter, "Feed my lambs." Our Lord still had a ministry for Peter to perform, but he could not perform it unless Christ had the proper place in his heart.

Jesus' second question was similar to the first, but without the comparison to the other disciples. Peter had to question the sincerity of his love, not in comparison to the others, but in relation to himself alone and his Master. Again he responded with the same word as before, and once more Jesus gave him a task: "Shepherd my sheep."

The third question employed the word Peter had been using: "Do you have affection (*phileis*) for me?" It made Peter examine even the fondness which he surely thought he had. Peter felt this probing keenly and appealed to Christ's omniscience to verify his claim. Again Jesus gave a responsibility "Feed my sheep." As Peter would carry out his apostolic ministry, he must deal with the spiritually mature "sheep" as well as the young and weaker "lambs." He must "feed" them as well as care for all their other pastoral needs. Love for Christ would be essential to keep him at his task. Later Peter passed this charge on to the elders of the church (I Peter 5:2-4).

The risen Christ then showed to Peter that his divine sovereignty was still being exercised. This prediction of Peter's martyrdom[25] was referred to by the apostle in II Peter 1:14. In the meantime Peter was to follow Christ as the director of his ministry. Seeing John nearby, Peter asked Jesus about John's future, and was told that whether John lived till Christ's return or died prior to it was dependent upon Christ's will for him. Peter's task was to be faithful in following his Master's orders.

This statement caused a false report to circulate among the brethren[26] about John's not dying. It seems clear that John must

[25]The prediction that Peter would "stretch out" his hands is regarded by some as a prediction of crucifixion. Although appropriate for this type of death, the words probably conveyed no more to Peter than that he would someday be seized and led to execution. Some ancient traditions do say that Peter was crucified head downward at Rome. Eusebius *Ecclesiastical History*, III.1, in *The Fathers of the Church*, trans. Roy J. Deferrari (Washington, D.C., 1965), p. 138.

[26]"Brethren" (*adelphous*) is used in 21:23 in the sense of disciples or believers, as in 20:17.

still have been alive when chapter 21 was written. Otherwise the report would have stopped spreading.

III. The Author's Concluding Testimony (21:24-25)

It is possible that the last two verses of the Gospel were written by someone else, perhaps by the elders of the church at Ephesus. This is the view of many, who feel that "we know" points to other persons who add their testimony to verify John's authorship of the rest of the Gospel. However, this is not the only way to understand these verses. It seems clear that the "disciple who testifies" (21:24) is the disciple whom Jesus loved (21:20-23). That the author should refer to himself in the third person is not surprising in view of his similar reference in 19:35. The argument that the use of the plural "we know" (21:24) points to writers or editors other than the author is offset by the employment of the singular "I suppose" in 21:25. All things considered, it is likely that even these concluding words were written by John. Because he was an eyewitness to most of the events described, and was so well known in the early church, his testimony would be accepted as true by the vast majority of his readers.

As John brought his narrative to its close, he was conscious of the inexhaustible riches from which he drew, and by a "delightful hyperbole"[27] he expressed the inability of the world itself to contain in books all that could be recorded. The encounter with Jesus had transformed his life. The impressions received during their years together had matured in the decades that followed and had never lost their wonder. The thesis with which the author began, that the Word had become flesh and had revealed the glory of God in order to make men children of God by faith, has been demonstrated. Even the shock of crucifixion was part of the divine plan, and the risen Christ still had the same concern for those who trusted him. He continues as the only one whom men must follow. He is the Light in the darkness.

---

[27]Leon Morris's apt phrase. *John,* p. 881.

Questions for Discussion

1. Why did Jesus tell Mary not to touch him?
2. Why didn't Mary recognize Jesus?
3. What relation did Christ's bestowing of the Spirit upon the disciples in 20:22 have to the promise of Pentecost?
4. How did the apostles forgive sins and retain sins?
5. What did Jesus mean by asking Peter if he loved him "more than these"?

Bibliography

Aharoni, Yohanan, and Michael Avi-Yonah. *The Macmillan Bible Atlas.* New York: The Macmillan Company, 1968.

Alexander, Archibald. "Logos." *The International Standard Bible Encyclopedia,* ed. James Orr.Grand Rapids: Wm. B. Eerdmans Publishing Co., 1939, 1946.

Andrews, Samuel J. *The Life of Our Lord Upon the Earth.* Grand Rapids: Zondervan Publishing House, reprinted 1954.

Arndt, William F., and Wilbur F. Gingrich. *A Greek-English Lexicon of the New Testament.* Chicago: University of Chicago Press, 1957.

Babylonian Talmud, trans, Michael L. Rodkinson. Boston: The Talmud Society, 1918.

Baker's Dictionary of Theology, ed. Everett F. Harrison. Grand Rapids: Baker Book House, 1960.

Barrett, C. K. *The Gospel According to St. John.* London:G S.P.C.K., 1967.

Bernard, J. H. *A Critical and Exegetical Commentary on the Gospel According to St. John,* in The International Critical Commentary series. New York: Charles Scribner's Sons, 1929.

The Biblical World, ed. Charles F. Pfeiffer. Grand Rapids: Baker Book House, 1966.

Blass, F., and A. Debrunner. *A Greek Grammar of the New Testament and Other Early Christian Literature,* trans. Robert W. Funk. Chicago: University of Chicago Press, 1961.

Boice, James M. *Witness and Revelation in the Gospel of John.* Grand Rapids: Zondervan Publishing House, 1970.

Borchert, Gerald L. "They Brake Not His Legs," *Christianity Today*, Vol. VI, No. 12 (March 16, 1962).

Brooke, A. E. *The Commentary of Origen on St. John's Gospel*. Cambridge: The University Press, 1896.

Brown, Raymond E. *The Gospel According to John*. Volumes 29 and 29A in The Anchor Bible series. Garden City: Doubleday and Co., Inc., 1966, 1970.

Bultmann, Rudolf. *The Gospel of John, A Commentary*, trans. G. R. Beasley-Murray. Philadelphia: The Westminster Press, 1971.

Calvin, John. *The Gospel According to St. John*, eds. David W. Torrance and Thomas F. Torrance, trans. T. H. L. Parker. Grand Rapids: Wm. B. Eerdmans Publishing Co., 1959.

Catchpole, David. "You Have Heard His Blasphemy." *The Tyndale House Bulletin*, No. 16 (April 1965).

Colwell, E. C. "A Definite Rule for the Use of the Article in the Greek New Testament." *Journal of Biblical Literature*, Vol. 52 (1933).

Cribbs, F. Lamar. "A Reassessment of the Date of Origin and the Destination of the Gospel of John." *Journal of Biblical Literature*, Vol. LXXXIX, Part I (March 1970).

Danby, Herbert. *The Mishnah*. New York: Oxford University Press, 1933.

Daniel-Rops, Henri. *Daily Life in Palestine at the Time of Christ*. Translated by Patrick O'Brian. London: Weidenfeld and Nicholson, 1962.

Daube, David. "Jesus and the Samaritan Woman: the Meaning of *sunchraomai*," *Journal of Biblical Literature*. Vol. LXIX, Part II (June 1950).

Dods, Marcus. "The Gospel of St. John." *The Expositor's Greek Testament*, ed. W. Robertson Nicoll. Volume I. Grand Rapids: Wm. B. Eerdmans Publishing Co., reprint edition.

Edersheim, Alfred. *The Life and Times of Jesus the Messiah*. New American Edition. Grand Rapids: Wm. B. Eerdmans Publishing Co., 1945.

_____. *The Temple, Its Ministry and Services as They Were at the Time of Jesus Christ*. Grand Rapids: Wm. B. Eerdmans Publishing Co., reprinted 1950.

Ellis, David J. "The Gospel According to John." *A New Testament Commentary*, eds. G. C. D. Howley, F. F. Bruce, H. L. Ellison. Grand Rapids: Zondervan Publishing House, 1969.

Eusebius Pamphili *Ecclesiastical History*. Translated by Roy J. Deferrari in *The Fathers of the Church*. Washington, D.C.: The Catholic University of America Press, 1953. Reprinted 1969.

Fee, Gordon D. "The Use of the Definite Article with Personal Names in the Gospel of John." *New Testament Studies*, Vol. 17, No. 2 (January 1971).

Filson, Floyd V. *The Gospel According to John* in The Layman's Bible Commentary series. Richmond, VA: John Knox Press, 1963.

Finegan, Jack. *The Archaeology of the New Testam* University Press, 1969.

Freed, Edwin D. "Did John Write His Go Samaritan Converts?" *Novum Testament* (July 1970).

Gaster, T. H. *The Dead Sea Scriptures*, in City: Doubleday and Co., Inc., 1956

Godet, Frederick Louis. *Commentary on the Gospel of John*, trans. Timothy Dwight. Grand Rapids: Zondervan Publishing House, reprint edition.

Gruss, Edmond C. *Apostles of Denial*. Newhall, CA: Presbyterian and Reformed Publishing Co., 1970.

Guthrie, Donald. *New Testament Introduction: Gospels and Acts*. Chicago: Inter-Varsity Press, 1965.

Haenchen, Ernst. "History and Interpretation in the Johannine Passion Narrative." *Interpretation*. Vol. XXIV, No. 2 (April 1970).

Harner, Philip B. "Qualitative Anarthrous Predicate Nouns: Mark 15:39 and John 1:1." *Journal of Biblical Literature*. Vol. 92, No. 1 (March 1973).

Harrison, Everett F. "The Gospel According to John," *Wycliffe Bible Commentary*, eds. Charles F. Pfeiffer and Everett F. Harrison. Chicago: Moody Press, 1962.

_____. *Introduction to the New Testament*. Grand Rapids: Wm. B. Eerdmans Publishing Co., 1964.

Hartley, John E. "Textual Affinities of Papyrus Bodmer XIV (P[75])," *The Evangelical Quarterly*, Vol. XL, No. 2 (April 1968).

Harvey, A. E. *The New English Bible Companion to the New Testament.* Oxford University Press, 1970.

liam. *Exposition of the Gospel According to John*, estament Commentary series. Grand Rapids: use, 1953.

n the Baptist and the Johannine Prologue." *dies*, Vol. 16, No. 4 (July 1970).

w Birth. Findlay, OH: Dunham Publish-

————. *Then Would My Servants Fight.* Winona Lake, IN: Brethren Missionary Herald Co., 1956.

Hunter, Archibald M. *According to John.* Philadelphia: The Westminster Press, 1968.

Inch, Morris, "Apologetic Use of 'Sign' in the Fourth Gospel." *The Evangelical Quarterly,* Vol. XLII, No. 1 (January 1970).

The Interpreter's Bible, ed. George Arthur Buttrick. New York: Abingdon Press, 1952.

The Interpreter's Dictionary of the Bible, ed. George Arthur Buttrick. New York: Abingdon Press, 1962.

Josephus *Jewish Antiquities,* trans. H. St. J. Thackeray, in The Loeb Classical Library. Cambridge: Harvard University Press, 1957.

————. *The Jewish War,* trans. H. St. J. Thackeray, in The Loeb Classical Library. Cambridge: Harvard University Press, 1956.

Kent, Homer A., Jr. "The Day of That Sabbath Was a High Day." Unpublished monograph, Grace Theological Seminary, 1950.

————. *The Epistle to the Hebrews.* Grand Rapids: Baker Book House, 1972.

————. "The Gospel According to Matthew." *Wycliffe Bible Commentary,* eds. Charles F. Pfeiffer and Everett F. Harrison. Chicago: Moody Press, 1962.

————. *Jerusalem to Rome.* Grand Rapids: Baker Book House, 1972.

Kittel, Gerhard, and Gerhard Friedrich. *Theological Dictionary of the New Testament,* trans. Geoffrey W. Bromiley. Grand Rapids: Wm. B. Eerdmans Publishing Co., 1964-1972.

Lenski, R. C. H. *The Interpretation of St. John's Gospel*. Columbus, OH.: Lutheran Book Concern, 1942.

Lindars, Barnabas. "Two Parables in John." *New Testament Studies*, Vol. 16, No. 4 (July 1970).

McClain, Alva J. "The Doctrine of the Kenosis in Philippians 2:5-8." *Grace Journal*, Vol. 8, No. 2 (Spring 1967).

_____. *The Greatness of the Kingdom*. Grand Rapids: Zondervan Publishing House, 1959.

Morgan, G. Campbell. *The Gospel According to John*. New York: Fleming H. Revell Co., n.d.

Morris, Leon. *The Gospel According to John*, in The New International Commentary on the New Testament series. Grand Rapids: Wm. B. Eerdmans Publishing Co., 1971.

_____. *Studies in the Fourth Gospel*. Grand Rapids: Wm. B. Eerdmans Publishing Co., 1969.

Mowry, Lucetta, "The Dead Sea Scrolls and the Background for the Gospel of John." *The Biblical Archaeologist*, Vol. XVII, No. 4 (December 1954).

The New Bible Dictionary, ed, J. D. Douglas. Grand Rapids: Wm. B. Eerdmans Publishing Co., 1962.

Orni, Efraim, and Elisha Efrat. *Geography of Israel*. Third revised edition. Jerusalem: Israel Universities Press, 1971.

Pancaro, Stephen. "'People of God' in St. John's Gospel." *New Testament Studies*, Vol. 16, No. 2 (January 1970).

Parnham, F. S. "The Miracle at Cana." *The Evangelical Quarterly*, Vol. XLII, No. 2 (April 1970).

Plummer, Alfred. *The Gospel According to St. John,* in The Cambridge Bible for Schools and Colleges. Cambridge: The University Press, 1906.

Reith, George. *The Gospel According to St. John.* Edinburgh: T. & T. Clark, 1899.

Roberts, Alexander, and James Donaldson, eds. *Ante-Nicene Fathers.* Reprint. Grand Rapids: Wm. B. Eerdmans Publishing Co., 1951.

Robertson, A.T. *A Harmony of the Gospels for Students of the Life of Christ.* New York: Harper & Brothers Publishers, 1922.

Rosscup, James E. "Fruit in the New Testament." *Bibliotheca Sacra,* Vol. 125, No. 497 (January 1968).

Smalley, Stephen S. "The Johannine Son of Man Sayings." *New Testament Studies,* Vol. 15, No. 3 (April 1969).

Scofield, C. I., ed. *Scofield Reference Bible.* New York: Oxford University Press, revised edition, 1967.

Scroggie, W. Graham. *A Guide to the Gospels.* London: Pickering & Inglis, Ltd., 1948.

Smith, Charles R. "The Unfruitful Branches in John 15," *Grace Journal,* Vol. 9, No. 2 (Spring 1968).

Tasker, R. V. G. *The Gospel According to St. John,* in The Tyndale New Testament Commentaries series. Grand Rapids: Wm. B. Eerdmans Publishing Co., 1965.

Taylor, Charles. *Sayings of the Jewish Fathers.* New York: Ktav Publishing House, 1969.

Tenney, Merrill C. *John: The Gospel of Belief.* Grand Rapids: Wm. B. Eerdmans Publishing Co., 1951.

Thomas W. H. Griffith. "The Plan of the Fourth Gospel." *Bibliotheca Sacra*. Vol. 125, No. 500 (October 1968).

_____. "The Purpose of the Fourth Gospel." *Bibliotheca Sacra*, Vol. 125, No. 499 (July 1968).

Trudinger, L. Paul. "The Seven Days of the New Creation in St. John's Gospel: Some Further Reflections." *The Evangelical Quarterly*, Vol. XLIV, No. 3 (July 1972).

Turner, George A., and Julius R. Mantey. *The Gospel According to John*, in The Evangelical Commentary series. Grand Rapids: Wm. B. Eerdmans Publishing Co., n.d.

Unger, Merrill F. *The Baptizing Work of the Holy Spirit*. Chicago: Scripture Press, 1953.

Walker, William O., Jr. "Postcrucifixion Appearances and Christian Origins." *Journal of Biblical Literature*, Vol. LXXXVIII, Part II (June 1969).

Wead, David W. "We have a Law." *Novum Testamentum*, Vol. XI, Fasc. 3 (July 1969).

Westcott, B. F. *The Gospel According to St. John*. Grand Rapids: Wm. B. Eerdmans Publishing Co., reprinted 1950.

_____. *Introduction to the Study of the Gospels*. Boston: Gould & Lincoln, 1869.

Wilkinson, John. "The Physical Cause of the Death of Christ." *The Expository Times*, Vol. LXXXIII, No. 4 (January 1972).

Wind, A. "Destination and Purpose of the Gospel of John." *Novum Testamentum*, Vol. XIV, Fasc. 1 (January, 1972).

The Wycliffe Historical Geography of Bible Lands, eds. Charles F. Pfeiffer and Howard F. Vos. Chicago: Moody Press, 1967.

Yadin, Yigael. *Bar-Kokhba*. New York: Random House, 1971.

The Zondervan Pictorial Bible Dictionary, ed. Merrill C. Tenney. Grand Rapids: Zondervan Publishing House, revised 1967.